CW00421967

CHILDHO
ABUSE

To
A. W. Berger

CHILDHOOD ABUSE

Effects on Clinicians'
Personal and
Professional Lives

Helene Jackson
Ronald Nuttall

Foreword by David L. Corwin

SAGE Publications
International Educational and Professional Publisher
Thousand Oaks   London   New Delhi

For information address:

SAGE Publications, Inc.
2455 Teller Road
Thousand Oaks, California 91320
E-mail: order@sagepub.com

SAGE Publications Ltd.
6 Bonhill Street
London EC2A 4PU
United Kingdom

SAGE Publications India Pvt. Ltd.
M-32 Market
Greater Kailash I
New Delhi 110 048 India

Printed in the United States of America

Library of Congress Cataloging-in-Publication Data

Jackson, Helene.
  Childhood abuse: Effects on clinicians' personal and professional
lives / authors, Helene Jackson, Ronald Nuttall.
     p.   cm.
  Includes bibliographical references and index.
  ISBN 0-8039-4780-1 (cloth).—ISBN 0-8039-4781-X (pbk.)
  1. Child sexual abuse—Diagnosis. 2. Child sexual abuse—
Investigation. 3. Psychotherapists—Attitudes. 4. Child welfare
workers—Attitudes. 5. Child sexual abuse—Public opinion.
6. Psychotherapist and patient. I. Nuttall, Ronald. II. Title.
RJ507.S49J33   1997
618.92'85836075—dc21   96-45839

This book is printed on acid-free paper.

97 98 99 00 01 02 10 9 8 7 6 5 4 3 2 1

Acquiring Editor:	C. Terry Hendrix
Editorial Assistant:	Dale Grenfell
Production Editor:	Sanford Robinson
Production Assistant:	Denise Santoyo
Typesetter & Designer:	Andrea D. Swanson
Indexer:	Will Ragsdale
Cover Designer:	Lesa Valdez

Contents

Part III: Sexual Abuse Allegations: What Do Clinicians Believe and Why Do They Believe It?

Part IV: Effects of Childhood Abuse on Personal Relationships and Professional Behavior

Foreword

During the past several decades, child maltreatment has become a major focus of public and professional concern. There is, however, nothing new about the abuse of children. Indeed, this is not even the first time that society has confronted physical and sexual child abuse. Our current attempt to address child abuse is actually the second major professional effort against child victimization within the past 150 years. The first began in France around the middle of the 19th century and was suppressed by the turn of the century by professionals impugning the credibility of child witnesses (Olafson, Corwin, & Summit, 1993). Between that period of professional concern and the present one, two psychiatrists, Sigmund Freud (1896/1989), and later his disciple, Sandor Ferenczi (1932/1955), described the psychological impact of child sexual abuse. Each was scorned and condemned by outraged colleagues. Ostracism probably contributed to Freud's retraction of his original hypothesis that early childhood seduction was the root of hysterical neurosis and the formulation instead of his theories of fantasized sexual involvement between children and their parents that he called the Oedipus complex. When Ferenczi reasserted his mentor's original thesis, based on the confessions of Ferenczi's adult patients about their current sexual involvements with children rather than the retrospective accounts of adult patients describing their childhood sexual abuse on which Freud had relied, Freud himself joined in the rebuke of Ferenczi.

It is the very importance and centrality of child maltreatment that stirs emotions and mobilizes powerful reactions to suppress its discovery. The uncovering of child abuse threatens those who misuse their authority to exploit and harm children. It challenges prevailing scientific authority and current theories of human development that have failed to control for and to account for child maltreatment's prevalence and psychological impact. Whether our society has evolved far enough to maintain the current effort on behalf of victimized children depends very much on the development of knowledge and skill in the accurate identification of abused children and their abusers while minimizing the harm to innocent adults and nonabused children.

This book, with its two studies by Jackson and Nuttall, takes us further down the path to that knowledge. Their findings and suggestions may improve professional efforts to recognize accurately the victims of child sexual abuse as well as to understand the impact of both physical and sexual abuse on the lives of the men and women who become mental health professionals. Contained in these pages are some startling revelations and several important recommendations for improving the training of mental health practitioners and refining professional decision making about suspected child abuse cases.

Using a very interesting and innovative research method (Taguchi, 1987), the authors' first study examines a number of factors that influenced the perceptions and conclusions of professionals who responded to the authors' survey regarding the likelihood of possible child sexual abuse in different vignettes. They discovered that many case attributes, including race, which have no empirically demonstrated value in discriminating true from false sexual abuse allegations, appeared to influence the respondents' likelihood ratings. Jackson and Nuttall also found that a number of clinician characteristics influenced their credibility ratings, including gender, age, theoretical orientation, and history of childhood abuse.

If the vignettes had been drawn from actual cases with independent proof of their validity or falseness, the findings might also have provided some insight into what case and clinician characteristics are associated with the most accurate categorization. Unfortunately, given the history of this field and the current backlash, attempts may be made to misuse the findings in this book to attack current professional efforts to identify and assist abused children. Some may misleadingly cite these data to assert that pediatricians, psychiatrists, psychologists, and social workers are unreliable decision makers in the assessment of suspected child sexual abuse. As the authors point out, such inference exceeds the scope of their study.

The unsupported assertion would be, at best, foolish and, at worst, dishonest. The real value of these findings, and this book, is to educate clinicians about the dangers of unwarranted bias and illustrate steps they can take to protect their professional decision making against these adverse influences. Indeed, other professionals who assess suspected child sexual abuse cases, including judges, lawyers, and investigators, would benefit from reading this book.

We are all subject to a variety of distorting influences when making judgments based on complex, sometimes ambiguous and confusing information. Bias is important but is not the only problem. For this reason, our adversarial justice system attempts to sort reliable from unreliable information using rules of evidence and cross-examination. The strength of professional opinions regarding possible sexual abuse (and many other professional judgments) is best measured by the thoroughness of the evaluation; the use of empirically validated methods; accurate documentation; and appropriate disclosure of the limitations of expertise, knowledge, and the methods used. One cannot, of course, extrapolate the findings of this study of a group of clinicians to predict or impeach the decision making of an individual clinician.

The second study presented in this book addresses the impact of childhood physical and sexual abuse on the lives and careers of the respondent professionals. These research findings are even more thought-provoking than those of the initial research. Perhaps most striking is the strong effect of childhood physical abuse in predicting self-reported adult abusive behavior among the male respondents. The markedly increased rates of admitted sexual involvement with patients by professionals who reported a childhood history of physical and sexual abuse is especially troubling. However, only a small minority of therapists, almost entirely males, who acknowledged childhood abuse experiences reported having engaged in inappropriate sexual contact with patients. This finding needs further study.

As the authors propose, efforts to help prevent sexual exploitation of patients by therapists should be undertaken in programs that educate and supervise clinicians and by professional societies and licensing organizations. More attention during clinical training programs on the effects and consequences of child and patient sexual and physical victimization might reduce some of this malpractice. Just as sexual abuse of children is uncomfortable to think about and difficult to address, the sexual abuse of patients by their therapists is in some ways even more disquieting for the mental health professions to confront. We must, however, find ways to prevent the sexual exploitation of patients without maligning the great majority of therapists, abused and not abused during their own childhood, who do not mistreat patients.

The use of multidisciplinary teams to assist professional decision making is a valuable and well-established approach in child abuse work. Jackson and Nuttall include this approach in their recommendations to minimize the dangers of individual bias while noting the possible difficulties associated with differential prestige and power within groups. However, many evaluations of suspected child sexual abuse are performed outside of the specialized assessment programs where it is less feasible to assemble six or seven different professionals to discuss each case. Nonetheless, it is still possible to develop smaller evaluation teams, perhaps including two or three individuals with different skills and perspectives and, ideally, both genders.

During 1983 to 1988, while in private practice in northern California, I met regularly with a group of six or seven other professionals who worked with sexually abused children and their families. We called it the Peer Review and Psychotherapy Group. The group provided an opportunity for peer consultation on particularly difficult treatment or evaluation cases and also provided emotional support that helped us cope with the stress of this work. In late 1993, Tasha Boychuk, an Arizona psychologist who has done research and much clinical work evaluating children in suspected abuse cases, told me that she and others in Arizona helped enact a state statute to support this form of peer review. Such groups may be particularly useful for the multidisciplinary review process Jackson and Nuttall recommend.

Another way to increase balance and objectivity in evaluating suspected abuse cases is to use a "competing hypotheses approach" (Corwin, 1995). This method makes explicit the most likely alternative explanations for a particular case to assist the evaluators in gathering observations and findings that support or detract from each of the competing hypotheses. Clinicians can thus avoid the trap of attending only to those facts that support a single hypothesis and thus decrease the risk of making false positive determinations.

The pervasive bias in human perception and judgment makes this book an important contribution to the growing child abuse literature. People look at the world through the lenses of their previous life experiences, emotions, values, knowledge, personalities, and cultures. Clinicians bring their own unique perspectives to the cases they evaluate. Only by acknowledging the existence of individual bias can professionals develop and use methods for limiting its possible adverse influence on their decision making. The research by Jackson and Nuttall presented and discussed here provides a constructive and healthy exploration of some difficult but very important issues for professionals who want to improve their response to child maltreatment.

DAVID L. CORWIN

Preface

There are no value-free processes for choosing between risky alternatives. The search for an "objective method" is doomed to failure and may blind the searcher to the value-laden assumptions they are making.

Douglas and Wildavsky (1983, p. 4).

The initial survey reported here arose from ideas generated between 1988 and 1990 when (supported by both National Institute of Mental Health and Boston College) the first author, Helene Jackson (HJ), worked with the Family Violence Unit and the Sexual Abuse Treatment Team at Children's Hospital, Boston, evaluating and treating cases of alleged physical and sexual abuse. HJ quickly became aware that team members, presented with the same data, often reached very different conclusions about the validity of sexual abuse allegations. It appeared that the emotionally loaded issue of sexuality, the characteristic inconclusiveness of medical evidence, the lack of witnesses, and the historical suspicion of children's credibility combined to render sexual abuse allegations vulnerable to the projection of personal and professional attitudes and biases. The Morgan case, highly publicized at that time, illustrates the nature of the problem.

In May 1989, the *New York Times Magazine* featured Dr. Elizabeth Morgan's charges that her ex-husband had sexually abused their 2½-year-old daughter Hilary (Szegedy-Maszak, 1989). Hilary had told her therapist that her father, Dr. Eric Foretich, had "poked his penis in my hiney." Subsequently, in Morgan versus Foretich, 75 witnesses presented testimony in one of the longest and most controversial domestic-relations suits on record.

Consistent with HJ's clinical experience, much of the testimony was contradictory. After evaluating Hilary over a 2-month period, Dr. David Corwin, a child psychiatrist and specialist in sexual abuse cases, testified on behalf of Dr. Morgan. Hilary's therapist also testified that Hilary had indeed been sexually abused. Her nursery school teacher testified that, consistent with sexual molestation, Hilary's behavior and mood had dramatically changed following visits with her father. A Baltimore pediatrician who specializes in sexual abuse cases reported that in his physical examination of Hilary, he had found a scarred vagina and an enlarged hymen that he believed were consistent with the alleged sexual abuse.

However, Dr. Elissa P. Benedek, a forensic psychiatrist, testified that after interviewing Hilary, she was not convinced that the child had been sexually abused. She speculated that, as a result of a series of positive reinforcements, Hilary may have been programmed to make her allegations. Undermining the pediatrician who found evidence consistent with sexual abuse, a pediatric gynecologist, Dr. Catherine DeAngelis, testified that the abnormalities observed during Hilary's physical exam were not necessarily attributable to sexual abuse.

The judge, after hearing the testimony, awarded unsupervised visitation rights to Dr. Foretich. Dr. Morgan, unyielding in her conviction that Hilary (by now 4½ years old) had been sexually abused by her father, refused to reveal Hilary's whereabouts. The judge then held Dr. Morgan in contempt of court and jailed her. When the *Times* article appeared, Dr. Morgan had been in jail for 21 months.[1]

Discussion of this publicized and controversial case with colleagues generated widely diverse opinions. After reading the *Times* article, some were of the opinion that sexual abuse had occurred. Dr. Morgan was a saint, a devoted mother willing to sacrifice her freedom to protect her child from further sexual abuse. Others were convinced that sexual abuse had not occurred. Dr. Morgan was a pathological liar, a mentally disturbed woman accusing her ex-husband falsely to obtain sole custody of her daughter. The contrast in the views of these witnesses led HJ to seek the sources of these strikingly different conclusions. To what extent do personal background, professional training, and other factors affect a person's perception of sexual abuse allegations?

Consequently, HJ formulated the hypothesis that differing perceptions of sexual abuse allegations are related to the backgrounds of the people making the evaluation (e.g., gender, age, and discipline) as well as to individual belief systems. At this point, she joined with Ronald Nuttall (RN) to develop and carry out a mail survey of a random national sample of professionals who, by virtue of their disciplines, were most likely to have major responsibility for the evaluation of sexual abuse allegations (clinical social workers, pediatricians, psychiatrists, and psychologists). An experimental design was constructed to determine, from the replies, what personal, professional, and case-related factors influence professionals' opinions of the validity of sexual abuse allegations.

Our results validate the hypothesis that evaluations of sexual abuse are both subjective and variable and depend on a variety of personal and case factors that may be irrelevant to objective analyses. Note, however, that our population of clinicians was not confined to "experts" in sexual abuse. Our data do not include information about our respondents' specialized training or education in the evaluation of childhood sexual abuse allegations. Thus, it should not be assumed that our results are representative of any population other than those in general practice. To our knowledge, no study to determine factors that influence clinicians' determination of the validity of sexual abuse allegations has been limited to an "expert" sample. Clearly, this is an important area for further study.

More objective evaluation of sexual abuse allegations will require much further research, education, and training. However, our report should alert professionals to the personal and professional biases that interfere with objective judgment. This book may thus serve to guide educators and practitioners of all the helping professions who are confronted daily with the responsibility of making the hard choice between maintaining a family's integrity and a child's safety.

Judging the Sexual Abuse Allegations Yourself

The 16 vignettes created for this research are given in Appendix A in the same order in which they appeared in the original questionnaire. Each case describes one allegation of child sexual abuse. We invite you to read and rate them (using the scale at the bottom of each page) according to your confidence that sexual abuse occurred. By rating each vignette before reading the book, you will participate in the same evaluation process as our professional respondents. You might have a colleague (or a class) also rate the vignettes. You will surely find, as we did, that people differ greatly in their ratings of the credibility of the allegations. You can compare your ratings of each vignette with the average ratings of our respondents given in Chapter 4, Table 4.1.

We encourage those of you who teach in undergraduate, graduate, or continuing education programs to use these vignettes as an experiential exercise to help students become aware of their idiosyncratic biases that can interfere with objectivity. We strongly believe that a combination of knowledge based on empirical research and self-awareness is needed to ensure more objective evaluations of sexual abuse allegations.

The results of our initial survey have led us to ask what other effects, if any, a childhood history of abuse may have on the professional and personal lives of our respondents. Thus, we designed, and included in this work, a follow-up survey to explore such effects in greater detail.

Note

1. On September 26, 1989, Dr. Morgan was released after 25 months in jail. Her release was the result of a congressional mandate that limits the time anyone can be incarcerated for civil contempt in the District of Columbia (Barringer, 1989). A determination that Hilary had been sexually abused was never made.

Acknowledgments

The work on which this book is based began in 1989. Support for the initial and follow-up surveys was awarded to Helene Jackson (HJ) by the National Institute of Mental Health and Boston College in the form of an Individual Clinical Faculty Scholar Award (MH Grant #MH19076-01) and from Children's Hospital, Boston.

First, we want to thank the almost 700 respondents who gave us their time and knowledge in judging the vignettes and completing two long, complex, and personal questionnaires. They have made a major contribution to the field of child abuse.

We are grateful to Beth Kemler, Eli and Caroline Newberger, and Suzanne Meyer who welcomed HJ as a colleague on the Sexual Abuse Treatment Team and Family Violence Unit at Children's Hospital. They provided a climate in which she could participate in and learn about the complex issues and challenges involved in evaluating sexual abuse allegations.

We want to thank Jason Aronson, David Finkelhor, Shirley Goldstein, Carol Hartman, and Carolyn Thomas, for their support, encouragement, and confidence in HJ's ability to develop and implement this research project, and David Corwin who validated the importance of empirically documenting the subjectivity of clinical evaluations of sexual abuse allegations. We are grateful to our colleagues at Columbia University, School of Social Work, and Boston College, School of Social Work and School of Education, whose support and encouragement were invaluable.

Many people have contributed to the final product presented here. Ronald Nuttall's (RN) daughter, Kim Nuttall-Vazquez, provided invaluable help and assistance during many phases of the data collection and analysis as well as editorial suggestions on various drafts of the manuscript. Jack Goldstein, Carolyn Thomas, and Lee Liberman applied their editorial expertise to the manuscript. Their constructive criticisms helped us to clarify our ideas, and make the book more reader friendly.

We would also like to acknowledge the assistance of our editors Dale Grenfell, Terry Hendrix, and Sanford Robinson, of Sage Publications, and the three anonymous reviewers who encouraged us and gave detailed suggestions for improving the manuscript.

We want to acknowledge the support, editorial assistance, and patience of RN's wife, Dr. Ena Vazquez Nuttall. HJ's husband, Abe Berger, was, as usual, a constant source of comfort, encouragement, and critique (an unusual and unbeatable combination). Throughout the seemingly endless and often painful process of reanalysis, reinterpretation, and rewriting, his superb editorial ability, his enthusiasm, optimism, and dedication to the scientific method were an inspiration.

Last, our thanks to HJ's two sons, David and Jonathan, and their spouses, Danielle and Karen. They and their children are a source of pleasure and pride and a constant reminder that parenting, although stressful, can be loving and nonabusive.

PART I

Sexual Abuse

1

Introduction
and Overview

In this book, we address one of the most perplexing and complicated of our current, acute social problems, child sexual abuse, and the personal and professional challenges it poses to those responsible for the evaluation, protection, and treatment of children and their families.

The deleterious psychological consequences of the abuse of children were clear to Freud, who, in his seduction theory, drew a causal connection between early sexual victimization of his patients and their emotional illnesses. His subsequent adoption of the Oedipus complex theory and his recantation of the original formulation (Freud, 1953) permitted post-Victorian society to deny the evidence of the rape, prostitution, and humiliation of its children. Despite later clinical observations (Ferenczi, 1949) and research findings that supported Freud's original theory (Kinsey, Pomeroy, & Martin, 1953), children's sexual abuse allegations continued to be ignored, attributed to fantasy (Bagley & Ramsay, 1986), or disbelieved (Bender & Blau, 1937). Today, some professionals continue to blame the victim, holding children responsible for their own victimization (Eisenberg, Owens, & Dewey, 1987; Frenken & Stolk, 1990). In modern democratic, industrial societies, it is generally accepted that children are different from adults, with feelings, thoughts, hopes, and fears of their own. However, evidence of the disregard of children's needs is reflected in the escalating reports of their maltreatment. According to Sgroi (1978), "sexual abuse of children is a crime that our society abhors in the abstract, but tolerates in reality" (p. xv). Our insensitivity to the exploitation of children, so passionately recorded by Dickens, has made possible the romanticized and idealized Broadway musical comedy *Oliver*. We have, perhaps, not moved as far from 19th-century sentimentality as we would like to believe.

Although many claim that ours is a "child-centered" society, we demonstrate our hypocrisy (or ignorance) by our unwillingness to support the well-being of our children (Grubb & Lazerson, 1982, as cited in Zelizer, 1985). Between 1980 and 1990, a period of great economic growth in the United States, the "safety nets of the social systems (created to serve children and adolescents) . . . frayed" (Moynihan, 1990, p. 52). During this time, "urban society in America . . . suffered a retrogression without equivalent" (p. 50). In 1990, it was reported that more than 20% of U.S. children were living below the official poverty line, an increase of more than 25% in the past decade (UNICEF, 1990), the highest child poverty rate of any major Western industrial country.

The historian deMause wrote that "the history of children is a nightmare from which we have only recently begun to awaken" (deMause, 1974, p. 1). Many children who have been sexually abused continue in the throes of the bad dream from which they have yet to be rescued. For some, the pain is a product of their sexual exploitation and victimization; others suffer from the indifference of a society that is either unwilling or unable to acknowledge or empathize with their anguish (Enzer, 1988). Still others are tormented by a fragmented legal and social service system whose policies often ignore their developmental and psychological needs.

Although we believe that our social policies are ostensibly created to protect children, these policies are often determined by the biased and inhumane belief that children and families who cannot care for themselves deserve to suffer (Brazelton, 1990). Many young people live in families or neighborhoods where poverty and its shared correlates of crime, fear, repetitive neglect, abuse, and trauma are pervasive (Garbarino, Schellenback, & Sebes, 1986). Abused children who perceive no alternative to running away (Burgess & Hartman, 1986) become vulnerable to further trauma and less able to accomplish the maturational tasks required to achieve productive lives.

Major changes in societal values and attitudes have occurred in the past two decades, however. The abuse of children that was hidden and tolerated not so long ago is now viewed (at least publicly) as illegal or unacceptable (Kempe, 1978). Increased media attention to dramatic allegations of the sexual victimization of children has fueled both public and professional debate over the actual incidence and prevalence of child and adolescent sexual victimization. Although some sensational accounts have triggered accusations of professional witch hunts, more responsible reports have generated legitimate concerns for both the protection of children and for those who may be wrongly accused.

The transfer of the concept of sexual abuse from the shadows into the light of public concern (DeJong & Emmet, 1983) in both the United States and internationally (Finkelhor, 1994) is reflected in the startling increase in the number of reported sexual abuse allegations. For example, the U.S. Department of Health and Human Services (USDHHS) reported a threefold increase in the rate of child abuse allegations between 1977 and 1992 (USDHHS, 1992, p. 10). Of the cases investigated, 54% were not substantiated, 32% were substantiated, with 9% indicated and 5% closed without a finding or other disposition (p. 11). It is not clear whether the rapid rise in reports of child abuse is a result of a real change in the rate of maltreatment of children, a shift in societal attitudes about the status and rights of women and young people (Gordon, 1988), or an increased likelihood that professionals will recognize and report abuse (DHHS, 1988). Although sexual abuse is a serious problem that often has major consequences for its victims (Browne & Finkelhor, 1986b; Haaken, 1994), cultural denial of its magnitude and effects continues (Henderson, 1983; Ramey, 1979, cited in Browne & Finkelhor, 1986b).

Accurate estimates of the numbers of sexually victimized children are made elusive by problems of definition (Finkelhor, 1994). Denial or skepticism is encouraged by the wide range of the reported prevalence rates of child and adolescent sexual abuse: 6% to 62% for females; 3% to 31% for males (Browne & Finkelhor, 1986a). These wide ranges may be explained by actual anomalies among different populations studied, differences in definitions, or hesitancy to report as a result of "less than optimal conditions for the disclosure of abuse" (Wyatt & Peters, 1986a, p. 242).

Reliable evaluation of an allegation has been made difficult by the aura of disbelief that surrounds childhood sexual abuse. This distrust has been reflected in the tendency of many parents and professionals to find children's retractions of sexual victimization more believable than their complaints (Goodwin, 1985) and in the resistance of the legal system to accept children's testimony as credible evidence (Conte, Sorenson, Fogarty, & Rosa, 1991; Corder & Whiteside, 1988). Children who make allegations of sexual abuse are often stigmatized and labeled malicious (Summit, 1983). Adults project onto children an adult model of behavior that implies the ability to "resist, to cry for help and to attempt to escape the intrusion" (p. 183). Clearly, negative responses to disclosure exacerbate the child's feelings of helplessness, alienation, and guilt and can be experienced as another trauma (Sauzier, 1989; Summit, 1983).

Disbelief that such outrageous, abusive acts are perpetrated on children by fellow human beings may encourage so-called clinician denial (Benedek, 1985). Despite the increased sensitization to sexual abuse among professionals (Berliner & Conte, 1993), internalized and often unconscious attitudes about sex role stereotypes, belief systems connected to professional training, and personal history are all likely to influence decisions about the data clinicians find important and how they are interpreted (Corwin, Berliner, Goodman, Goodwin, & White, 1987; Jackson & Ferguson, 1983; Jackson & Nuttall, 1993; Mayer, 1983; Nuttall & Jackson, 1994).

These are major challenges to clinicians who evaluate sexual abuse allegations (Berliner & Conte, 1993). For many professionals, determination of the validity of sexual abuse allegations is a relatively new responsibility (Faller, 1990).[1] Many professionals lack much of the knowledge and many of the skills required to identify and diagnose sexual abuse (Frenken & Stolk, 1990). Melton (1989) questions the ethics of mental health professionals' involvement as expert witnesses in sexual abuse cases, and underscores the need for clarity about the limits of their role and expertise. Despite these concerns, professionals are increasingly asked to distinguish reality from fantasy and authentic versus coached responses and to determine why a child may be making a false allegation (Berliner & Conte, 1993; Terr, 1986).

Although there is clearly a need for objective evaluation, verifying or refuting allegations of child sexual abuse is a difficult process (Benedek & Schetky, 1987a, 1987b; Bernet, 1993; Brekke, 1987; Corwin et al., 1987; deYoung, 1984; Green, 1986; Jackson & Nuttall, 1993; Nuttall & Jackson, 1994; Sgroi, Porter, & Blick, 1982). Attempts to provide guidelines for the evaluation of suspected childhood abuse (American Professional Society for the Abuse of Children [APSAC], 1990; deYoung, 1986) are impeded by the lack of an empirically based method for discriminating between abused and nonabused children (Bybee & Mowbray, 1993). Furthermore, workers may resist an empirically based assessment model that forces them to change from unstructured to structured interviewing (Doueck, Levine, & Bronson, 1993).

Unfortunately, there are usually large differences among professional judgments of sexual abuse allegations (Boat & Everson, 1988b; Jackson & Nuttall, 1993; Kendall-Tackett & Watson, 1991; Saunders, 1988). Some claim that professionals "always [find] sexual abuse where alleged" (Benedek & Schetky, 1987b, p. 912), whereas others express concerns that sexual abuse is too often unrecognized despite evidence of its existence. Not surprisingly, clinicians are also influenced by attitudes, fantasies, and belief systems that may or may not reflect reality (Gambrill, 1990). A commitment to a particular conceptual framework may interfere with the objective examination and sampling of data (Attias & Goodwin, 1985; Gambrill, 1990). Clinicians' initial perceptions of a disclosure may affect the entire course and outcome of an allegation of sexual abuse (Attias & Goodwin, 1985). The need to evaluate a sexual abuse allegation quickly and accurately is critical, not only because of the potential danger of further victimization or intimidation of the child (Hanson, 1988) but in cases of false accusations, to remove suspicion from innocent people. Surely, the consequences of allegations on parental relationships and family functioning should not be minimized (Benedek & Schetky, 1987b; Brant & Tisza, 1977).

Many factors may interfere with objective evaluation of alleged sexual abuse. The intense emotional reaction and the media attention aroused by this issue make objectivity difficult. Children rarely present sexual abuse as the initial complaint (DeJong, 1985). Most professionals have little knowledge about sexual abuse. Many hesitate to become involved in cases that can make excessive demands on their time, provide no financial reward, and impel them into a frustrating system that is fragmented among welfare, foster care, schools, health care, criminal and juvenile justice, and mental health (CSWE, 1994; DeJong, 1985).

Children are least likely to disclose purposely when the abuser is the biological parent (Anderson, Martin, Mullen, Romans, & Herbison, 1993). Because the majority of reported child abusers are related or known to the family, it is difficult for child victims to risk an exposure that could jeopardize relationships on which they are emotionally, financially, and physically dependent. Furthermore, there is some evidence that disclosure places added stress on children (Sauzier, 1989). When children do disclose sexual abuse, they may not be believed or be put under great pressure from parents and professionals to retract their accusations (Goodwin, 1985). A sense of loyalty combined with fear of rejection and anger from family members exacerbate the child's apprehension (Berliner & Barbierie, 1984; Boat & Everson, 1988a; DeJong, 1985).

In sexual abuse allegations, the ambiguity of the data (Yates, 1993), the usual absence of physical evidence (Berliner & Conte, 1993) or witnesses (Finkelhor, 1985), and parental ambivalence make verification and prosecution of sexual abuse far more difficult than for cases of physical abuse (White, Strom, Santilli, & Halpin, 1986). Decisions about what cases to bring to court often depend on the agency to which the case is initially referred and on the measure of the child's credibility. Consequently, only a small percentage of substantiated cases are litigated (Cross, De Vos, & Whitcomb, 1994).

Factors beyond the boundaries of clinical relevance may significantly influence professionals, thereby compromising their objectivity and accuracy (Corwin et al., 1987; Jackson & Nuttall, 1993, 1994; Kelley, 1990; Mayer, 1983; Nuttall & Jackson, 1994). For example, a professional's age and gender may influence child abuse reporting decisions and perceptions of the validity of allegations. Older practitioners are less likely to report abuse than are their younger colleagues, and women are more likely than their male colleagues to suspect and report sexual abuse (Finlayson & Koocher, 1991; Zellman & Bell, 1989).

Women may also judge symptoms of victimization more severely than do men (Howe, Herzberger, & Tennen, 1988; Jones & McGraw, 1987; Snyder & Newberger, 1986) and perceive intrafamilial abuse to be more prevalent than do males. More men than women, particularly psychiatrists, are likely to overestimate the role of fantasy in children's allegations of sexual abuse (Attias & Good-win, 1985). Furthermore, Attias and Goodwin found that more men than women would not report a case in which there had been a retraction of a child's allegation.

Multidisciplinary sexual abuse evaluation teams are generally considered most effective in achieving unbiased judgments because the biases of one member of the team may be canceled out by the biases of others (Gambrill, 1990). However, status differences among male and female team members of various disciplines may also influence team decision making and lead to "confirmation bias" (Gambrill, 1990, p. 78). Differences in personal background, perception of professional roles, and attitudes and values related to training are potential obstacles to reaching individual and group objectivity (Abramson, 1989). Furthermore, "clinical settings differ in terms of what behaviors are reinforced, ignored, or punished" (Gambrill, 1990, p. 41).

The relationship between a personal history of childhood abuse and subsequent clinical judgment has rarely been studied (Eisenberg et al., 1987; Kelley, 1990; Kendall-Tackett & Watson, 1991; Saunders, 1988). The omission of definitions of sexual abuse in some studies and, when given, differences in definitions make it difficult to generalize results or compare findings (Wyatt & Peters, 1986a). Despite methodological and definitional flaws, it is evident that personal and case factors do play a critical role in professional perceptions of sexual abuse allegations. For example, professional respondents who reported some form of personal childhood abuse were likely to evaluate examples of physical and emotional abuse more severely than those who did not report such a history (Howe et al., 1988).

Among case factors that have been shown to influence professional judgments of sexual abuse are the victim's and perpetrator's race (Hampton & Newberger, 1985), the relationship of the perpetrator to the victim (Browne & Finkelhor, 1986a), the victim's gender and age (National Center on Child Abuse and Neglect [NCCAN], 1988), and custody issues (Green, 1986).

Our initial nationwide study is the first to examine a large ($N = 656$), randomly drawn sample to determine (a) the prevalence rates and characteristics of childhood sexual and physical abuse among practicing professionals and (b) how and to what extent specific personal, professional, and case factors influence judgments about sexual abuse allegations. In our follow-up study, we examined the effects of a history of childhood abuse on respondents' mental health and on their personal relationships and professional behavior. In both studies, we provided respondents with specific definitions of both physical and sexual abuse (Giovannoni & Becerra, 1979; Kempe, 1978). Some data from the initial survey have been published elsewhere (Jackson & Nuttall, 1993, 1994; Nuttall & Jackson, 1994). Results of the follow-up survey have not been previously published.

In Chapter 2, we outline the methodology and design of the two projects: the initial survey and its follow-up. We discuss the limitations characteristic of the sexual abuse literature, such as definitional problems, lack of control or comparison groups, reliance on retrospective data, and sampling bias. We review other research with vignette designs and compare them to our study. Last, we describe the sample size, respondents, questionnaires, scale of measurement, construction of the vignettes, statistical analyses, and limitations for each study.

In Chapter 3, we give the prevalence rates of childhood abuse (to age 18) among the respondents to this study and describe some characteristics of the abused, the abuser, and the abuse (age at onset, peak vulnerability, duration, relationship to the abuser, and type of abuse).

In Chapters 4 and 5, we describe the personal and case factors that significantly influenced the respondents' credibility scores for the sexual abuse allegations as they were presented in the 16 vignettes. The effects of specific respondent and case factors on professional judgments about sexual abuse allegations are presented, discussed, and interpreted in the context of current, available literature

In Chapter 6, we present the effects of a childhood history of abuse on adult mental health. Specifically, we compare abused and nonabused respondents on their scores obtained from the Brief Symptom Inventory form of the Symptom Checklist-90-R (Derogatis, 1983, 1993; Derogatis, Lipman, & Covi, 1973; Derogatis, Rickels, & Rock, 1976) and the Mississippi Civilian Post Traumatic Stress Disorder (Keane, 1988). Our findings are discussed in the context of relevant literature.

In Chapter 7, we describe the effects of a childhood history of abuse on respondents' personal relationships and professional behavior. We compare our abused and nonabused respondents on marital status, child rearing, sexual satisfaction, quality of relationships, choice of work setting, career satisfaction, and therapist-client boundaries.

Last, in Chapter 8, we discuss the implications of our findings for the education, training, and practice of professionals responsible for the care and protection of children and their families. We make recommendations for education and training, practice, and future research.

Each chapter may be read and understood independently. Thus, the reader may choose to read every chapter or to select a specific chapter or chapters of interest. Those interested in methodology, experimental design, and statistics will find Chapter 2 particularly informative[2] Those who find the details of experimental design uninteresting may proceed to the remaining chapters where they will discover much that, we believe, can be applied to their practice.

In our initial survey, we find, not surprisingly, that there is need for more objective evaluations of sexual abuse allegations. In our follow-up survey, we find a history of childhood abuse can have major negative implications for personal relationships and professional behavior. Clearly, we do not imagine that the problems identified in these two studies can be significantly addressed without the development of major educational and training programs and much further research.

Notes

1. Throughout this book, the terms *professionals, clinicians,* and *practitioners* are used interchangeably.

2. Those particularly interested in the fractional factorial experimental design can read more about the methodology in Appendix D.

PART II

The Projects

2

Methodology

Overview

Our initial survey was the first study of a randomly drawn national sample of practicing professionals designed to determine the specific personal attributes and case factors that affect clinicians' responses to allegations of sexual abuse. We also examined the prevalence of a personal history of childhood (to age 18) maltreatment among clinicians and the effects of mediating variables, such as type of abuse and abuser characteristics on personal life choices.

Respondents evaluated 16 vignettes alleging sexual abuse in which 15 case factors were systematically varied in accord with a Taguchi fractional factorial design (Taguchi & Konishi, 1987). Significant case and personal factors were determined by regression analyses.

In a follow-up survey, we sought detailed information about the abuse histories of respondents who reported a history of childhood abuse. We compared them to their nonabused peers in mental health status, career and sexual satisfaction, and professional boundary violations. We also examined the effects of disclosure, types of abuse, abuser characteristics, and family factors on mental health status, career, and sexual satisfaction.

Although a response bias study found no significant differences between respondents and nonrespondents in the frequency of abuse, the relatively small number of those abused limited the power of some statistics.

Introduction

Historically, studies of sexual abuse have exhibited poor methodologies and weak data analyses (Conte & Schuerman, 1987) and have been severely limited by sampling biases and definitional confusion (Kalichman, Craig, & Follingstad, 1988). Research has been hampered by failure to use standardized instruments and lack of, or inappropriate use of, control groups. The distinction between intrafamilial and extrafamilial sexual abuse, and long-term and short-term effects, has in general been ignored, and there has been disagreement about the age range for childhood and adolescence (Russell, 1983; Tong, Oates, & McDowell, 1987).

Data obtained with imprecise or unclear definitions of sexual abuse can be misleading (Briere & Runtz, 1988; Doueck, Levine, & Bronson, 1993; Eisenberg, Owens, & Dewey, 1987; Fry, 1993; Kalichman et al., 1988; Kercher & McShane, 1984; Wyatt & Peters, 1986b). For example, in a review of four prevalence studies (Finkelhor, 1979b, 1984; Russell, 1983; Wyatt, 1985), Wyatt and Peters (1986b) found that, controlled for differences in definitions of sexual abuse, prevalence rates that had initially appeared widely disparate became more concordant. Differences in methodology can also influence apparent prevalence rates (Kendall-Tackett, Williams, & Finkelhor, 1993), and choice of methodology may be affected by training, discipline, and targeted audience (Briere & Elliot, 1994).

Major methodological limitations that have been noted in the literature are the use of clinical, deviant, and college populations not representative of the general population (Rosenfeld, Nadelson, & Krieger, 1979); small samples that do not possess the statistical power to detect real effects; chart reviews in which abuse may have gone unrecorded or been withheld or denied by the patient (Jenny & Roesler, 1993); and reliance on retrospective designs (Tajfel, 1969).

Rarely has there been control for contextual or mediating variables (Rosenfeld et al., 1979), such as family pathology; additional trauma (Bernet, 1993; Mikkelsen, Gutheil, & Emens, 1992); disclosure, type, duration, and age at onset of abuse; and relationship to the abuser. These weaknesses have led to inconclusive and contradictory results (deYoung, 1986; Morison & Greene, 1992). Consequently, the actual prevalence of child sexual abuse and its sequelae (Sirles, Smith, & Kusama, 1989) are poorly known, and the development of effective interventions has been delayed (Howling, Wodarski, Kurtz, & Gaudin, 1989).

Recently, however, sexual abuse research has moved from anecdotal, descriptive reporting to more empirical investigation (Mikkelsen et al., 1992). In the design of our two projects, we addressed many of the limitations noted above by obtaining a large sample, providing definitions of sexual and physical abuse, applying standardized instruments to measure the mental health of our respondents, and developing an experimental design that facilitates quantitative statistical analyses. Still, our findings are surely also biased by the limitations inherent in retrospective data, such as the subjectivity and social construction of memory, the expected reluctance to disclose abuse, the respondents' internal pressure for "political correctness" (Hibbard & Zollinger, 1990), lack of control for family dysfunction and additional trauma, and, of course, by our omission of additional personal and case variables.

For the initial study, we selected a survey methodology and a vignette design. Vignettes, like other research designs, possess both advantages and disadvantages. Although an improvement over the traditional questionnaire, vignette designs are limited to their constructed scenarios. It is thus difficult to deduce from the hypothetical, well-defined vignette how respondents would react to an actual, complex case (Deblinger, Lippmann, Stauffer, & Finkel, 1994; McPherson & Garcia, 1983). However, the vignette design allows presentation to each subject of complex, multifactorial stimuli of sexual abuse allegations while restricting all respondents' judgments to the same data. Vignettes are easy to administer and manage; all respondents can be given the same vignettes and the variables can be varied systematically, each providing its own control (Alexander & Becker, 1978; Bressee, Stearns, Bess, & Packer, 1986). Furthermore, a fractional factorial approach permits a small number of vignettes to represent a larger universe.

Ours is the first vignette study of a national sample of clinicians designed to determine specific factors that influence decisions about the credibility of sexual abuse allegations. Vignette designs have been used to examine the determinants of police and nurse attitudes toward rape (Giovannoni & Becerra, 1979), to identify public and professional definitions of sexual abuse (Finkelhor & Hotaling, 1984; Katz & Benjamin, 1960), to determine the effects of social class and personal acquaintance on reporting decisions, and to determine nurses' recognition of child abuse and their tendency to report (McPherson & Garcia, 1983)

Vignette designs have also been used to determine the factors that affect mental health professionals' decisions to report sexual abuse (Coons, 1986; Thoennes & Tjaden, 1990); the effects of religion on physicians' identification of, and response to, child abuse (Benson, Swann, O'Toole, & Turbett, 1991); the effects of victim, perpetrator, and respondent factors on students' responses to child sexual abuse (Gaertner, 1973); and students' attributions of causality and blame to victims of intrafamilial abuse (Collings & Payne, 1991). They have been used to compare professionals' personal versus professional expectations and responses to child sexual abuse (Deblinger et al., 1994), professional assignment of blame (Tajfel, 1969), and police and juror bias in recognizing and reacting to child abuse and neglect (Bressee et al., 1986). For a comprehensive overview of classical statistical design approaches to fractional factorials and vignette research, see Alexander and Becker (1978).

Finkelhor and Redfield's (Finkelhor, 1984) study of the public's definition of sexual abuse most resembles the vignette design used in our research. Using a factorial survey approach (Beck, 1990; Mukerjee, 1995; Tedeschi & Calhoun, 1995), they included two, two-level factors (victim gender and perpetrator gender) and one five-level factor (relationship of victim to the perpetrator) in 20 vignettes. In addition to the three fully crossed variables, another set of factors (victim age, perpetrator age, sex act, consent, and consequences) were randomly selected and included in each vignette. Thus, each respondent ($N = 521$) was given a different set of 20 experimental vignettes.

Our vignette design differs from that of Finkelhor and Redfield. We used (a) a standardized Taguchi style (L16) fractional factorial approach (Taguchi & Konishi, 1987; see Appendix D), (b) the same set of vignettes for all respondents, and (c) much longer vignettes that presented treatment combinations of many more factors (15 vs. 8).

Most important, our vignettes were designed to reflect the ambiguity characteristic of most sexual abuse allegations, thus eliciting projection and consequently, provoking a wide range of responses.

The Initial Survey

Sample

In 1989, we drew a random, stratified sample of 1,635 clinicians from the latest national directories of four disciplines: clinical social work, pediatrics, psychiatry, and clinical psychology.[1] We chose these four specialties as representative of professionals most responsible for the evaluation of child and adolescent sexual abuse allegations.[2] Experience with child sexual abuse was not a criterion for inclusion. Respondents were not asked to identify themselves either by race or ethnicity. We divided each discipline by gender and drew lists of 200 males and 200 females taking every kth respondent after a random start. The "k" was chosen to yield 200 respondents of each gender by discipline population. In addition to the initial sample of 400 social workers, 35 more were randomly drawn to correct a small discrepancy in sampling.[3]

Respondents

Many professionals, given assurance of anonymity, acceptable sponsors, and the opportunity to contribute to the field, are quite willing to make known intimate details of their life experiences (Green, 1993). We obtained a 42% response rate (N = 655; social workers, 39%; pediatricians, 32%; psychologists, 44%; and psychiatrists, 43%). Respondents ranged in age from 27 to 73 years with a mean age of 46 and a mode of 40. On average, they had been out of graduate programs for more than 15 years and had varied professional experience in child sexual abuse.

Those reporting direct experience working with sexually abused children (72%) spent an average of 8½ hours per week with sexual abuse cases and had worked with them, on average, slightly more than 7 years (about half the time the mean respondent had been out

Table 2.1 Characteristics of the Respondents to the Initial Survey

	Clinical Social Workers	Pedia-tricians	Psychol-ogists	Psychi-atrists	Total
Number of Respondents					
Total	169 (39%)	128 (32%)	176 (44%)	173 (43%)	646
Males	71 (42%)	57 (44%)	74 (42%)	83 (48%)	285 (44%)
Females	98 (58%)	71 (56%)	102 (58%)	90 (52%)	361 (56%)
Mean Age	48.3	42.0	47.0	46.3	46.2
Number sexually abused					
Total	36 (21%)	14 (11%)	32 (18%)	27 (16%)	109 (17%)
Males	15 (21%)	7 (12%)	8 (11%)	8 (10%)	38 (13%)
Females	21 (21%)	7 (10%)	24 (24%)	19 (21%)	71 (20%)
Number physically abused					
Total	12 (7%)	10 (8%)	17 (10%)	6 (3%)	45 (7%)
Males	5 (7%)	7 (12%)	5 (7%)	3 (4%)	20 (7%)
Females	7 (7%)	3 (4%)	12 (12%)	3 (3%)	25 (7%)
Theoretical orientation					
Psychodynamic	114 (67%)	13 (14%)	98 (56%)	135 (78%)	360 (56%)
Cognitive-behavioral	35 (21%)	37 (29%)	72 (41%)	35 (20%)	179 (27%)
Family system	83 (49%)	22 (17%)	43 (24%)	31 (18%)	179 (27%)
Psychosocial	87 (51%)	22 (17%)	25 (14%)	42 (24%)	176 (27%)
Biological	4 (2%)	59 (46%)	11 (6%)	89 (51%)	163 (25%)
Child development	33 (20%)	63 (49%)	27 (15%)	40 (23%)	163 (25%)
Social Learning	12 (7%)	1 (1%)	27 (15%)	1 (1%)	41 (6%)
Feminist	5 (3%)	3 (2%)	11 (6%)	4 (2%)	23 (3%)

NOTE: Of the total of 655 cases, 8 were missing designation of discipline and 1 was missing designation of gender, leaving a total of 646 for this table.

of school).[4] A summary of the characteristics of the respondents is presented in Table 2.1.

We did not ask if respondents had received specialized training in evaluating sexual abuse. We thus cannot assume that, as a group, our clinicians are experts in the field of sexual abuse. Clearly, research to identify factors that influence expert evaluations of sexual abuse allegations would be an important addition to our study of the "universe" of clinicians.

The Survey

We designed a booklet to include 16 vignettes (see Appendix A) and a demographic questionnaire (See Appendix B). In the cover letter asking subjects to participate, we described the research, its sponsors (National Institute of Mental Health [NIMH],[5] Boston College, and Children's Hospital), and its likely contribution to clinical practice (see Appendix C). As an incentive to return and complete the questionnaire, we included a self-addressed postage-paid card offering respondents the choice of a free professional book and the option of requesting a summary of the study results.[6,7] The questionnaires were not identifiable by name or number. To protect anonymity, we requested that respondents mail the card separately. A modification of the Total Design Method (Dillman, 1978) was used in preparing and conducting the survey. Two follow-ups were sent: (a) a reminder postcard and (b) a packet with another letter and a second copy of the questionnaire.[8]

The Questionnaire

To obtain the respondents' reports of their own childhood history of abuse, we defined sexual abuse as "the involvement of dependent, developmentally immature children and adolescents in sex acts that they do not fully comprehend and to which they are unable to give informed consent or that violate the social taboos of family roles" (Kempe, 1978, p. 382). To obtain the respondents' reports of their own childhood history of physical abuse, we defined physical abuse as an act "being inflicted non-accidentally . . . which causes or creates a substantial risk of causing disfigurement, impairment of bodily functioning, or other serious physical injury" (Giovannoni & Becerra, 1979, p. 83).

We chose 12 personal variables for classification of the respondents (see Table 2.2). These variables were chosen either because they had been demonstrated in the literature to have an effect on clinical judgments, such as gender (Broussard & Wagner, 1988; Broussard, Wagner, & Kazelskis, 1991) or discipline (Daniel, Hampton, & Newberger, 1983; Johnson, Owens, Dewey, & Eisenberg, 1990; Reidy & Hochstadt, 1993), or they had been observed by the first author, Helene Jackson (HJ), to influence clinical judgments (childhood history of abuse, age, marital status, number of children, work role and setting, type and length of experience, and theoretical orientation).

Table 2.2 Respondent Factors

Age
Gender
Marital status
Number of children
Work role
Work setting
Type of experience
Length of experience
Discipline
History of childhood sexual abuse
History of childhood physical abuse
Theoretical orientation
  Psychodynamic
  Cognitive-behavioral
  Family systems
  Psychosocial
  Child development
  Biological
  Social learning
  Feminist

Scale of Measurement

We asked subjects to read 16 vignettes, each of which contained an allegation of sexual abuse, and to rate how confident they were that sexual abuse had occurred. The credibility scale ranged from 1 (very confident sexual abuse did not occur) to 6 (very confident sexual abuse did occur; see Table 2.3).[9] We constructed the vignettes to test the null hypotheses that the 15 case factors would not affect respondents' judgments about the credibility of the sexual abuse allegations. Thus, a credibility score of 3.5 is a null score, reflecting belief as likely as disbelief. Any score significantly different from 3.5 reflects the difference from the null.

Construction of the Vignettes

We created 16 vignettes in which allegations of child sexual abuse were depicted and in which we systematically varied 15 two-level case factors (see Table 2.4). Like the respondent variables, the case factors were chosen either because they had been shown in the

Table 2.3 Scale of Measurement for Rating the Credibility of Case Vignettes

On a scale of 1 to 6, how confident are you that the sexual abuse did occur?

Please circle one number:

1. Very confident it did not occur
2. Fairly confident it did not occur
3. Slightly confident it did not occur
4. Slightly confident it did occur
5. Fairly confident it did occur
6. Very confident it did occur

Table 2.4 Fifteen Vignette Factors

Factor	Level 1	Level 2
Alleged Victim		
A Gender	Male	Female
B Age	3 to 8 years	13 to 16 years
C Race	Minority	White
D Behavioral changes	Yes	No
E Affect about event	No affect	Affect
Alleged Perpetrator		
F Socioeconomic status	Professional	Nonprofessional
G Relationship to alleged victim	Familial	Nonfamilial
H Age	16 to 25 years	26+ years
I Race	Minority	White
J History of violence	Yes	No
K History of substance abuse	Yes	No
Alleged Victim's Caretaker(s)		
L Childhood history of sexual abuse	Yes	No
M History of psychiatric illness	Yes	No
Family		
N Prior contact with protective service agencies	Yes	No
O Child custody-visitation issues	Yes	No

literature to be predictive of sexual abuse or, from clinical observations by HJ, to influence clinical judgments.

Factors were organized within four categories: the alleged victim, the victim's nonoffending caretaker(s), the alleged perpetrator,[10] and family background. The individual factors were (a) victim and perpetrator race (Hampton & Newberger, 1985); (b) behavioral changes of the victim (Browne & Finkelhor, 1986a); (c) victim gender and age

(National Center on Child Abuse and Neglect, 1988); (d) victim affect (Goodwin, 1985); (e) perpetrator's relationship to the victim; (f) perpetrator's age, socioeconomic status (SES), and history of substance abuse and violence (Finkelhor, 1984); (g) caretaker's history of sexual abuse and history of psychiatric illness; (h) family's prior contact with protective services; and (i) custody issues (Green, 1986). Factors known to be exceptionally powerful in their effect on credibility, such as medical-physical findings and a perpetrator's confession, were excluded, as were factors that are found in only a small percentage of reported cases (e.g., female perpetrators).

The 15 two-level case factors were organized in the 16 vignettes using a fractional orthogonal Taguchi style experimental design (Taguchi & Konishi, 1987). The vignettes were constructed to follow the patterns shown in Table 2.5.

Where a "1" is shown, the first level of the factor was used; where a "2" is shown, the second level of the factor was used (see Table 2.4 for the definitions of Levels 1 and 2 for each case factor). The asterisks in Table 2.5 designate factor levels where, as a result of a clerical error, the wrong level (according to the L16 experimental design) was assigned. This had only minor effects on the orthogonality of the design, essentially causing the factors of "Family Prior Contact with Protective Service Agencies" and "Family Child Custody-Visitation Issues" to correlate +/- 0.126 with the other factors (the planned correlation was, of course, 0.00).

Each row shown in Table 2.5 is a blueprint for the construction of one vignette. For example, the case vignette "David" (see Appendix A, Vignette #16) was created by following the eighth row of the design matrix.

Thus, David is at level 1 for the first factor, A (i.e., he is male). Note that the next four factors (B through E) require level 2 (i.e., David is an adolescent who is Caucasian). Although David's behavior does not change following the alleged abuse, he does show negative affect when talking about the event. Continuing along row eight, the next two factors (F and G) require level 1; the alleged perpetrator is both a professional and a family member.

The two factors H and I require level 2; the alleged perpetrator is over 26 years old and is Caucasian. According to the design matrix, the next four factors (J through M) are at level 1; the alleged perpetrator has a history of violence and substance abuse; the nonoffend-

Table 2.5 Vignette Factor Levels by Case

							Case								
Factor[a]	A	B	C	D	E	F	G	H	I	J	K	L	M	N	O
Billy	1	1	1	1	1	1	1	1	1	1	1	1	1	1	1
Juan	1	1	1	1	1	1	1	2	2	2	2	2	2	2	2
Eddie	1	1	1	2	2	2	2	2*	2*	2*	2*	1*	1*	1*	1*
Joey	1	1	1	2	2	2	2	2	2	1*	1*	1	1	1	1
Jeff	1	2	2	1	1	2	2	1	1	2	2	1	1	2	2
Scott	1	2	2	1	1	2	2	2	2	1	1	2	2	1	1
Harry	1	2	2	2	2	1	1	1	1	2	2	2	2	1	1
David	1	2	2	2	2	1	1	2	2	1	1	1	1	2	2
Jean	2	1	2	1	2	1	2	1	2	1	2	1	2	1	2
Linda	2	1	2	1	2	1	2	2	1	2	1	2	1	1	2
Jenny	2	1	2	2	1	2	1	1	2	1	2	2	1	2	1
Donna	2	1	2	2	1	2	1	2	1	2	1	1	2	1	2
Paula	2	2	1	1	2	2	1	1	2	2	1	1	2	2	1
Rose	2	2	1	1	2	2	1	2	1	1	2	2	1	1	2
Rita	2	2	1	2	1	1	2	1	2	2	1	2	1	1	2
Nancy	2	2	1	2	1	1	2	2	1	1	2	1	2	2	1

NOTE: The asterisk (*) indicates items in which, as a result of a clerical error, the incorrect level was used. Where a 1* appears, the Taguchi L16 level should be a 2, where a 2* appears the L16 level should be a 1. See text for discussion of the effects of these errors.
a. See Table 2.2 for the description of the factors and levels.

ing caretaker was sexually abused as a child and has a history of psychiatric illness. The last two factors in row eight (N and O) require level 2; David's family has had no prior contact with protective services nor are custody-visitation issues involved in the case.

The vignettes were constructed to minimize the correlation among the 15 case factors (zero or nearly zero for all 15 factors). This allowed the independent measurement of the effects of each of the 15 factors (see Appendix 4 for discussion of the Taguchi style experimental design in the construction of vignettes).

Guided by the current abuse literature, we initially hypothesized that the following variable levels would elicit high credibility values: female victims (Margolin, 1994; Russell, 1983, 1984, 1986), older victims (German, Habenicht, & Futcher, 1990; Thoennes & Tjaden, 1990), victims whose behavior had changed following the alleged abuse (Bressee et al., 1986; DeJong, 1985; Deltaglia, 1990; Koverola, Pound, Heger, & Lytle, 1993; Murphy et al., 1991), older perpetrators, perpetrators who were family members (Anderson et al., 1993; Margolin, 1994; Pierce & Pierce, 1985), perpetrators who had a history of substance abuse or violence (Gelinas, 1983; Kameen & Thompson, 1983; Margolin, 1994; Murphy et al., 1991; Sirles et al., 1989; Waterhouse & Carnie, 1992), nonoffending caretakers with a childhood history of sexual abuse or psychiatric illness (Pierce & Pierce, 1985), and families with prior contact with protective services (Murphy et al., 1991; Pierce & Pierce, 1985). Variables we initially expected (or hoped) to have little effect on credibility were (a) race of the victim (Cross et al., 1994; Laumann, Gagnon, Michael, & Michaels, 1994; Wyatt, 1985) and perpetrator, (b) the victim's affect when disclosing the abuse, (c) socioeconomic status of the perpetrator[11] (Sedney & Brooks, 1984), and (d) family custody-visitation issues (Thoennes & Tjaden, 1990).

Statistical Analysis

Two distinct multiple-regression approaches were used to analyze our data.

Regression #1: Case Factors. The multiple regression used in this study is different from the usual multiple regression where individuals are the units of analysis. In this regression analysis, the 15 case factors (see Table 2.4) were the independent variables. The unit of analysis was the vignette as rated by a particular group of respondents. We designed our survey with eight independent samples divided by gender and discipline to yield eight groups: one group each of male and female clinicians for each of the four disciplines. For each of these eight populations, we obtained the average credibility rating for each of the 16 vignettes.

There were thus 128 units of analysis (16 vignettes by two genders by four disciplines). The dependent variable was the average credibility rating for each vignette for the respective group. The independent variables were the 15 vignette factors plus the gender of the rating group.

Regression #2: Respondent Factors. In this regression, the units of analysis were individual respondents. The dependent variable was the average credibility score of each of the 655 respondents averaged across all 16 vignettes. Consequently, there were 655 respondent units of analysis for these regressions. The dependent variable measured the clinicians' average level of belief or disbelief of the allegations across the different sexual abuse allegations.

For this analysis, the average credibility score may be viewed as a 16-item scale within which each vignette is one item. The Cronbach alpha reliability coefficient of the scale was .87, a highly respectable value (DeVellis, 1991). A factor analysis of the 16 vignettes showed that the first principal axis solution accounted for 29.9% of the variance and the Cattell Scree test indicated only one factor (Cattell, 1966). The dependent variable, then, is reasonably unifactorial and highly reliable.

The independent variables for these analyses were the 12 characteristics of the respondents (see Table 2.2) thought to have an effect on the extent to which clinicians believe or disbelieve sexual abuse allegations.

Limitations

In contrast to previous studies, we sought to determine the bases on which professionals determine the credibility of sexual abuse allegations. It was not the purpose of this study, nor was it feasible within its methodology, to measure the accuracy of clinicians' judgments. As Berliner and Conte (1993) point out, there is no method currently available that can establish the absolute validity of sexual abuse allegations.

This study provides the prevalence rates of childhood sexual and physical abuse among clinicians between the ages of 27 to 73 years. However, it does not give the current incidence of abuse. Studies of 18-year-olds are required to yield an estimate of the rates of abuse, particularly sexual abuse, over the past 10 to 15 years.

The use of different definitions of sexual and physical abuse continues to cause confusion in the interpretation of relevant statistics. The Kempe (1978) and Giovannoni (Giovannoni & Becerra, 1979, p. 83) definitions used in this study were a reasonable choice for our research purposes. However, as Briere (1992), in his recent review of sexual abuse research, notes, "Until researchers settle on a standard definition of what does and does not constitute sexual abuse, findings regarding abuse (prevalence) and its correlates must be evaluated in terms of the specific definition being used" (p. 198), thereby limiting its generalizability.

The fractional factorial design we used does not allow independent measurement of interaction effects between two or more factors. Experimental research seeking such interactions is an important area for further study. Although the personal and case factors were chosen carefully, inclusion of a different set of variables would probably change the relative effects of each of the factors.

Vignette methodologies have the disadvantage that subjects are asked to respond to simulated and narrowly defined events. Thus, the association between respondents' reactions to vignettes and their reactions in the "real world" of clinical practice is unclear. Recent attempts to validate vignette studies have been difficult and inconclusive (Lanza, 1990; Lanza & Carifo, 1992). Clearly, research in this area is important.

Although our overall sample was large ($N = 655$), the number of abused respondents was relatively small. This limited our statistical power when examining mediating variables, such as duration, frequency, and type of abuse and relationship of perpetrator to victim. A larger sample of those abused may have shown significant effects for these variables. This is an important area for future research.

The 42% response rate obtained, although respectable, does limit the generalizability of the findings. However, the similarity of our findings to results from other studies of professionals (Kelley, 1990; Kendall-Tackett & Watson, 1991; Saunders, 1988) supports the presumption of reasonable reliability. The sample used in this study includes clinicians from various disciplines responsible for the evaluation and care of sexually abused children and their families. They do not, however, represent experts in the field. This research should be extended to a sample of professionals who have had extended, specialized education, training, and experience in evaluating sexual abuse allegations. In addition, other populations that evaluate child sexual abuse allegations, such as protective service workers, teachers, judges, lawyers, and police investigators, should be studied.

Response Bias Study

To examine a possible response bias for abuse history, we conducted a survey of nonrespondents to determine if there were significant differences in the prevalence of childhood abuse histories between respondents and nonrespondents. Three hundred single-page questionnaires were sent to a random sample of nonrespondents to the first survey; 102 responses were received (a 34% response rate). We limited our inquiry to five questions to minimize the time required to complete the questionnaire and to maximize the response rate (see Appendix E). Applying the same definitions of abuse used in the initial questionnaire, we asked if the respondent (to age 18) had (a) been sexually abused, (b) been physically abused, (c) witnessed sexual abuse, or (d) witnessed physical abuse (or a combination of these).

Because the original questionnaire was anonymous, we could distinguish nonrespondents from respondents only by identifying clinicians who had not returned the postcard to request a free book. However, when we compared the postcard return rate with that of the questionnaire, we found we had received fewer postcards than questionnaires. Clearly, some individuals classified as nonrespondents had responded but had not returned the postcard. To control for this potential duplication bias, we asked a fifth question: had respondents to the follow-up study completed and returned the original questionnaire.

In this substudy, we did not survey by discipline. Consequently, the data we obtained can be compared only in the aggregate (i.e., with the entire sample of the four disciplines included in the initial survey: clinical social workers, pediatricians, psychiatrists, and psychologists). We found no statistically significant differences between the respondents and nonrespondents in the frequency of either their sexual or physical abuse histories. Nonrespondents reported a 12% incidence of childhood sexual abuse, whereas respondents reported 17%. This difference is not statistically significant. The rates of physical abuse were 5% for nonrespondents and 7% for respondents: again, not a statistically significant difference. Furthermore, there was no statistically significant difference for witnessing sexual abuse (3% of nonrespondents, 4% of respondents). There was, however, a significant difference between the two groups in the frequency of witnessing physical abuse (8% for nonrespondents vs. 19% for respondents; $\chi^2 = 5.62$; 1 df; $p < .05$). We concluded that possible response bias (the abused more likely to reply than the nonabused) did not threaten the validity of the study.[12]

The Follow-Up Study

Sample

To obtain more detailed information about the respondents' childhood history of abuse and to identify other, perhaps more subtle effects of childhood victimization, we conducted a follow-up study to compare those who (in the initial survey) reported a childhood history of abuse to those who did not report abuse. We mailed a follow-up questionnaire to the 655 respondents to the initial survey who had returned the postcard requesting a free book. A cover letter asking subjects for their participation, assuring anonymity, and describing the research and its potential contribution to clinical practice was mailed as part of the packet (see Appendix F). The questionnaires were not identifiable by name or number. Again, we offered a summary of the study results and the choice of a free professional book as an incentive to participate in the study. To protect anonymity, we requested that respondents mail the postage-paid book choice card separately.

Respondents

A total of 392 clinicians responded, yielding a 60% response rate. Of the 392 respondents, 220 (56%) were female, 169 (43%) were male (3 respondents did not identify their gender). By discipline, 122 (31%) were clinical social workers, 56 (14%) were pediatricians, 96 (24%) were psychiatrists, and 107 (27%) were clinical psychologists (11 respondents did not identify their discipline). Ages ranged from 31 to 82 years; the mean age of the respondents was 48.1 years (SD = 10.7). Regarding marital status, 74% were married; 8% had never married; 8% were with a significant other; and 8% were divorced, separated, or widowed. No information was available on the marital status of 2%. The percentage who had or were raising children was 76%; 23% had not.

These demographic descriptions were similar to the first sample, with an increase of the percentage of social workers (26% of the initial study; 31% of the follow-up) and a decrease in the percentage of pediatricians from 20% to 14%. The follow-up sample was, of course, 2 years older; average age 48.1 years compared to 46.1 years in the initial study. The same fractions were female (56%), married (74%), and had raised one or more children (76%). Of the respondents, 91% reported a heterosexual orientation, 4% a homosexual orientation, 2% identified themselves as bisexual, and 1% asexual; 2% did not declare their sexual orientation.

The Follow-Up Questionnaire

In the follow-up questionnaire, we again asked clinicians if they had experienced or witnessed abuse as children (see Appendix G). If they responded affirmatively, we asked about the abuse in greater depth. For example the abuse had been accompanied by force or threat, and had they told anyone about the abuse? If they had, we wanted to know if they were believed and if they had received help. Our questions were guided by the abuse literature that suggests these factors may affect the sequelae of child abuse, either positively or negatively.

To determine possible associations between a childhood history of abuse and mental health status, we asked each respondent to complete the Derogatis Brief Symptom Inventory (BSI; Derogatis, 1993) and the Mississippi Civilian Post-Traumatic Stress Disorder (MCPTSD) scale (Keane, 1988).

The BSI is a shortened form of the SCL-90-R instrument (Derogatis, 1983; Derogatis et al., 1973; Derogatis, Rickels, & Rock, 1976), containing 53 items that measure nine primary symptom scales and a Global Severity Index. To examine the relationship between a childhood history of abuse and post-traumatic stress disorder, we used the 39-item MCPTSD.

From the sexual abuse literature and HJ's clinical experience, we expected that a childhood history of abuse would have an impact on various aspects of respondents' personal and professional lives. Therefore, we asked questions about career satisfaction, sexual functioning, sexual preference, personal relationships, and professional boundaries. Vignettes were not employed in the follow-up questionnaire.

Limitations

Our follow-up and initial surveys share the limitations of all self-reported, retrospective research. The data are necessarily dependent on the meaning our respondents have made of their experiences and their willingness to report honestly their life events as they remember them. The sensitive nature of the questions and the secrecy typically associated with sexual abuse suggest that the results reported in the initial survey and the follow-up probably underestimate both the prevalence of childhood abuse and its effects on the personal and professional lives of our respondents.

Summary and Conclusions

We conducted the initial and follow-up surveys to determine the prevalence and effects of a childhood history of abuse among practicing clinicians. In the initial study, we used both an experimental vignette design in which 15 factors were systematically varied among 16 hypothetical vignettes and a self-administered questionnaire. In the follow-up study, we used a more detailed self-administered questionnaire to measure the effects of childhood abuse on personal and professional experiences and two standardized instruments to measure mental health status. The results, in some aspects very surprising, are presented and discussed in the following chapters.

Notes

1. We drew from *The NASW Register of Clinical Social Workers* (5th ed., 1987); *The 1989 Fellowship Directory*, American Academy of Pediatrics; *The Biographical Directory, 1989*, Washington, DC: American Psychiatric Association; and *The 1987-1988 Directory of the American Psychological Association.*
    Because the sampling frame was defined by these registers, professionals who were not members of these associations are not represented in our sample. This may be a particular problem with the social work register because many qualified social work practitioners choose not to be included in the social work clinical register.
2. Although pediatricians are not mental health professionals, they are usually included as members of sexual abuse evaluation teams.
3. As a result of a miscalculation of the number of professionals in the social work register, the sample of 400 was completely drawn using names beginning with "A" to "T" (i.e., before the register was completed). To ensure representation of all NASW members, an additional 35 were randomly selected from listings between "U" and "Z."
4. The high (72%) rate may reflect a sampling bias. However, the substantial prevalence rates reported in both inpatient and outpatient mental health settings

suggest that any clinician with a caseload of more than 24 clients will see at least one client who has a childhood history of sexual abuse.

5. NIMH Grant #MH19076-01.

6. We gratefully acknowledge assistance from Jason Aronson, Inc., for providing us with the professional books and processing the requests.

7. We speculate that the pediatricians' lower response rate, compared to the other disciplines, may, in part, have resulted from the books that we offered. All were on psychological or psychiatric topics.

8. Dillman reports survey responses up to 80%. Possible reasons for our lower response rate are the length of time required to read and rate the vignettes and complete the demographic portion of the questionnaire (approximately 90 minutes). Furthermore, economic constraints precluded the extensive telephone and telegram follow-up recommended by Dillman.

9. We used this set of scale alternatives because our focus was on determining the credibility of an allegation, not on whether it should be reported.

10. Henceforth, "victim" and "perpetrator" stand for the vignette factors "alleged victim" and "alleged perpetrator".

11. Evaluation of the relative risk of child sexual abuse as a fuction of the SES of the perpetrator is complicated by the inconclusiveness of the literature on the subject, and by the nature of the design of our study (See Chapter 5).

12. A larger sample size might find a statistically significant tendency towards greater response by those with a childhood history of abuse, making our prevalence rates somewhat inflated. However, as discussed in Chapter 3, our prevalence rates are consistent with those reported in other non-clinical samples.

3

Prevalence and Characteristics of Abuse Among Clinicians

Overview

For the initial sample of clinicians, we found the following reported rates of childhood abuse:

21% physically abused, sexually abused, or both
14% sexually abused only
4% physically abused only
3% both physically and sexually abused

According to our respondents' reports,

The occurrence of either physical or sexual abuse increased the probability of the other abuse.

Women were more likely than men to have been abused (20% vs. 13%).

Men and women in the youngest age cohorts (under 46 years) on average report the same rates of sexual abuse (15% for both males and females).

Women born prior to 1934 (age 56+ years) and between 1934 and 1943 (age 46 to 55 years) were more likely than their younger cohorts to report a childhood history of sexual abuse.

Men born prior to 1934 were less likely than their younger cohorts to report a childhood history of sexual abuse.

We also found the following:

The modal age at which respondents were sexually abused was 8 years.

The modal age at which respondents were physically abused was about 10 years.

Abused respondents in this study differed from abused clinical populations by a later age at onset, a shorter duration of abuse, and a lower rate of abuse by a family member.

Introduction

In this chapter, we present the prevalence rates for childhood sexual and physical abuse (to age 18 years) reported by the clinical social workers, pediatricians, psychiatrists, and psychologists who participated in our initial survey. We also present some characteristics of the abused, the abuser, and the abuse.[1] The data presented here are derived solely from anonymous responses to our questionnaire. We have no independent evidence for the validity of the self-reports of our respondents. Our findings are dependent on the respondents' willingness to disclose their abuse, their retrospective recollections, and their application of the Kempe (1978) and Giovannoni and Becerra (1979) definitions to their childhood experiences (see discussion to follow). However, because much childhood abuse is concealed due to the secrecy, fear, and shame that surround it (Laumann et al., 1994), we believe that our prevalence rates are probably underestimates.

Sexual and Physical Abuse

Sexual abuse prevalence rates found in other studies range from 19% to 38% for girls (Browne & Finkelhor, 1986a; Russell, 1983) and 3% to 15% for boys (Finkelhor, 1984), depending on the definitions of abuse, the population sampled, and methodology. In both our initial and follow-up surveys, we defined sexual abuse as "the involvement of dependent, developmentally immature children and adolescents in sex acts that they do not fully comprehend and to which they are unable to give informed consent or that violate the social taboos of family roles" (Kempe, 1978, p. 382). We asked each respondent, "Within this definition, were you ever the victim of sexual abuse?"

Of our initial sample of 655 clinicians, 110 (about 17%) reported a childhood history of sexual abuse. Included in the 17% sexually abused were 3% (of the total) who reported both sexual and physical abuse (i.e., about 18% of the sexually abused had also been physically abused; see the following discussion for the definition of physical abuse).

Our findings confirm previous reports that a history of childhood sexual abuse is not uncommon among practicing professionals. For example, Howe et al. (1988), in their study of mostly social workers, psychologists, and psychiatrists, found an overall rate of abuse higher than ours (33% vs. 21%). However, the percentage of their respondents reporting sexual abuse was significantly lower (8% vs. 17%). Our rate is closer to Kelley's (1990) finding that 13% of the respondents in her sample of child protective workers, nurses, and police officers reported a personal history of childhood sexual abuse. The discrepancy between the Howe et al. study and ours may be attributed to their lack of a clear definition of abuse. A comparative summary of reported prevalence rates of childhood sexual abuse is given in Table 3.1.

In our study, only 7% reported a history of physical abuse. Clinical samples of reported abuse (American Association for Protecting Children [AAPC], 1988; U.S. Department of Health and Human Services, 1988) show a ratio of physical to sexual abuse the reverse of our finding. Of all children in this country reported as maltreated, about twice as many are reported for physical abuse as for sexual abuse.[2]

Table 3.1 Reported Prevalence of Sexual Abuse

Study	Sexual Abuse Prevalence	Sample
Professional Samples		
Elliott and Briere (1992)	26.9% of women	Randomly drawn mail survey of female professionals (N = 2,963)
Feldman-Summers and Pope (1994)	26% of women, 17% of men	Randomly drawn sample of psychologists (N = 500)
Howe et al. (1988)	9.4% of women, 5.6% of men	Nonprobability sample of professionals (N = 106): social workers, psychologists, and psychiatrists
Kelley (1990)	13% of both males and females	Nonprobability sample of child protective workers, nurses, and police officers (N = 228)
Jackson and Nuttall (1993)	20% of women, 13% of men	Randomly drawn national sample of professionals (N = 655): clinical social workers, clinical psychologists, pediatricians, and psychiatrists
Community Samples		
Anderson et al. (1993)	32% of women	Randomly drawn community sample of women in New Zealand (N = 500)
Finkelhor, Hotaling, Lewis, and Smith (1990)	27% of women, 16% of men	Randomly drawn national telephone survey (N = 2,626)
Goldman and Goldman (1988)	28% of girls, 9% of boys	Nonprobability community sample in Australia (N = 991)
Janus and Janus (1993)	23% of women, 11% of men	Nonprobability community sample surveyed by telephone (N = 2,689)
Laumann, Gagnon, Michael, and Michaels (1994)	17% of women, 12% of men	Randomly drawn national survey of face-to-face interviews (N = 3,432)
Moore and Schussel (1995)	30% of mothers, 9% of fathers	Randomly drawn national sample surveyed by telephone (N = 1,000)
Clinical Samples		
Kolko, Moser, and Weldy (1988)	78% of children (ages 5-14)	Nonprobability sample of child psychiatric inpatients (N = 103) and their parents
Swett and Halpert (1993)	81% of women	Nonprobability sample of women in an inpatient psychiatric facility (N = 88)

It is not surprising that the highest rates of abuse are found among psychiatric inpatient populations (Anderson et al., 1993; Bryer, Nelson, Miller, & Krol, 1987; Carmen, Reiker, & Mills, 1984). For example, Swett and Halpert (1993), in their study of 88 women hospitalized in an inpatient psychiatric facility, found that 81% reported histories of either physical or sexual abuse or both. Similarly, a sample of 103 child psychiatric inpatients and their parents (Kolko et al., 1988) yielded a 78% rate of abuse.

This high incidence of sexual abuse is not unique to this country. Available data suggest that the sexual maltreatment of children is a general problem, at least in the industrial, democratic societies that value scientific, objective reporting (or consider childhood sexual abuse a problem). In a community sample in New Zealand, about one third of 500 women reported a history of sexual abuse prior to age 16 (Anderson et al., 1993). In another study of the prevalence and nature of child sexual abuse in Australia, Goldman and Goldman (1988) replicated Finkelhor's (1979a) survey of U.S. college students. The Goldmans found that 28% of girls and 9% of boys reported a sexual experience before age 13 with a person at least 5 years older.

As part of a community survey on sexual behavior, Janus and Janus (1993) conducted a telephone survey of 2,689 men and women (males = 1,318; females = 1,371) to determine the prevalence of child sexual abuse.[3] They report a prevalence rate similar to ours: 11% for men and 23% for women. Using a nationally representative random-digit phone approach, the Gallup Organization (Moore & Schussel, 1995) interviewed 1,000 parents about their own and their children's abuse.[4] They found that 20% of the respondents had been physically abused as children (26% of fathers; 17% of mothers). Similar to the results of the Anderson et al. study, 23% of the parents (30% of mothers; 9% of fathers) reported a childhood history of sexual abuse. Based on a random selection of one child per family, parents in the Moore and Schussel study reported that 5.7% of their children had been sexually abused prior to the time of the study (6.1% of boys; 5.3% of girls). The difference in the rates of abuse for parents and those reported for their children may be due to the hesitation children have to disclose their victimization, either to their parents or to authorities. An alternative explanation may be that parents are reluctant to acknowledge that their children have been victims of sexual abuse in general and of intrafamilial abuse in particular. Finkelhor (1994), in his review of international studies of child sexual abuse, also found prevalence rates similar to those reported in this country. He notes that more sophisticated studies are needed to allow meaningful comparison of rates between different cultures—a difficult but critically important task.

Gender and Sexual Abuse

The sexual abuse literature overwhelmingly supports the conclusion that more females than males are sexually abused (American Association for Protecting Children, 1988; Browne & Finkelhor, 1986a, 1986b; DeJong & Emmet, 1983; Ellerstein & Canavan, 1980; Finkelhor, 1980; Finkelhor & Hotaling, 1984; Finkelhor et al., 1990; Murman, Dorko, Brown, & Tolley, 1991; Russell, Russell, 1984, 1986; Sansonnet-Hayden, Haley, Marriage, & Fine, 1987; U.S. Department of Health and Human Services [USDHHS], 1988). It is interesting that the USDHHS (1992) reports that the ratio of reported female to male sexual abuse increases with age, ranging from two to one in infancy to about seven to one by age 14 years, suggesting that boys may become more reluctant to report with age because of increasing concerns about sexuality or that they become less vulnerable (perhaps as a function of their size and strength). In contrast, girls become more vulnerable (perhaps as a function of their more visible sexual characteristics).

The rates of sexual abuse reported in our study show that females, on average, suffer sexual abuse at a significantly greater rate than do males. However, between-gender differences were smaller than expected. Of the 287 male respondents, 13% ($N = 38$) reported sexual abuse as children; 20% ($N = 72$) of the 365 female respondents reported such abuse.[5] Thus, applying Kempe's (1978) definition of sexual abuse, about one fifth of the female clinicians and about one in seven to one in eight of the male clinicians reported that they had been sexually abused as children. This difference was significant at the alpha .05 level (χ^2 analysis).

We analyzed our data to determine if the gender differences in prevalence rates were correlated with profession. The reported frequencies for sexual abuse were 21% for social workers, 11% for pediatricians, 18% for psychologists, and 16% for psychiatrists. Chi square analysis of gender differences across all four disciplines for sexual abuse was not statistically significant. However, post-hoc comparisons between female pediatricians (low rates) and all other women and between male social workers (higher rates) and all other men showed significant differences at the .05 level (see following discussion).

When we examined a childhood history of sexual abuse by gender within the disciplines, we found a gender difference in the

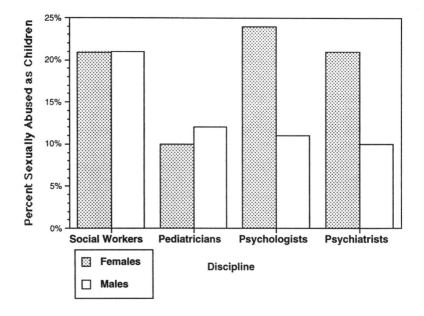

Figure 3.1. Childhood Sexual Abuse by Discipline and Gender

psychologist and psychiatrist cohorts (see Figure 3.1). In these two disciplines, women were twice as likely to have been sexually abused as were men (21% for female psychiatrists vs. 10% for male psychiatrists; 24% female psychologists vs. 11% for male psychologists). For social workers (21% for both genders) and for pediatricians (12% and 10%), the rates for sexual abuse showed no gender difference.

Another perspective on these differences is that the rate for females was about 22% for all disciplines, except for pediatricians where it was about half, or 10%. Males show about half the female base rate (11%) for all disciplines, except social work, where it is twice as great and equal to the female rate.

Although the overall ratio of three sexually abused females to two males found in our study is lower than that typically reported in clinical populations (DeJong & Emmet, 1983; Ellerstein & Canavan, 1980; Lanktree, Briere, & Zaidi, 1991; Sansonnet-Hayden et al., 1987; USDHHS, 1988), it is consistent with studies of other professional and nonclinical samples (Feldman-Summers & Pope, 1994; Finkelhor et al., 1990; Goldman & Goldman, 1988; Laumann et al., 1994) that place the male-to-female ratio anywhere from three to two to two to one.

In one of the early surveys of the prevalence of sexual abuse, Finkelhor (1980) found, in a nonprobability sample of 800 college students, that women were twice as likely as men to report a childhood history of sexual abuse. In 1990, Finkelhor et al. (1990) conducted the first national survey of a randomly drawn community sample of men and women to determine the prevalence, characteristics, and risk factors of sexual abuse. Improving on previous methodologies, they gave respondents repeated opportunities to disclose sexual abuse. Their findings confirm earlier results obtained from community samples in which women reported a prevalence rate not quite twice that of men (27% for women; 16% for men).

In a landmark study of a national, randomly drawn community sample (N = 3,432) designed to examine sexual practices in the United States, University of Chicago researchers (Laumann et al., 1994) found prevalence rates for men and women consistent with previous studies of nonclinical samples. They used a relatively narrow definition of sexual abuse that excluded reports of voyeurism or exhibitionism. Respondents were asked "whether they had been touched sexually by anyone before puberty or when they were twelve or thirteen years of age" (p. 340). Women reported a 17% rate; men, 12%.

Consistent with the community surveys cited above, Howe et al. (1988), in their sample of 106 professionals, found that females in all groups were more likely to have been sexually abused than were males (9.4% for females; 5.6% for males). In a recent study of a random sample of psychologists, Feldman-Summers and Pope (1994) examined memory recall in abused respondents. The prevalence rate of childhood sexual abuse was 26% for women and 17% for men.

Because the female-male abuse ratio is higher for clinical samples (about 2.5 females abused to 1 male abused), compared to nonclinical samples (about 1.5 to 1), male victims may be underrepresented among reported (clinical) cases of sexual abuse (Finkelhor, 1984). Various explanations have been offered for the disproportionate numbers of females reported as abused. From a sociological perspective, Finkelhor (1984) suggests that female vulnerability to abuse is a negative consequence of societal attitudes that place women and children in powerless positions, making them targets for male predators.

From a systems perspective, Finkelhor (1984) also proposes that the male-female ratio may be an artifact of agency service patterns. Organizations such as child welfare and other protective service agencies account for the majority of reported cases of child abuse and neglect. Because their sexual abuse referrals are primarily cases of intrafamilial abuse, they will, accordingly, have higher case loads of girls, because boys are more likely to be victims of extrafamilial abuse (see following sections). In addition, hospitals are more likely to provide services for intrafamilial or rape cases where the possibility of pregnancy makes the need for medical evaluation more urgent.

Another explanation for the between-gender discrepancies in prevalence rates is that boys, on average, are less likely than girls to disclose their sexual abuse. In our follow-up study, only 52% of the sexually abused men, but 73% of the sexually abused women, had disclosed the sexual abuse ($p <60 .05$). In contrast, there was no significant gender effect on disclosure of physical abuse; 59% of the men and 63% of the women revealed their physical abuse. As a partial explanation, Finkelhor (1984) proposes that the male socialization process emphasizes independence, discouraging and stigmatizing behaviors that may be viewed as evidence of weakness. Because most sexually abused boys are abused by males, the anxieties that all young victims have of exposing their victimization is exacerbated by the additional fear of being labeled homosexual (Faller, 1990; Johnson & Shrier, 1985; Nasjleti, 1980).

Cohort Age

The obvious question about the enormous recent increase in reported sexual abuse is, "Is it real?"—or does it result from increased awareness and reporting laws? In search for an answer, we analyzed the percentage of respondents reporting sexual and physical abuse by age cohort.[6]

We found an interesting interaction between age and gender for sexual abuse (see Figure 3.2). Women born before 1934 and between 1934 and 1943 were more likely to report sexual abuse (29% and 26.5%, respectively) than those born between 1944 and 1953 (12%) and those born after 1953 (18%). Thus for women, there is a direct relationship between age and incidence, with a declining rate of sexual abuse from a mean of 28% in the two oldest cohorts to 15% in the two youngest cohorts—a decrease by a factor of almost two.

For men, the picture is quite different. The three youngest cohorts are fairly equivalent, averaging about 17%. However, the oldest male cohort (born prior to 1934) has a significantly lower rate;

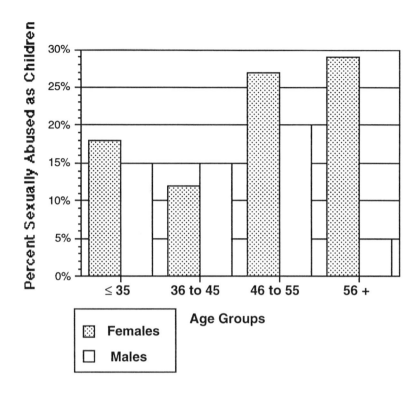

Figure 3.2. Childhood Sexual Abuse by Age Group and Gender

only 5% of this group reported having been sexually abused. It is surprising that men and women in the two youngest cohorts report the same mean rates of sexual abuse (15% for both genders).

The longitudinal view of the incidence of sexual abuse in this sample shows strikingly different reporting trends in the male and female cohorts. Rates of sexual abuse among the professional women who participated in our study have been sharply reduced in 30 to 40 years. In contrast, rates of sexual abuse among the men who participated in our study show a rate that has remained fairly constant (15% to 20%) since 1936, after a sudden increase from a low of 5%. We found no significant differences by age cohort for respondents who reported a history of physical abuse.

Finkelhor et al.'s (1990) national survey of adults for history of childhood sexual abuse is consistent with our findings for men but not for women. They found that men over 60 years of age reported a lower rate of childhood sexual abuse than did their younger cohorts. However, reversing our trend, they found that women in the 60+ age cohort reported significantly lower rates of abuse than did women in the younger cohorts, suggesting an increase rather than a decrease in abuse among younger women. Finkelhor suggests that their findings may be attributed to the older group's inability to remember the abuse. This speculation is consistent with their data (although one might disagree with its underlying assumption) but not with our results. Similarly, the suggestion that the increased rate of sexual abuse he finds among the younger female cohort may be a result of lessened stigma and consequently, less reluctance to report may be a plausible explanation for his data but not for our results.

Contrary to Finkelhor et al.'s (1990) findings, we show a significant decline in sexual abuse in recent years, at least as reported by these professional women. Furthermore, we find that recent rates of sexual abuse are about equal for both genders. We speculate that the increase in reports of male sexual abuse may reflect greater willingness on the part of younger rather than older men to disclose their abuse. We might expect older men to be more likely than younger men to fear the label of homosexuality and therefore, to be reluctant to disclose their victimization. As a result of increased tolerance and acceptance of differences in sexual orientation, younger men, particularly the more educated and those in the helping professions, may not have the same anxieties or experience the same constraints.

One possible explanation of the discrepancy between Finkelhor et al.'s (1990) data for the female cohorts and ours may be the differences between professional and community samples. Because women in our sample who had a childhood history of physical or sexual abuse were less likely than their peers without such a history to have raised children, they may have been disproportionately represented in the older cohorts (see Chapter 7). In contrast to a community sample, all our respondents had completed a graduate level of education and were actively involved in their profession. Prior to the 1950s, the challenges of pursuing a graduate education were formidable for mothers raising small children. As a result of the women's movement, marital and family roles became less rigid. For mothers whose options had previously been limited by societal expectations, graduate education and careers became feasible; they were no longer mutually exclusive. Thus, having children was no longer a major impediment for professional women. This societal change may account, in part, for the greater numbers of sexually abused female professionals in the older cohorts and the reduction in the proportion of women professionals who had been sexually abused as children in the younger cohorts.

Increased awareness, education, and prevention programs may also have effectively reduced the rates of sexual abuse for women, at least among professionals. At the same time, these factors may, paradoxically, produce an increase in reports among men by giving them permission to be more candid about their victimization.

Note, however, that the four disciplines in our sample were not similarly distributed by age and gender.[7] We, therefore, conducted a chi square analysis and found significantly different discipline distributions by age (p <60 .00001 for females; p = .019 for males). Among the oldest women respondents (56+ years), social workers were overrepresented, whereas pediatricians were underrepresented. In contrast, female pediatricians and psychiatrists were overrepresented in the two youngest age categories (under 36 years and 36-45 years). Among the men, psychiatrists were overrepresented among the oldest and youngest age categories and underrepresented in the middle category (36 to 45 years old).

To see if the differences in age distribution by discipline affected the rates of sexual abuse by age category, we collapsed the four age categories into two: "Younger" (under 46) and "Older" (over 46) to obtain a large enough sample for the analysis. For males as a whole, and for each of the four disciplines, we found no significant relationship between age and the rate of sexual abuse. About 15% of the men in the Younger group (N = 154) and about 11% of the men in the Older group (N = 133) reported they had been sexually abused as children.

As expected from our earlier results, we found a strong relationship between age and likelihood of sexual abuse for all women in the sample. About 28% (N = 153) of the women in the Older group compared to 14% (N = 212) of the women in the Younger group reported they had been sexually abused as children (η = .16,[8] p = .002).[9] Thus, the age effect (older women more likely to have been sexually abused than younger women) remains for the total female sample. The magnitude of the effect is about the same for social workers, pediatricians, and psychologists but not for psychiatrists.

Clearly, the basic question, whether the rapid increase in reports of abuse is attributable to societal and attitudinal changes or to real increases in the rates of incidence of abuse, requires much additional work to resolve.

Physical Abuse

Gender and Physical Abuse

We defined physical abuse as an act being "inflicted non-accidentally . . . which causes or creates a substantial risk of causing disfigurement, impairment of bodily functioning or other serious physical injury" (Giovannoni & Becerra, 1979, p. 83). We asked each respondent, "Within this definition, were you ever the victim of physical abuse?" In contrast to the national abuse prevalence data (National Center on Child Abuse and Neglect, 1988), our respondents reported physical abuse at a significantly lower rate than sexual abuse. Although their rates were much higher, Elliott and Guy (1993) also found significantly lower rates of physical abuse (13.8% physical abuse vs. 43.3% sexual abuse) in a group of female mental health professionals ($N = 340$).

Consistent with data from the USDHHS (1988), men and women in our study were equally likely to report a childhood history of physical abuse, although at a much lower rate. We find 7% for both genders, whereas USDHHS reports 44% for males and 54% for females. Gil (1973), in his national survey of reported cases of maltreatment, also found equivalent rates by gender (52.6% of males vs. 47.4% of females). However, in contrast to our findings (but consistent with USDHHS, 1992), he did find significant gender differences related to age. In his sample, boys younger than 12 years of age were more likely than girls to be physically abused; during adolescence, girls were more likely than boys to be so abused (63.3% of girls vs. 36.7% of boys). A comparative summary of reported prevalence rates of childhood physical abuse is given in Table 3.2.

It is not clear why the rates of physical abuse reported by our respondents are so much lower than those found in reported cases, community populations, and in Elliott and Guy's professional sample. Possible explanations may be found in the effects of population selection or, as noted earlier, in the relatively restrictive definition used in this study. This is another area for further research.

Although we found no statistically significant main effects on prevalence rates of reported childhood physical abuse for age cohort

Table 3.2 Reported Prevalence of Physical Abuse

Study	Physical Abuse Prevalence	Sample
Jackson and Nuttall (1993)	7% of women, 7% of men	Randomly drawn national sample of professionals (N = 656): clinical social workers, clinical psychologists, pediatricians, and psychiatrists
Moore and Schussel (1995)	17% of mothers, 26% of fathers	Randomly drawn national sample surveyed by telephone (N = 1,000)
Elliott and Guy (1993)	13.8% of women	Randomly drawn mail survey of female mental health professionals (N = 340)
U.S. Department of Health and Human Services (1988)	54% of women, 44% of men	Among those reported abused
Gil (1973)	47% of women, 53% of men	Among those reported physically abused

or discipline, we did observe that the psychiatrist cohort had a much lower rate of physical abuse than the other three disciplines (see Figure 3.3). On average, one in 12 social workers, pediatricians, and psychologists reported a personal history (to age 18 years) of physical abuse, whereas only one in 33 psychiatrists reported such a personal history. A post-hoc comparison of psychiatrists with the other three disciplines combined found chi square significance ($p <60$ .05). Because this was a post-hoc analysis, suitable caution should be exercised until the result is replicated in another sample.

For pediatricians, fewer females than males were physically abused; for psychologists, more females than males were physically abused. These effects were not quite statistically significant, only reaching the $p = .055$ level for an analysis that examined the interaction for psychologists and pediatricians by gender. With a larger sample size, such gender by discipline interactions may prove to be significant in future research.

Association Between Prevalence of Physical and Sexual Abuse

Consistent with the literature (Bryer et al., 1987; Chu & Dill, 1990; Deblinger, McLeer, Atkins, Ralphe, & Foa, 1989; Ogata et al., 1990; Silver, Boon, & Stones, 1983; Sirles et al., 1989; Swett & Halpert,

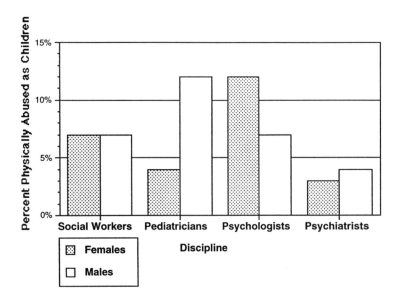

Figure 3.3. Childhood Physical Abuse by Discipline and Gender

1993), we found a strong association between physical and sexual abuse (χ^2, $1_{df} = 17.5$; $p <60$ .0001). About 3% of the total sample (14% of those abused) reported both types of abuse; 14% reported sexual abuse only, whereas 4% reported physical but not sexual abuse. Respondents who had been physically abused were more than twice as likely as those with no history of childhood physical abuse to have been sexually abused. Moreover, respondents who reported a childhood history of sexual abuse were more than 3 times as likely to also report physical abuse as those who had no childhood history of sexual abuse. This relationship held for both genders. Boys and girls who experienced one type of abuse were more likely than the nonabused to have experienced the other.

Although some reports (AAPC, 1988; Finkelhor & Hotaling, 1984) show no close relationship between the occurrence of physical and sexual abuse, Howe et al. (1988), in their survey of professionals, found that 10% of those who reported an abuse history reported more than one type of abuse. Note, however, that Howe and her colleagues requested information about four loosely defined types of abuse (emotional, physical, sexual, and neglect), whereas we limited our questions to physical and sexual maltreatment as they were clearly defined in the questionnaire. Other reports of frequencies of overlapping abuse (Bryer et al., 1987; Chu & Dill, 1990; Deblinger et al., 1989; Ogata et al., 1990; Swett & Halpert, 1993) have been obtained from samples of convenience drawn from psychiatric populations. Frequencies of overlapping abuse reported in these studies are high, ranging from 17% to 67% (see Chapter 6).

Abuse Characteristics

To design and develop effective preventive interventions, it is important to identify the mean age at which abuse is first likely to occur and the ages at which children are most likely to be abused. It is also necessary to determine if there are any associations between these ages and the severity of the sequelae of abuse. Unfortunately, the reliability of reports of the ages at which child abuse begins and most often occurs is difficult to assess. The task of determining the relationship of these abuse characteristics to the degree of initial or later impairment is complicated because workers do not usually report these factors. Those who do, often do not differentiate between intrafamilial and extrafamilial abuse or control for mediating variables, such as duration, relationship to perpetrator, family dysfunction, and so forth. Furthermore, available data are often constrained by sample age, definitional restrictions (Finkelhor, 1986), and time elapsed between disclosure and the first abuse incident (Kendall-Tackett, Williams, & Finkelhor, 1993).

Despite these caveats, a number of abuse factors have been identified in the literature that ameliorate or aggravate the damaging effects of sexual and physical abuse. In the following sections, we discuss some of these factors as reported by our respondents.

Age at Onset of Abuse

We asked each respondent who had reported physical abuse, sexual abuse, or both to circle the age(s) at which they were abused (see Appendix B, Q. 13 and Q. 20). Of the respondents who reported sexual abuse, more than 50% were first abused between the ages of 6 and 10 years (mean age = 8.5 years; SD = 3.5). The age of first abuse

Table 3.3 Reported Age of First Sexual Abuse

Study	Age of First Sexual Abuse	Sample
Nonclinical Samples		
Anderson, Martin, Mullen, Romans, and Herbison (1993)	Between ages 8 and 12 years	Randomly drawn community sample of women in New Zealand (N = 500)
Briere and Runtz (1988)	Mean age 9 years	Nonprobability sample of college women (N = 278)
Elliott and Briere (1992)	About age 9 years	Randomly drawn mail survey of female professionals (N = 2,963)
Feldman-Summers and Pope (1994)	About age 7 years	Randomly drawn sample of psychologists (N = 500)
Jackson and Nuttall (1993)	Between ages 6 and 10 years, mean age 8.5 years	Randomly drawn national sample of professionals (N = 655): clinical social workers, clinical psychologists, pediatricians, and psychiatrists
Clinical Samples		
Aiosa-Karpas, Karpas, Pelcovits, and Kaplan (1991)	Mean age 10.5 years	Nonprobability sample of incestuously abused and nonabused adolescents aged 12 to 19 years (N = 31)
Cosentino, Meyer-Bahlburg, Alpert, and Gaines (1993)	Mean age 6.8 years	Nonprobability sample of sexually abused girls from an outpatient program (N = 20)
Frenken and Stolk (1990)	Between ages 6 and 9 years	Nonprobability survey of professionals and adults incestuously victimized as children (N = 150 professionals; N = 50 adults)
German, Habenicht, and Futcher (1990)	Mean age 10 years	Nonprobability sample of female adolescents (N = 40) abused by biological or surrogate father and were in therapy
Johnson and Schrier (1985)	Between 5 and 12 years	Nonprobability sample of male outpatient adolescents reporting prepuberty sexual abuse (N = 40)
Kendall-Tackett and Simon (1987)	Mean age 7.5 years	Nonprobability chart review of adults who had been sexually victimized as children (N = 365)
Lanktree, Briere, and Zaidi (1991)	Mean age 7.3 years	Randomly selected child outpatient records (N = 64)
Lindberg and Distad (1985)	Between ages 4 and 22 years	Nonprobability outpatient sample of adult women entering therapy (N = 17)

(continued)

Table 3.3 Continued

Study	Age of First Sexual Abuse	Sample
Nash, Zivney, and Hulsey (1993)	Between ages 3 and 15 years (more than half under age 7 years)	Randomly selected records of girls whose sexual abuse had been substantiated ($N = 103$)
Rowan, Foy, Rodriquez, and Ryan (1994)	Mean age 5 years	Nonprobability sample of adults currently in psychotherapy who were sexually abused prior to age 16 by someone 5 years or more older ($N = 47$)
Silver, Boon, and Stones (1983)	Mean age 8 years	Nonprobability volunteer sample of women survivors of incest ($N = 77$)
Swett and Halpert (1993)	Mean age 4 years	Nonprobability sample of women in an inpatient psychiatric facility ($N = 88$)

was similar for the physically abused; over 50% were first abused between the ages of 5 and 10 years (mean age = 8.2 years; $SD = 4.6$). There was no significant difference by gender in mean age at which respondents reported their first abuse for either physical or sexual abuse. A comparative summary of reported age of first sexual abuse is given in Table 3.3.

Our findings are consistent with other reports of the age at onset of abuse for professional and community samples. Elliott and Briere's (1992) investigation of the long-term effects of early childhood sexual abuse on professional women placed their first sexual abuse experience, on average, at about age 9 years. Feldman-Summers and Pope (1994), in their random sample of 500 psychologists, found that age at onset for both physical and sexual abuse was about 7 years. In a randomly drawn community sample of about 500 women in New Zealand, Anderson et al. (1993) asked respondents whether they had experienced unwanted sexual approaches prior to age 16. They found that those who had been so abused reported the first incident between ages 8 and 12 years. Similarly, women in the Briere and Runtz (1988) college sample ($N = 278$) who had been abused prior to age 15, reported that abuse first occurred, on average, at age 9 years.

Studies of psychiatric outpatient samples are less consistent. Reports of age at first abuse range from 4 years to beyond adolescence. For example, Aiosa-Karpas, Karapas, Pelcovitz, and Kaplan (1991) found the mean age at onset of abuse as 10.5 years ($SD = 2.8$)

in their controlled study of a group of incestuously abused and nonabused adolescents who had received psychotherapy (N = 31; ages 12-19 years). Lindberg and Distad (1985), in their outpatient sample of 17 adult women entering therapy (24-44 years old) who had experienced incest as children, found that the age of reported onset ranged from 4 to 22 years.[10]

In an investigation of randomly selected records of 103 girls (ages 5-16) whose sexual abuse had been substantiated and referred to a child guidance clinic, Nash, Zivney, and Hulsey (1993) found that onset ranged from age 3 to 15 years, with more than half under 7 years of age. Cosentino, Meyer-Bahlburg, Alpert, and Gaines (1993), in their study of 20 sexually abused girls (ages 6-12 years) from an outpatient program, found that the mean age of onset was 6.8 years.

In a review of 64 randomly selected child outpatient records (mean age 12.1; SD = 3.87) to determine the impact of direct inquiry about sexual abuse on case finding, Lanktree et al. (1991) found that, among boys and girls who had been abused, the mean age at onset was 7.3 years (range = 3-14 years). In a sample of 40 female adolescents (12-18 years old) who had experienced abuse by a biological or surrogate father and were in therapy (German, Habenicht, & Futcher, 1990), the average age at which abuse had first occurred was 10 years. Johnson and Shrier (1985) found that the age at onset of sexual abuse among 40 male outpatient adolescents who had reported a prepuberty sexual abuse experience was between 5 and 12 years.

For 365 adults who had been sexually victimized as children and were seeking treatment, Kendall-Tackett and Simon (1987) found that the average age of onset was 7.5 years (range 0-20 years). Rowan, Foy, Rodriguez, and Ryan (1994), in their study of 47 adults (ages 20-51 years) sexually abused prior to age 16 by someone 5 or more years their senior, and who were currently in psychotherapy, found that the mean age of onset was 5 years. A survey of a volunteer sample of women survivors of incest (Silver et al., 1983) placed the mean age at which abuse had first occurred at 8 years.

In a study conducted in the Netherlands to examine the quality of professional help incest victims had received (Frenken & Stolk, 1990), respondents reported that abuse had first occurred between the ages of 6 and 9 years. However, in a sample of 88 women in a psychiatric hospital (mean age 33.7; SD = 10.6 years), Swett and Halpert (1993) found much younger mean ages at which abuse had first occurred: age 4 years for sexual abuse; age 5 for physical abuse.

Taking each report at equivalent value,[11] we find that there are no significant differences in the mean age at onset between professional, community, and clinical populations with a grand mean at onset of about 8 years. Within these limits, we conclude that the age of onset does not discriminate between clinical and nonclinical populations.

Ages of Peak Vulnerability for Abuse

Although children are at risk for abuse at any age, the modal age at which respondents in this study were sexually abused was 8 years (SD = 3.5). For both males and females, over 50% of sexual victimization occurred between the ages of 7 and 13 years. The modal age for physical abuse was about 10 years (SD = 3.5).

Consistent with our data, Finkelhor (1979a), in his sample of 796 "normal" college students, found that sexual abuse occurred most often between the ages of 8 and 12 years. These findings were further supported in a later study of a randomly drawn community sample (Finkelhor et al., 1990) in which the median age of sexual abuse was 9.9 years for boys and 9.6 for girls. In another study of a randomly selected community sample of women (N = 500), Anderson et al. (1993) found the greatest risk of sexual abuse to be in preadolescence (age 11). In a large, randomly drawn, community sample to examine sexual practices in the United States (Laumann et al., 1994), sexual contact (defined in the study as sexual touching prior to age 13) was found to occur most often between the ages of 7 and 10 years.

Moore and Schussel (1995), in their telephone interviews of a random sample of parents, found that rates of reported sexual abuse (in the year prior to the study) varied with age. For children to age 4, parents reported a sexual abuse frequency of 0.5%; between the ages of 5 and 8 years, 2.9%; between the ages of 9 and 12, 0.4%; and between the ages of 13 and 17, 3.8%. The possibility that there may be two periods in which children are at peak vulnerability for sexual abuse (early childhood and adolescence) is not unreasonable but requires further investigation. The ages at which respondents in this study reported physical abuse most likely to occur (between ages 4-15 years) are somewhat older than the 3-to-9-years range reported by Gil's (1973) sample of children abused prior to age 18.

Duration of the Abuse

We found no statistically significant gender difference in the mean duration of sexual abuse[12] (males 1.8 years, SD = 3.0; females 1.7 years, SD = 2.6). For both males and females, however, the modal duration of sexual abuse was just one incident (55.3% of the abused males, 54.1% of the abused females). Thirteen percent of the abused men, 13% and 8% of the abused women reported multiple incidents of sexual abuse within 1 year; 32% of the abused men and 38% of the abused women reported a duration of greater than 1 year.

In contrast, 75% of those who reported physical abuse were abused over a period of more than 1 year. The duration of physical abuse was between 2 and 3 times greater than the duration of sexual abuse (males = 4.4 years for physical abuse [SD = 4.3] vs. 1.8 for sexual abuse; females = 5.8 years for physical abuse [SD = 3.7] vs. 1.7 for sexual abuse). The great majority of both men and women reported physical abuse durations of 2 or more years (61% for men; 84% for women). A comparative summary of reported duration of sexual abuse is given in Table 3.4.

Not surprisingly, sexual abuse by a family member continued, on average, longer than abuse by a nonfamily member (about a year). The longer mean duration for a family member was 2.35 (SD = 3.19) years; for those abused by a nonfamily member, the mean was 1.38 (SD = 2.40) years. Whereas the differences in duration between the familial and nonfamilial groups are substantial, the large standard deviations (attributed to the occasional very long durations [10-15 years] reported by some respondents) reduce statistical significance. The average duration of familial sexual abuse reported in our study is somewhat lower than the 3½-year mean duration of incest reported in the literature (Meiselman, 1978).

Consistent with our findings, Cosentino et al. (1993), in their sample of sexually abused outpatient girls (ages 6-12), 90% of whom had been victims of familial sexual abuse, found that the mean duration of abuse was 2.2 years. Lanktree et al. (1991), in their chart review of children seen in an outpatient clinic, who had been abused prior to age 16, found that the average duration of sexual abuse was 2.1 years (82% of cases were intrafamilial).

However, Feldman-Summers and Pope (1994) found that the professionals in their study experienced, on average, more prolonged abuse (about 4 years).

Table 3.4 Reported Duration of Sexual Abuse

Study	Sexual Abuse Duration (In Years)	Sample
Cosentino, Meyer-Bahlberg, Alpert, and Gaines (1993)	2.2	Nonprobability sample of sexually abused girls from an outpatient program (N = 20)
Feldman-Summers and Pope (1994)	About 4	Randomly drawn sample of psychologists (N = 500)
Jackson and Nuttall (1993)	1.7 for girls, 1.8 for boys	Randomly drawn national sample of professionals (N = 655): clinical social workers, clinical psychologists, pediatricians, and psychiatrists
Kendall-Tackett and Simon (1987)	Range from 0 to 24	Nonprobability chart review of adults who had been sexually victimized as children (N = 365)
Lanktree, Briere, and Zaidi (1991)	2.1	Randomly selected child outpatient records (N = 64)
Lindberg and Distad (1985)	About 7	Nonprobability outpatient sample of adult women entering therapy (N = 17)
Nash, Ziveny, and Hulsey (1993)	Mean 2+	Randomly selected records of girls whose sexual abuse had been substantiated (N = 103)
Rowan, Foy, Rodriguez, and Ryan (1994)	6	Nonprobability sample of adults currently in psychotherapy who were sexually abused prior to age 16 by someone 5 years or more older (N = 47)

Lindberg and Distad (1985) examined symptoms in 17 women who reported childhood histories of incest and found average duration to be 7 years. Rowan et al. (1994) reported that among the 47 adults in their clinical outpatient sample who had been sexually abused as children, the modal duration of abuse was 6 years. Kendall-Tackett and Simon (1987), analyzing intake interviews of 365 adults sexually molested as children, found that the persistence of abuse ranged from 0 (single incident) to 24 years. Nash et al. (1993), in their randomly drawn record review of 102 sexually abused girls, found that the duration of abuse ranged from one day to 10 years (mean, 2+ years).

The lower average duration of sexual abuse in our population probably reflects the relatively low rate of incest reported by our respondents. The longer duration of physical abuse reported by women as compared to men in this study is not surprising. Once

Table 3.5 "Other" Types of Sexual Abuse Reported by Males

Shown pictures—talked to about sexual things
Made to watch adult masturbate
Anal sex
Attempted fondling
Penile touch, rectal area
A school teacher masturbated while talking to me
Shown pornographic pictures of young boys by an adult male
Female relative used me to obtain sexual pleasure by having my genitals rub hers

NOTE: Types of abuse are reported in respondents' own words.

males reach puberty, their body size limits their vulnerability to abuse. Because girls continue to be physically vulnerable to those stronger than themselves, their safety remains precarious.

Type of Abuse

In our initial survey, we asked respondents who reported a childhood history of physical or sexual abuse or both to note the ages during which the abuse had occurred. In the follow-up survey, we also requested descriptions of the type of sexual contact they had experienced. According to both male and female respondents, fondling of private parts was the most common type of sexual abuse (73% of males, 71% of females). For males, the next most common type of abuse was oral sex (33%), followed by attempted penile penetration (18%), completed penile penetration (15%), and digital penetration (6%). About 6% of sexual abuse reported by males was summarized as "other" (see Table 3.5 for descriptions).[14]

For women, after fondling of private parts, the second largest category (31%) was "other" (see Table 3.6), followed by digital penetration (20%), attempted penile penetration (11%), oral sex (9%), and actual penile penetration (6%).

The most common types of physical abuse reported by males were (a) hitting with and without an object (65% for each), (b) beating with and without an object (59% for each), and (c) pinching (18%). Next most common were burning and smothering (12% for each) and biting (6%). Four men reported "other" types of physical abuse (see Table 3.7).

The most common types of physical abuse reported by females were similar to those reported by males: hitting with an object (81%);

Table 3.6 "Other" Types of Sexual Abuse Reported by Females

Remove clothes
Viewing pornographic pictures
I masturbated the man to ejaculation
Genital contact
Male exposed penis and rubbed it against me, attempted to kiss me
Exposure by workman
Genital contact; no penetration
Voyeurism
Relative in household hiding in bedroom or bathroom to watch me undress.
Orthodontist "tickling" me, which in retrospect was fondling me.
French kissed by close relatives
Touch abuser's penis
My brother had me undress
Rubbing penis against vagina; no penetration
Watched older boy masturbate
Intrusive genital medical procedure
Inappropriate holding
Kiss on mouth not culturally accepted
Being rubbed against by a man from behind
Telephone threats repeatedly
Fondling of breasts by father and dentist

NOTE: Types of abuse are reported in respondents' own words.

Table 3.7 "Other" Types of Physical Abuse Reported by Males

Yardsticks, belts, washing mouth with soap
Father beat me in outbursts of anger
Verbal and emotional abuse; demeaning talk and shouting with threats of
   abandonment
Hot water poured on hand

NOTE: Types of abuse are reported in respondents' own words.

without an object (63%); beating with or without an object and pinching (31% for each); strangling (19%); and biting (6%). "Other" types accounted for 12% of physical abuse reported by females (see Table 3.8).

Relationship of Perpetrator to Victim by Gender

Not surprisingly, males committed the largest number of sexual offenses against both boys and girls (Finkelhor, 1980; Reinhart,

Table 3.8 "Other" Types of Physical Abuse Reported by Females

---

Iron gate slammed on finger and tip cut off; stoning, beated [sic] with broom
Pushed into wall, shaken by the arms so I could not control my head motions
Hair pulling
As a child, I was spanked by mother with a hairbrush
Slapped in face, pulling hair or ears

NOTE: Types of abuse are reported in respondents' own words.

1987). In our study, for both genders, men known to their victims or to their families (50% for males; 38% for females) made up the largest group of sexual offenders. The next largest group for both genders were male strangers (16% for men; 22% for women).

In the remaining categories, the relationship of the perpetrator to victim varied with the gender of the victim. Male respondents reported that the next largest group of offenders, after acquaintances and strangers, was brothers (13%), followed by other male family members (8%), female acquaintances (8%), mothers (5%), other female family members (5%), and female strangers (3%). Only one male respondent (3%) reported having been sexually abused by his father; none reported having been sexually abused by his grandfather.

Female respondents reported that the largest group of offenders, after male acquaintances and male strangers, were authority figures (16%), such as teachers, priests, and scout leaders. Fathers, brothers, and uncles formed the next largest groups (11%, 11%, and 12%, respectively). Grandfathers (7%) and other male family members (5%) accounted for the remaining significant abusers. Female family members were not reported as perpetrators. There was only a single report of a stepfather as abuser (1.4%).

Men who reported a childhood history of physical abuse were most likely to have been abused by their fathers (53%) and next most frequently by their mothers or male strangers (33% each). Women were most likely to have been physically abused by their mothers (50%) and next most frequently by their fathers (40%).

The prevalence of father-daughter incest found in our study (2% of the total sample of women; 11% of the abused females), and in other nonclinical populations, is significantly lower than that found in clinical populations.[15] For example, Bryer, Nelson, and Miller (1978) found that close to 40% of the 39 female inpatients (N = 15) who reported physical or sexual abuse or both reported an incestuous experience, primarily with fathers, stepfathers, or brothers (Bryer et al., 1978; Sansonnet-Hayden et al., 1987). Sansonnet-Hayden et al. (1987) found that more than half of 17 sexually abused psychiatric male and female adolescents were incest cases.

In general, our results support the findings of Finkelhor (1979a). In a nonclinical sample of 796 male and female undergraduate students, he found that less than 1% of the women reported sexual abuse by fathers and less than 0.5% by stepfathers (no such reports were made by the men). Only 2% of the respondents in Finkelhor's study of sexual abuse in Boston families (Finkelhor, 1984) reported that their children had been sexually abused by a parent. However, Russell (1986), in her study of 930 San Francisco women, found a 16% rate of incest, using a far broader definition than did Finkelhor. Russell defined incest as "any kind of exploitive sexual contact or attempted sexual contact that occurred between relatives, no matter how distant the relationship, before the victim turned eighteen years old" (p. 41).

In our study, when we define incest to include stepfathers and grandfathers as well as fathers, we find that 5% of the total sample of women (19% of the abused females) had experienced incestuous relationships. When we include all family members, the frequency of incest increased to 9% of the total sample of women (47% of the abused females). The incest rate for males for all family members is 5% of the total sample of men (28% of the sexually abused).

When we expand Finkelhor's definition of incest to include all relatives, as did Russell, then we find that about 25% of the males and females (23% and 28%, respectively) sampled by Finkelhor had experienced incest, a rate close to 1.5 times greater than Russell's 16%. Applying the expanded criteria of incest to the Laumann et al. (1994) national random survey of a community sample, we find that, of the total sample, 1.3% of the men and 3% of the women (19% of the men and 52% of the women who reported childhood abuse) meet the Russell definition for incest.

Janus and Janus (1993), using the category of "relatives" (similar to Russell's category of incest), found that 4.7% of the men and 14.4% of the women in the total sample reported having been sexually maltreated as children (44% of the men and 62% of the women who reported having been sexually maltreated as children). Thus, using broad but consistent criteria for incest across these five studies, we find a wide range of prevalence rates among the populations being considered: 9% (Jackson & Nuttall, 1993) to 25% (Finkelhor,

Table 3.9 Reported Rates of Intrafamilial Sexual Abuse

Study	Intrafamilial Sexual Abuse Percentages	Sample
Finkelhor (1979a)	< 1.5% of women	Nonprobability sample of college students (N = 796)
Finkelhor (1984)	2% of children	Randomly drawn survey of parents in Boston area (N = 521)
Jackson and Nuttall (1993)	2% of women; 11% of the abused females	Randomly drawn national sample of professionals (N = 656): clinical social workers, clinical psychologists, pediatricians, and psychiatrists
Janus and Janus (1993)	14.4% of women, 62% of abused women; 4.7% of men, 44% of abused men	Nonprobability community sample surveyed by telephone (N = 2,689)
Laumann, Gagnon, Michael, and Michaels (1994)	3% of women, 52% of the abused women; 1.3% of men, 19% of the abused men	Randomly drawn national survey of face-to-face interviews (N = 3,432)
Russell (1986)	16% incest	Randomly drawn sample of women in San Francisco (N = 930)

1979a). A comparative summary of reported rates of intrafamilial sexual abuse is given in Table 3.9.

Summary and Conclusions

The 21% combined prevalence of physical and sexual abuse found in this study is within the range reported in other nonclinical populations but lower than those obtained from clinical populations. Of our respondents, 14% reported a history of childhood sexual abuse only; 4% reported a history of childhood physical abuse only, and 3% (14% of those abused) reported histories of both physical and sexual abuse. Depending on the definition, prevalence rates of incest in the total population of professionals range from close to 5% to 9% for women and about half that for men. Of those abused, incest rates range from 9% to 45% for women and 8% to 35% for men, again depending on the definition of incest.

Although we found no gender differences in prevalence of physical abuse, on average, significantly more women (20%) than men (13%) reported a childhood history of sexual abuse. It is interesting that the between-gender differences occurred only in the oldest cohorts. Although both men and women in the youngest cohorts reported similar prevalence rates of childhood sexual abuse (15% and 17%), the rates have opposing long-term trends. Sexual abuse of girls appears to have decreased over the past 30 to 40 years, but male sexual abuse has apparently increased. For the two younger female cohorts, the rate has been reduced about twofold (28% to 15%). The 15% rate for the younger male cohorts is the same as the younger female rate and is 3 times greater than the 5% rate of the oldest male cohort.

Male social workers were more likely to have been sexually abused as children than males from pediatrics, psychiatry, and psychology. In contrast, female pediatricians were less likely to have a history of childhood sexual abuse than females in clinical social work, psychiatry, or psychology.

We found a strong association between reports of physical and sexual abuse. Of the physically abused, 39% also reported a history of sexual abuse; 16% of the sexually abused also reported a history of physical abuse. The peak vulnerability reported for both sexual and physical abuse was about 8 years of age. Most perpetrators of sexual abuse for both genders were males who were either acquaintances or strangers rather than relatives. Whereas the mean duration of sexual abuse reported by both genders was approximately 1 year, sexual abuse by family members was, on average, longer. Both males and females were most likely to have been physically abused by a same-sex parent and to have been abused for a longer duration than the sexually abused. However, females reported a significantly longer duration of physical abuse than did males.

Our abused professionals differ from clinical populations in a number of factors, suggesting that they may be among the "fortunate abused." We speculate that the greater age at onset, the relatively short duration of sexual abuse, and the lower rate of incest reported by our abused respondents may be among the factors that prevent the more extreme and damaging sequelae of childhood sexual abuse so often found in clinical populations.[16]

Notes

1. Unless otherwise indicated, data reported in this chapter were obtained in the initial study.

2. This disparity may be attributed to the use of a relatively narrow definition of physical abuse that requires the potential for serious risk or injury (see Giovannoni & Becerra, 1979).

3. In their national survey, Janus and Janus did not provide a definition of sexual abuse. Respondents were asked to respond "yes" or "no" to the statement, "I was sexually molested as a child."

4. Moore and Schussel (1995) used a relatively narrow definition of sexual abuse: "Before the age of 18, were you personally ever touched in a sexual way by an adult or older child, when you did not want to be touched that way, or were you ever forced to touch an adult or older child in a sexual way—including anyone who was a member of your family, or anyone outside your family? (p. 20).

5. Total is less than 656 because one respondent did not indicate gender and two did not indicate whether they had been abused.

6. We assigned the respondents by gender to four groups: (a) younger than 36, (b) 36 to 45, (c) 46 to 55, and (d) 56 and older. These ages correspond to birth after 1954, during the periods of 1944 to 1953 and 1934 to 1943, respectively, and before 1934.

7. For both studies, our samples were drawn by discipline and gender without regard to age.

8. η is a measure of association between two variables independent of linearity. η^2 is the proportion of the variance of one variable accounted for by the other variable (Glass & Hopkins, 1996).

9. When we examined this effect by discipline, the smaller Ns reduced the significance obtained and the relationship between age and likelihood of sexual abuse was significant only for the women psychologists ($p < 60$ .01). However, the relationship was in the same direction for female scoail workers and pediatricians. The relationship was not present for the women psychiatrists. The overall η coefficient for women predicting secual abuse was .16 ($p = .002$).

10. The age range extending up to 22 in this study illustrates the problems of defining *child* and *adolescent* in the child abuse literature.

11. We have not attempted to obtain "best values" by evaluation of the quality of the reports.

12. We analyzed these data as follows: When abuse was reported as one time only, we recorded its duration as "0." When abuse was reported more than once within a 1-year period, we recorded its duration as "1." When abuse was reported over a period of years, we recorded its duration as the number of years from the first to the last abuse inclusive. Thus, if the respondent reported abuse occurring between ages 5 and 10, we recored the abuse as having occurred for 6 years.

13. The relatively short duration for an outpatient sample may be explained by the early age cutoff.

14. Totals exceed 100% because some respondents specified multiple types of abuse.

15. Note that on average 20% of both the sexually abused males and females reported abuse by more than one perpetrator. The prevalence of incestuous abuse given is the mean percent of the abused who suffered this relationship. As a fraction of all abuse (rather than those abused) these rates become 20% smaller.

16. For analysis of these data, see Chapter 6.

PART III

Sexual Abuse Allegations: What Do Clinicians Believe and Why Do They Believe It?

4

Credibility Ratings of Sexual Abuse Allegations: Effects of Respondent Factors

Overview

We found very wide variation in the credibility ratings of the sexual abuse allegations. However, respondents, on average, were more likely than not to believe the allegations in the vignettes. The mean credibility score for all respondents over all vignettes was about one standard deviation greater than the design null (about 0.5 scale unit, or 10% of the total span).

The following respondent factors were significantly associated with clinicians' credibility scores at the .05 level:

Younger clinicians found the allegations more credible than their older colleagues.

Women were more likely than men to find the allegations credible.

Clinical social workers were more credulous than their peers in the other three disciplines.

Family-systems-oriented clinicians were more credulous than their colleagues who reported other theoretical orientations.

Clinicians who reported a personal history of physical or sexual abuse found the allegations more credible than their peers without such a history (two factors).

Respondents who had raised children found the allegations less credible than those who had not raised children.

Clinicians engaged in client-patient care or administrative duties related to child sexual abuse found the allegations more credible (two factors).

Years of experience (like age) were negatively associated with belief in the allegations.

Introduction

We selected 12 respondent factors as independent variables, either because they had been reported in the abuse literature to have an effect on clinical judgment or because they had been so identified by the first author, Helene Jackson (HJ), in her practice. The 12 respondent factors were age, gender, marital status, number of children, work role and setting, type and length of experience, discipline, personal history of childhood abuse (physical and sexual), and theoretical orientation (psychodynamic, cognitive-behavioral, family systems, psychosocial, child development, biological, social learning, and feminist).

Our hypotheses that the personal factors of age, gender, raising children, discipline, theoretical orientation, and history of abuse significantly influence clinical judgments about sexual abuse allegations were validated. In contrast, we found no significant effects on credibility ratings for the factors of marital status and number of children.

Several variables that were found to be significant in the univariate analysis (viz. work role and setting, and type and length of experience) were, apparently, highly intercorrelated with other factors found significant in the stepwise multiple regression analysis. They were not included in the final regression model.

Scale of Measurement

As a major part of our initial study, we requested each participant to read 16 vignettes in which an allegation of sexual abuse was made and to rate each for credibility (see Appendix A). Each respondent was asked, "On a scale of 1-6 how confident are you that the sexual abuse did occur?" Six choices were allowed for the degree of confidence that the sexual abuse described in the vignette had taken place, resulting in the following scale:

1	2	3	4	5	6
Very confident it did not occur	Fairly confident it did not occur	Slightly confident it did not occur	Slightly confident it did occur	Fairly confident it did occur	Very confident it did occur

We constructed the vignettes to test the null hypotheses that the 15 case factors would not affect respondents' judgments about the credibility of the sexual abuse allegations. Thus, a credibility score of 3.5 is a null score, reflecting belief as likely as disbelief. Any score significantly different from 3.5 reflects the difference from the null.

Variability of the Credibility Scores

One of the most significant findings of this study is the great variability demonstrated in the clinicians' credibility ratings of the sexual abuse allegations. For each of the 16 vignettes, individual scores ranged over the full scale of confidence, from *very confident it did not occur* to *very confident it did occur*. These vast differences of opinion demonstrate that, even among professionals, there is only a weak objective basis for the determination of the validity of sexual abuse disclosures.

Table 4.1 Means and Standard Deviations for 16 Vignettes (Ordered by Average Credibility Score)

Case	Total Mean	SD	Females Mean	SD	Males Mean	SD	Gender t Test Significance
Paula	4.97	0.90	5.07	0.87	4.83	0.90	< .001
Joey	4.67	1.10	4.81	1.07	4.49	1.11	< .001
Jean	4.48	1.15	4.57	1.08	4.37	1.22	.034
Billy	4.36	1.15	4.52	1.10	4.15	1.19	< .001
Eddie	4.35	1.06	4.51	1.00	4.15	1.11	< .001
Juan	4.25	1.02	4.21	1.03	4.31	1.01	NS[a]
Rose	4.25	1.15	4.30	1.10	3.95	1.19	< .001
David	4.10	1.08	4.28	1.05	3.88	1.07	< .001
Jenny	4.08	1.18	4.12	1.18	4.02	1.18	NS
Rita	3.95	1.16	4.06	1.13	3.81	1.18	0.007
Scott	3.94	1.11	4.03	1.07	3.82	1.15	.020
Donna	3.84	1.23	4.00	1.19	3.63	1.26	< .001
Linda	3.77	1.24	3.90	1.23	3.60	1.24	.002
NULL	3.50	—	3.50	—	3.50	—	—
Harry	3.38	1.15	3.48	1.16	3.26	1.14	.014
Nancy	3.10	1.10	3.13	1.08	3.07	1.12	NS
Jeff	3.05	1.19	3.11	1.16	2.98	1.22	NS
Average	4.03	0.61	4.13	0.61	3.89	0.59	< .001

a. NS means not significant.

The subjectivity of clinical decision making and its implications for the identification, management, treatment, and outcome of abuse cases is well-documented (Daniel, Hampton, & Newberger, 1983; Gomez-Schwartz & Horowitz, 1984; Johnson, Owens, Dewey, & Eisenberg, 1990; Reidy & Hochstadt, 1993). The ambiguities characteristic of these cases make clinical judgments particularly vulnerable to biased, often unconscious thoughts and feelings (Berliner, 1988; Berliner & Conte, 1993; Corwin, Berliner, Goodman, Goodwin, & White, 1987). Our study provides empirical evidence that major differences exist among clinicians evaluating sexual abuse disclosures.[1]

Another major finding is that, on average, clinicians believed the allegations presented in the study. Table 4.1 presents the means and standard deviations of the credibility scores for all 16 vignettes by gender.

Mean Credibility Ratings

In this study, the total range of the credibility scale is five units (from 1 to 6). The average credibility rating for all clinicians over the

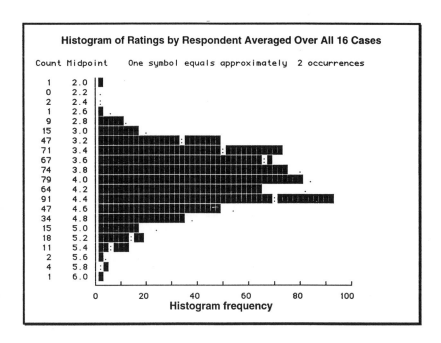

Figure 4.1. Histogram of Ratings by Respondent Averaged Over All 16 Cases

NOTE: Approximately normal distribution, mean = 4.03, SD = 0.61. The normal curve of the above mean and SD is shown by the dot notations.

16 vignettes was 4.03, with a standard deviation of 0.61 (see Table 4.1, bottom line). Because a mean score of 3.5 indicates disbelief as likely as belief, the difference between 3.5 and 4.03 is more than one tenth of the whole scale and almost a whole standard deviation. Thus, the mean of 4.03 demonstrates the respondents' overall tendency to believe the allegations depicted in the vignettes.

Figure 4.1 presents the histogram of frequencies for the average credibility ratings by respondent over all 16 case vignettes. Note that this is approximately a normal distribution with a mode of 4.4.

The mean credibility ratings of all 16 vignettes by gender and discipline are presented in Table 4.2 and in Figure 4.2. In contrast to males, females in all disciplines demonstrated a greater degree of belief that sexual abuse had occurred. An analysis of variance shows that the effect of gender was statistically significant across disciplines

Table 4.2 Mean Credibility Ratings by Gender and Discipline for All Vignettes

Gender		Social Workers	Psychologists	Pediatricians	Psychiatrists
Males	Mean	3.98	3.94	3.95	3.74
	(SD)	(.59)	(.58)	(.64)	(.53)
Females	Mean	4.26	4.11	4.06	4.06
	(SD)	(.59)	(.57)	(.62)	(.65)

NOTE: SD = Standard deviation.

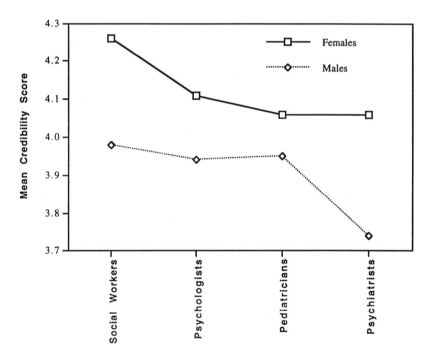

Figure 4.2. Mean Credibility by Discipline and Gender

(F = 4.76 with 1 and 120 df; $p < .05$). However, the four disciplines did not significantly differ in their mean credibility scores.

Overall, mean credibility ratings for individual cases ranged from a high of 4.97 for vignette "Paula," where 5 is *fairly confident it*

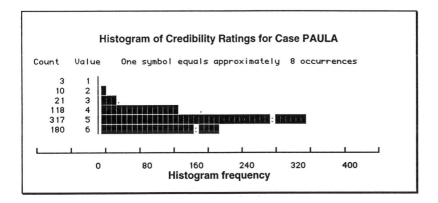

Figure 4.3. Histogram of Credibility Ratings for Case "Paula"
NOTE: Highly skewed to the high side due to ceiling effect; mean = 4.97, *SD* = 0.90.

did occur, to a low of 3.05 for "Jeff," where 3 is *slightly confident it did not occur* (see Table 4.1).

Two of the 16 vignettes had mean scores close to 5 ("Paula," 4.97 and "Joey," 4.67); three had average ratings close to 3 ("Jeff," 3.05; "Nancy," 3.10; and "Harry," 3.38). Ratings for the remaining vignettes were close to 4 (*slightly confident it did occur*).[2] The histograms of the distribution of scores for "Paula" and "Jeff" are presented in Figures 4.3 and 4.4 as examples of high and low credibility vignettes.[3] Note that both the mode and mean for these extreme case scores differ by almost two scale units.

The standard deviations of the individual vignettes ranged from a low of 0.90 for "Paula" to a high of 1.24 for "Linda," with most around 1.10 scale units. The mean value of the standard deviation of an individual vignette is > 1.0 scale unit, a significant fraction of the five-unit scale span. Table 4.1 presents the mean credibility scores and standard deviations for each vignette by gender and discipline. Female raters averaged higher credibility scores than did males for 12 of the 16 vignettes. There were no statistically significant differences in the ratings by gender for four of the vignettes ("Juan," "Jeff," "Jenny," and "Nancy").[4] The average score across all 16 vignettes was 4.13 for females and 3.89 for males. This difference of 0.24 represents about four tenths of a within-group standard deviation.

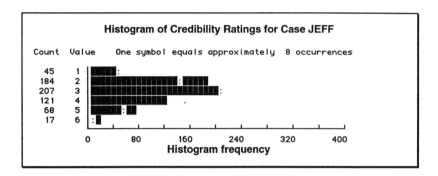

Figure 4.4. Histogram of Credibility Ratings for Case "Jeff"
NOTE: Fairly normal distribution with a low mean; mean = 3.05, *SD* = 1.19.

Univariate Analysis of Credibility From Respondent Variables

We used Pearson product-moment correlation coefficients to examine the relationships between respondent factors and the average credibility rating of each subject over the 16 vignettes. A number of personal factors significantly influenced clinicians' credibility ratings. Specifically, a childhood history of physical or sexual abuse was related to belief in the sexual abuse allegations ($r = .10$; $p < .01$ and $r = .09$; $p < .05$, respectively). Witnessing physical abuse was also related to greater belief in the allegations ($r = .10$; $p < .01$). Both gender ($r = .19$) and age ($r = -.18$) were significantly related to the degree to which clinicians believed the allegations ($p < .01$). Respondents who had raised children found the allegations less credible ($r = -.12$; $p < .01$). Of the four disciplines, social workers had the greatest confidence in the credibility of the allegations ($r = .11$; $p < .01$), whereas psychiatrists had the least confidence ($r = -.11$; $p < .01$). Similarly, clinicians whose theoretical orientation was family systems ($r = .13$; $p < .01$) or feminist ($r = .09$; $p < .05$) found the sexual abuse allegations more believable, whereas clinicians with a biological orientation ($r = -.12$; $p < .01$) found them less so.

Where respondents worked and how many hours they worked did not affect the degree of credibility. However, clinicians who engaged in client-patient care or administrative-supervisory duties

Table 4.3 Multiple Regression Analysis of Respondent Variables on Mean Credibility Ratings Over 16 Vignettes

Variable	B	SE B	β	t Ratio	Significance of t Ratio
Age (Years)	−.010	0.002	−.18	−4.58	< .001
Gender: 1 = Male,					
2 = Female	0.216	0.048	0.17	4.53	< .001
Family System Orientation:					
1 = Yes, 0 = No	0.136	0.054	0.10	2.51	< .05
Clinical Social Worker:					
1 = Yes, 0 = No	0.137	0.056	0.10	2.46	< .05
Personal History of					
Physical Abuse: 1 = Yes,					
0 = No	0.222	0.092	0.09	2.42	< .05
Personal History of					
Sexual Abuse: 1 = Yes,					
0 = No	0.126	0.064	0.08	1.97	< .05
(Constant)	4.04	0.135		30.01	< .0001

NOTE: Dependent variable is mean credibility over 16 vignettes; units of analysis are 624 respondents (only 624 respondents had complete data on these variables).
Multiple R 0.33
R^2 10.9%
Adjusted R^2 10.1%
Standard Error 0.587
F = 2.64185; Signif F = < .0001

related to child or adolescent sexual abuse had greater confidence in the allegations' credibility ($r = .13$; $p < .01$ and $r = .09$; $p < .05$, respectively) than those who did not. Years of experience beyond the final degree (working with clients and patients) was, like age, negatively associated with belief in the abuse allegations ($r = -.17$; $p < .01$). Because age and length of experience were highly intercorrelated, only age was used for the multiple regression analysis. Although the correlations are statistically significant, they are relatively small. Taken individually, they are not likely to have clinical significance.

Multiple Regression on Credibility From Respondent Variables

Because many of the respondent factors were intercorrelated, we used a stepwise multiple regression analysis to determine the joint effects of individual respondent factors on clinicians' credibility scores. Table 4.3 presents the results where the units of analysis are the respondents and the dependent variable is the mean credibility score for each respondent averaged across the 16 vignettes. This analysis predicts how credible the clinician found the sexual abuse allegations as a function of the six significant respondent factors.

The details of the regression analysis are presented in Table 4.3. About 10% of the variability in mean credibility scores can be predicted from six respondent-specific factors: age, gender, discipline, theoretical orientation, and personal history of sexual and physical abuse. Although highly significant, this small fraction of "explained" variance reflects the great variability found in individual respondent credibility ratings of sexual abuse allegations.

The Age Factor

Younger professionals found the allegations more credible than did their older counterparts (see Table 4.3). The B weight shows an inverse relationship between age and credibility scores (i.e., with every additional age year of the respondent, the credibility score decreases by .010). For example, the average credibility scores of a 30-year-old and a 60-year-old clinician would differ by 0.300 scale units. Thus, the older the clinician, the lower the confidence in the allegations' credibility.

In our review of the literature, we located few articles relevant to these results. However, there is some evidence that supports our finding that older professionals are less credulous than younger professionals.[5] For example, in their study to assess the various factors that influence reporting patterns among mandated reporters, Zellman and Bell (1989) found older practitioners less likely to report abuse than their younger colleagues. In the United Kingdom, Davey and Hill (1995) interviewed 60 professionals to investigate how education and training affect differences in perception of symptoms suggestive of sexual abuse. They found that older respondents (medical-psychological and social worker groups) were less likely to endorse symptoms as indicative of sexual abuse than were their younger colleagues (residential care workers and police officers).[6]

Why older clinicians found the allegations less credible than did their younger cohorts is not clear. However, the reluctance to report among older professionals may be explained by their higher level of disbelief. For example, Kalichman, Craig, and Follingstad (1990), in their study of professional reporting patterns, found a positive correlation between level of belief in the validity of given allegations and the likelihood of reporting. The differences found in the degree of credibility and reporting patterns with age may result from lack of knowledge, on the one hand, or may be a product of maturity and practice experience (Morison & Greene, 1992), rather than simply age.

Older clinicians may be more likely to be influenced by the Freudian "myth of the seductive child" than are younger, more recently trained practitioners. On the other hand, with experience, clinicians may become more cautious and conservative in their practice. Major shifts in educational values and societal attitudes related to sexuality and femininity that have occurred over the past 30 to 40 years may also be contributing to this finding. This is clearly an important area for further exploration.

The Gender Factor

Women, on average, rated the credibility of sexual abuse allegations about .216 scale units higher than did men. Cognitive, emotional, and attitudinal differences by gender have been well documented in the feminist, relational, and victimization literature (Gilligan, 1982; Jordan, Kaplan, & Miller, 1991; Stiver, 1990; Surrey, 1985). Studies of professionals show that women judge manifestations of maltreatment more severely than do males (Howe et al., 1988; Jones & McGraw, 1987). Snyder and Newberger (1986), in their vignette study of 295 professionals in an urban teaching hospital, found that female psychologists (N = 24) judged parental neglect far more severely than did their male colleagues and that female physicians (N = 23) interpreted physical abuse much more seriously than did their male counterparts. Attias and Goodwin (1985), in an attitude survey of professionals in private practice (N = 108), found that women perceived incest as more prevalent than did men and that more men than women, particularly psychiatrists, overestimated the role of fantasy in children's allegations of sexual abuse. Similarly, in a survey of psychology interns (N = 11; Cohen, 1993), male therapists were more likely to perceive sexual abuse allegations as fantasy than were females.

Studies of professional reporting patterns have yielded similar results. Zellman and Bell (1989), in their survey of mandated reporters in 15 states and interviews of child protective agencies in 6 states, found that women were more likely to indicate their intention to report sexual abuse than were their male colleagues. Other research suggests that more women than men would report a case in which a child had retracted an allegation and that women were less likely than men to have an exaggerated view of the proportion of children who make false allegations of sexual abuse (Attias & Goodwin, 1985).

Recently, researchers who have examined the relationship between gender and assignment of blame in sexual abuse cases have found that professional men and women attribute blame differently. Johnson et al. (1990) used a hypothetical case history of an adolescent incestuously abused by her father to examine determinants of attribution of blame in a study of a nonprobability sample of 99 teachers and 162 social workers in England. Although they found no gender differences in their respondents' attribution of blame, they did find that women were more likely than men to predict negative consequences for the incest victim.

Reidy and Hochstadt (1993) also examined assignment of blame in father-daughter incest cases in a study of a nonprobability sample of 101 mental health professionals in California. They report that respondent gender is one of the most important factors influencing attribution of blame. Though most of the licensed psychologists, psychiatrists, social workers, and counselors who responded to the study attributed major blame to the perpetrator, female respondents were less likely than males to attribute some responsibility to the victim. Seventy-six percent of females assigned no blame to the victim, whereas only 51% of males assigned no blame.

The allocation of blame by professionals in cases of childhood sexual abuse may affect the choice of intervention and its outcome (Reidy & Hochstadt, 1993). Kalichman et al. (1990) explored the relationship between clinicians' resolve to report child sexual abuse and their beliefs about who was responsible for the abuse. Using an experimental 2 × 2 factorial vignette design (and a nonprobability sample), they surveyed 467 licensed psychologists from two southern states. Each respondent was given a vignette in which a child discloses sexual abuse; the victim's gender and father's reaction to the child's disclosure were systematically varied. Kalichman et al. (1990) show that attribution of blame differed by respondent gender.

Females were less likely to assign responsibility to the father than were males, and were more likely to place responsibility for the abuse on the mother. Contrary to Reidy and Hochstadt's (1993) findings, they did not find a relationship between respondents' attribution of blame and intention to report.

Gender differences in perception are not limited to professionals. For example, Broussard, Wagner, and Kazelskis (1991), in their vignette study of 30 male and female undergraduates, found that women were likely to ascribe more serious harm to abuse victims than were men.

The generality of these findings leads us to speculate that, on average, women as nurturers and protectors of children (whether culturally or biologically determined or both) may develop a greater capacity for empathy than men. Pervasive discrimination against women and children may make women more sensitive to the victimization of others and more likely to believe children's allegations of sexual abuse. Ironically, these same factors may make them less forgiving of women who apparently do not protect their children.

The Discipline and Theoretical Orientation Factors

In the multiple regression of the respondent characteristics (see Table 4.3), social workers demonstrated greater belief in the sexual abuse allegations than did clinicians of the other three disciplines. Regardless of theoretical orientation, social worker's credibility ratings averaged .137 scale unit greater than their non-social-work peers. There was no statistically significant interaction between gender and discipline; females were more credulous than males across all four disciplines. Clinicians who reported a family systems orientation, compared to all other theoretical orientations, rated the allegations, on average, .136 scale units higher on the credibility scale.

Saunders (1988), in his study of attitudes toward sexual abuse, found professional attitudes and belief systems to be compatible with the roles expected of them. Among a nonprobability sample of 132 legal and social work professionals, Saunders found (not surprisingly) that district attorneys and social workers were most likely to believe children's allegations of sexual abuse, and public defenders were least likely to have confidence in a child's credibility. Public defenders and social workers were less likely than public prosecutors, judges, or police to favor penalizing the perpetrator, whereas police and judges were most punitive in their approach to sex offenders.

Reidy and Hochstadt (1993), in their sample of 101 mental health professionals in California, sought to determine how blame is assigned in incest cases. Data obtained from the Jackson Incest Blame Scale (Jackson & Ferguson, 1983) showed that allocation of blame may be a function of professional discipline as well as gender. Psychiatrists and psychologists were more likely than social workers[7] and counselors to attribute blame to situational factors, such as broken homes and poverty, rather than to victim or perpetrator factors. Similarly, Johnson et al. (1990), in their study of teachers' and social workers' ($N = 261$) attribution of blame in father-daughter incest cases, discovered both professional and gender differences. Teachers were more likely to attribute blame to the victim than were social workers.

Gomez-Schwartz and Horowitz (1984) surveyed 790 professionals prior to their attendance at workshops or seminars on child sexual abuse. Their nonrandom sample included social workers, psychiatrists, psychologists, nurses, and physicians. Using a hypothetical case of a child's incestuous relationship with her stepfather, they found that the wide variations in the respondents' choice of intervention were often based more on the respondents' work setting than on their profession.

Attitudes about sexual abuse may be a function of professional roles and responsibilities (Gomez-Schwartz & Horowitz, 1984). Because multiple systems and various disciplines must work together on sexual abuse cases, there is a compelling need to identify training and value differences to provide effective and integrated services (Saunders, 1988).

Although multidisciplinary sexual abuse evaluation teams are considered most effective in achieving unbiased judgments, this approach has its own pitfalls. Wide disparities in personal background, perception of professional role, and attitudes and values acquired in training are potential obstacles to reaching individual and group objectivity (Abramson, 1989; Gambrill, 1990). Professional commitment to a particular perspective can "compromise the ability to weight evidence and sample data objectively" (Gambrill, 1990, p. 246). Status and gender-related differences among team members of different disciplines may also affect team decision making.

In most health-care settings, physicians are the designated or implicit team leaders. Thus, they may significantly influence team process, problem solving, evaluation, and choice of intervention. Furthermore, the perceived need of lower status members to conform and to maintain positive relationships with their higher status colleagues may be intimidating. Reluctance to express different or unpopular perceptions may result in "group think" (Abramson, 1989; Gambrill, 1990). To obtain more objective evaluations of sexual abuse allegations, members of interdisciplinary teams should be aware of the differences that may exist in attitudes and value systems (Abramson, 1993) and the extent to which these may be affecting clinical judgments.

The Personal History of Abuse Factors

As a supplement to the multiple regression analysis, we conducted a two-way analysis of variance with the mean credibility score as the dependent variable and a personal history of sexual abuse and a personal history of physical abuse as independent variables. We found a significant effect for both sexual abuse history ($p = .027$) and a history of physical abuse ($p = .045$). However, the interaction was not statistically significant ($p = .759$). Averaged across all 16 vignettes, there are significant differences in average credibility scores between sexually abused (4.16) and nonabused respondents (4.00). We found similar differences for physical abuse. The nonabused rated the credibility of the sexual abuse allegations at 4.01; the physically abused, at 4.16, slightly higher.

The personal history of abuse factor effects are independent and additive. Thus, professionals who reported histories of either sexual or physical abuse or both found the sexual abuse allegations more credible than did their peers who reported no such history.

In the only other systematic attempt to estimate the association between professionals who have childhood histories of abuse and clinical judgment, Howe et al. (1988) found that respondents who reported some form of childhood maltreatment evaluated physical and emotional abuse more severely than clinicians who did not report such a history (sexual abuse was not a factor in the Howe et al. vignettes). Studies of professionals do not usually address the possi-

Table 4.4A Susan, the Most Credulous Clinician

Predicted mean credibility (Susan) = 4.04 - 0.010 (age = 30)
  + 0.22(sex = 2) + 0.14(FS = 1) + 0.14(SW = 1) + 0.22(PA = 1) + 0.13(SA = 1)

Predicted mean credibility (Susan) = 4.04 - 0.30 + 0.44 + 0.14 + 0.14 + 0.22 + 0.13
  = 4.81

4.4B George, the Least Credulous Clinician

Predicted mean credibility (George) = 4.04 - 0.010 (age = 65)
  + 0.22(sex = 1) + 0.14(FS = 0) + 0.14(SW = 0) + 0.22(PA = 0) + 0.13(SA = 0)

Predicted mean credibility (George) = 4.04 - 0.65 + 0.22 + 0.00 + 0.00 + 0.00 + 0.00
  = 3.61

---

bility of respondents' childhood history of abuse (Reidy & Hochstadt, 1993). A single study of the long-term effects of an early history of sexual abuse on female professionals (Elliott, 1994) did not address the impact of such a history on clinical judgment.

In sharp contrast to our findings, Herzberger and Tennen (1988) found that in the general population, those who reported abuse histories were less likely to recognize abuse than those who had not. These disparate findings may be an indication that adult professionals abused as children are more likely than those in the general public to seek psychotherapy and to resolve the issues of their victimization. If so, they would be less likely to deny or block out the abuse of others and, consequently, might be particularly sensitive and responsive to victims of abuse.

Two Hypothetical Clinicians[8]

Using the B coefficients found in the multiple regression analysis of respondent variables (Table 4.3), we can predict clinicians' mean credibility scores by the equation summarized in Tables 4.4A and 4.4B. Based on the prediction equation, we can create profiles for the most and least credulous clinicians.

To understand the prediction equation, let us assume two hypothetical clinicians, George and Susan, the least and most credulous clinicians.

> Susan is a 30-year-old female MSW social worker whose practice is guided primarily by a family systems orientation. As a child, Susan was subjected to both physical and sexual abuse.

The equation predicts that her average rating of the credibility of sexual abuse vignettes would be 4.81 or very close to *fairly confident it did occur*.

> George, our least credulous clinician, is a 65-year-old male clinician with no history of childhood abuse. He may be a pediatrician, psychiatrist, or psychologist whose clinical practice is not guided by a family systems orientation.

Solely on the basis of George's personal attributes, we expect him to be neutral when evaluating a sexual abuse allegation (predicted rating, 3.61, or very close to the score of 3.5, the null response, neither believing nor disbelieving the allegation;[9] see Table 4.4B).

Solely on the basis of these personal attributes, we expect that clinicians such as Susan will have more confidence in the credibility of sexual abuse allegations than will clinicians such as George. The difference between George's and Susan's predicted credibility scores (from 3.61 to 4.81) is 1.20 units, about one fourth of the five-point scale (1 to 6), and about two within group standard deviations.

Summary and Conclusions

In this chapter, we have reported the significant differences in clinician responses to the allegations of sexual abuse depicted in the 16 vignettes presented in this study. The wide range of credibility scores for each vignette demonstrates that evaluations of sexual abuse lack objectivity and reliability. The personal factors of age, gender, discipline, theoretical orientation, and history of childhood abuse significantly affect clinicians' evaluations of the validity of the allegations, providing further evidence that clinically irrelevant factors influence clinicians' views of an allegation. Our findings are consistent with other studies examining professional beliefs about victim credibility (Saunders, 1988) and interpretation of sexual abuse (Boat & Everson, 1988a; Kendall-Tackett & Watson, 1991). Note again, our sample of professionals, on average, are in general clinical practice and are not representative of a sample of experts in the field of sexual abuse.

In general, females, social workers, the relatively young, and those who reported a childhood history of abuse demonstrated more confidence in the credibility of the sexual abuse allegations than did their colleagues in the other three disciplines who are male, relatively older, and do not report a childhood history of childhood victimization. There was no statistically significant interaction between gender and discipline; females were more credulous than males across all four disciplines.

About 10% of the variability in mean credibility scores can be predicted from the respondent-specific factors of age, gender, discipline, theoretical orientation, and a personal history of abuse. Thus, whereas a given individual could be scored on his or her personal attributes (see Tables 4.4A and 4.4B) and a predicted tendency calculated to belief in the sexual abuse allegations, the prediction is relatively imprecise. However, even such tentative or inexact predictions can be useful in minimizing the potentially harmful effects of unbalanced composition, particularly when selecting members for sexual abuse and family violence teams. Clearly, there is need for further research on the influence of personal factors that were not measured in this study, such as training differences, ethnicity, and race, among others.

Notes

1. Note that our sample is drawn from the general population of clinicians who may not have had training specific to sexual abuse.

2. Note that these are mean scores. The range of individual scores for every vignette covered the entire scale.

3. Because some few respondents did not rate every vignette, the totals vary slightly in the histograms of Figures 4.3 and 4.4.

4. We have yet to determine what case factors produced these gender-independent scores.

5. In this book, the terms *professionals, clinicians,* and *practitioners* are used interchangeably.

6. It is possible that the differences may be due to discipline rather than age or to a combination of the two.

7. We found this surprising given the "person-in-environment" approach of graduate social work education.

8. These regression coefficients need to be replicated in another study.

9. These are based solely on personal factors. As shown in Chapter 5, these credibility ratings are substantially modified when combined with significant case factors.

5

Credibility Ratings of Sexual Abuse Allegations: Effects of Case Factors

Overview

Of the 15 case factors systematically varied in the 16 vignettes, 9 significantly affected clinicians' credibility ratings: 7 at the .001 level, 1 at the .01 level, and 1 at the .05 level. These factors are given in order of the size of their effect (with note of our prior expectations for each):

> Caucasians were more probable perpetrators than minorities (a major surprise!).

Family members were more probable perpetrators than nonfamily members (as expected).

Minority children were more likely victims than Caucasians (also a surprise).

Victims who showed negative affect were more believable than those who showed positive or flat affect when reporting the alleged abuse (not expected).

Children were judged more credible victims than adolescents (not expected).

Victims whose behavior changed following the alleged abuse were more believable than those whose behavior showed no change (as expected).

Perpetrators with a history of substance abuse were viewed as more likely offenders than those without such a history (as expected).

Children or adolescents whose families had a prior history with protective services were more believable victims (as expected).

Nonprofessionals were more likely than professionals to be perceived as perpetrators (unexpected).

Introduction

In this chapter, we present the effects of specific case factors on clinicians' credibility ratings of the sexual abuse allegations illustrated in the 16 vignettes. We discuss those case factors that had significant effects on decisions about the validity of the allegations, as well as those that did not, and place our findings in the context of other empirical research.

Some factors, as expected, given current knowledge, influenced credibility ratings; however, other factors, such as the alleged perpetrator's history of violence and the caretakers' sexual abuse history, did not. Factors such as race, perpetrators' socioeconomic status (SES), and the victim's lack of affect that again, given current knowledge, would not be expected to influence clinical judgments, did so, and in the race factor, in a surprising manner.

To demonstrate vividly how a combination of case and personal factors can influence the outcome of clinical decision making, we developed a prediction equation to create two hypothetical vignettes (the least and most credible), scored by our least and most credible clinicians (see Chapter 4, Tables 4.4A and 4.4B).

Effects of Vignette Factors

Following the fractional factorial design described in Chapter 2, we varied 15 two-level case factors among 16 vignettes. We chose specific case factors, either because they had been identified in the literature to be associated with sexual abuse or because the first author, Helene Jackson (HJ), found them to be influential in clinical judgments of abuse cases. The selected factors were victim and perpetrator race (Hampton & Newberger, 1985); relationship of victim to perpetrator; behavioral changes of the victim (Browne & Finkelhor, 1986a); victim gender, age (National Center on Child Abuse and Neglect [NCCAN], 1988), and affect (Goodwin, 1985); perpetrator's SES, history of substance abuse (Kameen & Thompson, 1983), and history of violence (Finkelhor, 1984); custody issues (Green, 1986); family's prior contact with protective services (Pierce & Pierce, 1985); and the nonoffending caretaker's history of sexual abuse (Elwell & Ephross, 1987; Sansonnet-Hayden et al., 1987) and history of psychiatric illness (Finkelhor, 1980; see Table 5.1).

As noted in Chapter 2, factors known to be exceptionally powerful in their effect on credibility, such as medical-physical findings and a perpetrator's confession, were excluded, as were factors found in only a small percentage of reported cases (e.g., female perpetrators).

The 15 case factors and their two levels are shown in Table 5.1. Predictions of what level would lead to greater credibility ratings were based on an analysis of the literature and HJ's clinical experience and are indicated by asterisks (*). Where the two levels were expected to be equivalent, we have marked both levels with a number sign (#).

Multiple Regression Analysis on Credibility From Vignette Factors

We conducted a regression analysis of the 15 vignette factors to determine the effects of each on the credibility ratings of the respondents. The plan separately sampled eight populations: four disciplines (clinical social workers, psychiatrists, clinical psychologists, and pediatricians) each divided into gender groups.

For the analysis, we divided the respondents into the eight groups (2 genders times 4 disciplines) and averaged their ratings of

Table 5.1 Vignette Case Factors

Factor	Level 1	Level 2
Alleged Victim		
A Gender	Male	Female *
B Age	3 to 8 years	13 to 16 years *
C Race	Minority #	White #
D Behavioral changes	Yes *	No
E Affect about event	No affect #	Affect #
Alleged Perpetrator		
F Socioeconomic status	Professional #	Nonprofessional #
G Relationship to alleged victim	Familial *	Nonfamilial
H Ages	16 to 25 years	26+ years *
I Race	Minority #	White #
J History of violence	Yes *	No
K History of substance abuse	Yes *	No
Alleged Victim's Caretaker(s)		
L History of childhood sexual abuse	Yes *	No
M History of psychiatric illness	Yes *	No
Family		
N Prior contact with protective service agencies	Yes *	No
O Child custody-visitation issues	Yes	No *

NOTE: Levels marked with an asterisk (*) were expected to have higher credibility ratings based on the literature or clinical observations. Levels marked with # were expected to have equal credibility ratings.

the credibility of each vignette. For each group, there were 16 vignettes for (8 X 16) 128 units of analysis. Thus, we obtained eight average scores for each of the 16 vignettes. Our units of analysis were these averages across respondents in each subgroup for each vignette. The independent variables were the 15 vignette factors (see Table 5.2), each coded "1" or "2." The dependent variable was the average credibility rating averaged across the respondents in each of the eight groups. This regression was highly significant, accounting for 84.4% of the variance.

Of the 15 case factors, 7 were significant (see following discussion) at better than the $p < .001$ level, one at the $< .01$ and one at the $< .05$ level. The race of the perpetrator was the most powerful predictor (vignettes alleging sexual abuse by Caucasians were more believable than those in which the perpetrator was black or Hispanic). Other major factors included (a) the relationship of the alleged perpetrator to the victim (where the perpetrator was a family member the allegations were more credible), (b) the victim's race

Table 5.2 Multiple Regression Analysis of Vignette Case Factors on Mean
Credibility Ratings

Variable	Coefficient	Significance of t Ratio
Alleged Victim		
A Gender	0.086	NS
B Age	- 0.279	< .001
C Race	- 0.326	< .001
D Behavioral changes	- 0.251	< .001
E Affect about event	0.293	< .001
Alleged Perpetrator		
F Socioeconomic status	0.143	< .01
G Relationship	- 0.335	< .001
H Age	- 0.119	NS
I Race	0.589	< .001
J History of violence	- 0.090	NS
K History of substance abuse	- 0.232	< .001
Nonoffending Caretaker		
L Childhood history of sexual abuse	- 0.115	NS
M History of psychiatric illness	0.052	NS
Family		
N Prior contact with protective service agencies	- 0.170	< .05
O Child custody-visitation issues	- 0.002	NS
Constant	5.093	< .001

Note: These regression coefficients assume the case factor levels are coded "1" and "2."
a. NS means not significant.
Dependent variable is: Mean Credibility
Units of Analysis: 16 Vignettes as rated by 8 discipline samples by gender (total 128).
$R^2 = 86.3\%$; R^2(adjusted) = 84.4%.

(allegations of sexual abuse of a minority child were more credible),
(c) the victim's affect (vignettes where the child showed negative
affect were more credible), (d) the victim's age (the alleged sexual
abuse of a young child was more credible than the abuse of an
adolescent), (e) the victim's behavior (vignettes in which a child
showed behavioral changes were more credible), and (f) the perpetrator's history of substance abuse (a prior history of substance abuse
made the allegations more credible).

Two other factors were significant at $p < .05$: the SES of the
perpetrator (alleged sexual abuse by nonprofessionals had higher
credibility scores than those allegations in which the perpetrator
was a professional) and the family's relationship with protective
services (prior protective service intervention made the allegations
more believable).

Of the 15 factors, 6 were not significant (t values less than 2.0): (a) custody issues; (b) the nonoffending caretaker's history of child sexual abuse or history of psychiatric illness; (c) the victim's gender; (d) the perpetrator's history of violence; (e) and the age of the perpetrator.

Figure 5.1 graphically presents the regression effects on the credibility scores for each of the 16 vignettes. The regression coefficients in the graph are arranged by magnitude, allowing determination at a glance of those factors that had the greatest impact on the clinicians' ratings of credibility of sexual abuse allegations.

Note that the bars on the left indicate lower credibility, whereas those on the right indicate higher credibility. In this graph, the effects are coded so that zero corresponds to halfway between the two levels. Thus, the sizes of the effects are (+ and -) one half the values of the regression coefficients in Table 5.2.

Significant Case Factors

Perpetrator Race

The largest positive effect on credibility scores occurs in vignettes in which a Caucasian was the perpetrator (+.295 units above the grand mean; see Figure 5.1). Respondents were far more likely to believe sexual abuse allegations when the perpetrator was Caucasian than when he was black or Hispanic.[1] Conversely, we see the largest negative effect on credibility scores in vignettes where the perpetrator was a minority member (-.295 units above the grand mean). Thus, the effect of the perpetrator's race is impressive, increasing or decreasing the credibility score by .59 (2 × .295) scale units.

When we first examined our findings on race, we were both astonished and suspicious. We recalled physical scientist Jacob Bronowski's comment about startling observations to the effect that if, while exploring the Antarctic, you see a horselike animal with black and white stripes playing on the ice, you probably should look again to make sure that what you think you see is really there. Accordingly, we went back to our data to look again. To our amazement, we found the zebra was still there!

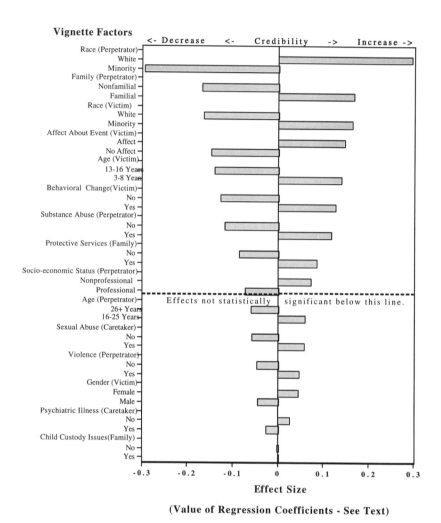

Figure 5.1. Effects of Vignette Factors on Credibility Scores
NOTE: For values of regression coefficients, see text.

Over 50 years ago, Myrdal (1944) wrote, "race . . . continue[s]
. . . to gnaw at the American conscience" (p. 169). Unfortunately, his
statement is as valid today as it was then. Despite evidence that
perpetrators may come from any racial or ethnic group (Dembo,
Williams, & Schmeidler, 1993; Finkelhor, 1984; Laumann, Gagnon,

Michael, & Michaels, 1994; Russell, 1983; Sedney & Brooks, 1984), in this study, the race of the perpetrator was the most powerful predictor of credibility and in what, at first, appeared to be a paradoxical direction. Clinicians had more confidence in the credibility of sexual abuse allegations made against Caucasians than those made against blacks or Hispanics.

Our results contradict studies of physical abuse in which allegations involving ethnic minority families have been disproportionately reported and substantiated (Hampton & Newberger, 1985; Jason, Andereck, Marks, & Tyler, 1982). However, our findings are consistent with results of a study that identified factors that influence the decision to prosecute cases of child sexual abuse (Cross, DeVos, & Whitcomb, 1994). Of 431 cases referred for possible court action, Cross et al. found that Caucasian perpetrators were more likely to be prosecuted than were African American or Hispanic perpetrators. Because interracial abuse is relatively rare, the vast majority of sexual abuse offenders are likely to be of the same racial group as the victim (DeJong & Emmet, 1983). Thus, the observation that the courts do not take the abuse of blacks and Hispanics as seriously as the abuse of Caucasians may be a reflection of reverse racism, or another form of systemic racism.

Reviewing the social science literature on racism from the 1950s to the 1970s, Fajardo (1985) found that conceptualizations of racism shifted from viewing prejudice as personal, attitudinal bigotry, independent of the actual situation, to an environmental phenomenon that considers a more complex model of "social costs, rewards, belief congruence, values, conformity pressures, status, and the type of social/physical relationship between the subject and the stimulus person" (Amir, 1976, cited in Fajardo, 1985, p. 256).

According to Crosby, Bromley, and Saxe (1980), "discrimination exists when individuals from one group . . . receive significantly more help than individuals from the other group" (p. 546). Thus, prejudice may imply both negative and positive bias. According to Dutton and Lake (1973), "reverse discrimination (positive bias) refers to interactions between a white person and a minority group member where the white behaves more favorably toward the minority group member than he would behave toward another white in the same . . . situation" (p. 94).

Dienstbier (1970) was the first to study situations in which whites may behave more favorably toward minority members than

toward other whites. He proposes the term "positive racial prejudice" as "favoritism toward [black] stimulus persons over white
stimulus persons of identical personality descriptions" (p. 214). He
postulates four conditions for positive prejudice. The subject (a) is
not bound into an irrevocable relationship with the person involved,
(b) has a personal commitment to demonstrate opposition to the
notion of racial deficiency, (c) wishes to appear egalitarian, and (d)
has a need to attenuate guilt about negative prejudice.

Elaborating on Dienstbier's (1970) findings, Dutton (1976) labels this a "special case of altruistic behavior" whereby individuals
are reassured that they are egalitarian and nondiscriminatory (Gaertner, 1973). Ironically, in an attempt to be fair, people may overreact
to unduly favor minority or disadvantaged group members and thus
unfairly indict the majority[2] (Fajardo, 1985). Dutton (1976) proposes
criteria similar to those of Dienstbier as prerequisites for reverse
racism to occur: (a) the majority member must believe in the concept
of racial equality and view racial discrimination as unfair; (b) the
nonminority person must view the minority person as a potential
victim of racial discrimination, and (c) interaction between the nonminority and minority individuals must be limited, allowing the
social boundaries between them to remain fixed.

In our study, respondents had nothing to lose or gain by giving
the benefit of the doubt to the minority member accused of sexual
abuse. As noted earlier, it is likely that most respondents surveyed
in this study view themselves as liberals. Thus, we expect them to
feel remorse about racial inequity and, consequently, to empathize
with a minority member. We speculate that the motivation to view
oneself as egalitarian and nondiscriminatory may be a manifestation
of an internalized mental representation of the social pressure to be
"politically correct."

Our research population fulfills both Dienstbier's and Dutton's
requirements: the professionals who participated in this study are
certainly overwhelmingly white[3] and probably view themselves as
liberal and egalitarian. Their involvement in the study was a time-
limited, simulated, "pseudo" interaction that had no personal or
professional cost. That is, the anonymity of the respondents and the
social distance between them and the people described in the vignettes
was neither threatened or compromised.

Another explanation of our result may be found in Katz's (1970)
view that prejudice may be expressed either in discriminatory or

reverse discriminatory behavior, the outcome of which will depend on three categories of psychological factors: self-interest (whether the behavior will result in a loss or gain to the majority member), cognitive-emotional predispositions (the tension among the majority member's level of discrimination, "sympathy for the underdog, and guilt over racial injustice," p. 74), and social-conformity pressures (disapproval or approval).

According to Fajardo (1985), Katz places the psychological etiology of prejudice and reverse prejudice in the context of psychodynamic theory. Using the concepts of ambivalence and identification, Katz suggests that individuals who have unresolved conflicts toward authority will have more intense reactions to members of minority groups. Accordingly, negative contact between an ambivalent individual and a minority member will result in the ambivalent individual's identification with the predominant culture; when an ambivalent individual's contact with a minority member is positive, identification will be with the victim of oppression. Thus, depending on the quality of the contact with the minority member, the ambivalent individual may display either racism or reverse racism.

The concepts of *blame analysis* (Felsen, 1991), *social desirability* (Tierney, 1992), and a *special case of altruistic behavior* (Dutton, 1976; Dutton & Yee, 1974; May, 1974) have been used to describe reverse prejudice. Felson suggests that social scientists are particularly vulnerable to the need to protect certain groups by avoiding assignment of blame; Tierney proposes that some people feel compelled to conceal their racial hostility, because relatively few middle-class U.S. citizens wish to be seen as prejudiced.

Tajfel (1969) moves beyond the unconscious as an explanation of prejudice, which, he believes, is "laid down" very early. Framing the etiology of prejudicial judgments in the context of adaptive cognition, he proposes three cognitive processes operative in prejudice: "categorization," "assimilation," and a "search for coherence" (p. 82). According to Tajfel, categorization is the process by which individuals seek to reduce complex and ambiguous cognitions to clearly defined, comprehensible terms. Assimilation is the process by which prejudice is channeled through societal judgments that are internalized very early and continue throughout life. The search for coherence is an attempt to make meaning of events; its direction will depend on the extent to which the individual can maintain self-esteem and principle.

Marlowe, Frager, and Nuttall (1965), like Tajfel, use the theory of cognitive dissonance (Festinger, 1957) as a basis for understanding reverse racism. They propose that the act of favoring minorities may serve two functions: first, to reassure individuals of their egalitarian beliefs, and second, to alleviate the discomfort arising from their, or others', perception of themselves as prejudiced.

Larsen (1974), integrating Tajfel's three cognitive processes, proposes an explanation of racism based on three factors: (a) social cost, (b) cognitive consistency, and (c) categorization. He found that social cost was the most powerful variable predicting preference or rejection. According to Larsen (1974), the concept of social cost includes the variables of "pressure of the social environment, the status attributed by the group, the need to be socially accepted, or fears of being rejected" (p. 266).

Perhaps, favoring the perpetrators depicted as minority members reinforced our respondents' self-concepts as egalitarian and warded off threats of self-perception as prejudiced. However, as Crosby et al. (1980) emphasize, behavior that is not costly, or is easy to accomplish, is a flimsy basis from which to deduce an individual's attitudes. Although our findings may reflect the subjects' compliance with an egalitarian, nonprejudicial philosophy (Crosby et al., 1980) and a response to the subject's "private value system" (Dutton & Yee, 1974, p. 339), they do not necessarily predict the respondents' behavior in practice. This is a critical area for future research.

Relationship of the Perpetrator to the Victim

Our hypothesis that the "familial" level of the variable for relationship of the victim to the perpetrator (familial vs. nonfamilial) would elicit greater credibility was supported.[4] Figure 5.1 shows that the second largest effect on credibility is the relationship of the victim to the perpetrator. In the eight vignettes in which the perpetrator was a family member, the average credibility score was about +.17 units above the grand mean. In the eight vignettes in which the perpetrator was not a family member, the average credibility score was about -.17 units below the grand mean. On average, clinicians had more confidence that sexual abuse had occurred when the perpetrator was a family member.

As reports of familial abuse continue to escalate, earlier assumptions that most sexual abuse is perpetrated by strangers has increasingly been challenged. Researchers consistently show that most offenders are males known to their victims (Ellerstein & Canavan, 1980; Finkelhor, Hotaling, Lewis, & Smith, 1990; Kendall-Tackett & Simon, 1987).

Recent investigations of both clinical and nonclinical populations (Daro, 1988; Gale, Thompson, Moran, & Sack, 1988; Haugaard & Reppucci, 1988; Lanktree, Briere, & Zaidi, 1991; Mennen, 1993; Ryan, Warren, & Weincek, 1991) suggest that male family members or acquaintances are the primary perpetrators of sexual abuse, whereas male strangers account for a relatively small proportion of offenders (Sauzier, 1989). In DeJong and Emmet's (1983) record review of 566 predominantly black male and female children who presented at a sexual assault crisis clinic, 50% of offenders were known to their victims—either acquaintances or relatives.

In our initial study where we defined incest to include mothers, stepfathers, and grandfathers in addition to biological fathers, only 19% of the abused females and 8% of the abused males had reported incestuous relationships. When we included all family members, the frequency of incest increased to 47% of the abused females and 35% of the abused males.

In Laumann et al.'s (1994) community sample, the majority of each gender sexually touched as children were abused by individuals who were familiar to them (i.e., relatives and friends). In a chart review study, Pierce and Pierce (1985) compared 25 substantiated cases of sexual abuse of boys with 180 substantiated cases of sexual abuse of girls. They found that abuse took place within the home for both male and female children, suggesting that most offenders were known to the victims. Unlike our findings, the offender was most often the stepfather for both boys and girls. However, as in our findings, girls were more likely than boys to be sexually abused by their biological fathers.

Although both men and women in our study were most likely to be abused by men who were familiar to them (see Chapter 3), some reports suggest that boys are more likely than girls to be abused by strangers (van der May, 1988). Ellerstein and Canavan (1980) reviewed charts of 145 patients coming to an emergency room with the complaint of sexual abuse. They found that the majority of female victims had been abused at home or in other familiar settings but that most male victims were abused in a public setting. In a telephone survey of a large, randomly drawn community sample of males and females (1,145 males; 1,481 females), Finkelhor et al. (1990) found that women who had been sexually molested as children were likely to have been abused by family members, whereas boys were likely to have been victimized by strangers (Finkelhor et al., 1990).

As a consequence of the rapid growth of child day care, interest has developed in the incidence of nonfamilial abuse in out-of-home placements (Nunno & Motz, 1988) by care providers (Bybee & Mowbray, 1993; Finkelhor, Williams, Burns, & Kalinowski, 1988), babysitters, and other nonrelated live-in or transient individuals in the caretaking role (Margolin, 1991). The incidence rate of sexual abuse of children under the age of 6 years attending day care centers is estimated at 5.5 per 10,000, compared to an estimated incidence rate of 8.9 per 10,000 children abused at home (Finkelhor et al., 1988). The accuracy of these estimates is certainly questionable, because allegations of sexual abuse in day care centers are particularly difficult to investigate due to the youth of the victims (Bybee & Mowbray, 1993). Clearly, objective research in this area is badly needed.

Victim Race

The third most powerful predictor of credibility scores was the victim's race. (Sexual abuse allegations were more convincing when the victim was a minority member.) Thus, our expectation that this factor would have little or no effect on respondents' credibility ratings was disproved.

Despite reports that minority children are more vulnerable to sexual (Tzeng & Schwarzin, 1990) and physical abuse (Daniel, Hampton, & Newberger, 1983), other studies (Laumann et al., 1994; NCCAN, 1988) have found no consistent relationship between a child's race or ethnicity and the incidence of sexual abuse. Thus, our finding that race (perpetrator and victim) represents two of the three most powerful factors in clinicians' ratings of credibility of sexual abuse allegations is both disappointing and discouraging to those seeking objectivity.

Victim Affect

Our hypothesis that the victim variable "lack of affect" would have little or no effect on credibility was not supported. We see in

Figure 5.1 that the fourth most powerful predictor of credibility scores was the victim's affect when describing the alleged abuse. Those vignettes in which victims expressed negative affect were more credible (+.16); vignettes in which victims showed no affect were less credible (-.16).

The clinicians' conviction that allegations in which children did not show negative affect were less believable than those in which children did show such affect is consistent with Green's controversial evaluation paradigm of true and false allegations (Green, 1986). Green claims that a child's disclosure is usually accompanied by disturbed and saddened affect and that lack of such negative emotion can be viewed as indicative of a false allegation.

Indeed, most children, when disclosing sexual abuse, do show affect congruent with the description of the incident (Jones & McGraw, 1987). However, as Corwin, Berliner, Goodman, Goodwin, and White (1987) note, professionals routinely encounter the reverse. As early as 1933, the psychoanalyst Ferenczi (1949) reported the defenses of dissociation and repression among the sequelae of sexual abuse. He wrote, "the overpowering force and authority of the adult makes [children] dumb and can rob them of their senses" (p. 162). Many studies since have reported that children who have been seriously traumatized may, in a desperate effort to adapt, dissociate or retreat into emotional numbness (Jones & McGraw, 1987). Furthermore, children subjected to multiple interviews "may begin to recount their experience with muted emotions" (Jones & McGraw, 1987).

Goodwin (1985), addressing this issue, writes that "partial amnesia or mild dissociation (often found in children who have been sexually abused) can be associated with dream-like, stereotyped, affectless, impersonal accounts which [may] vary with each retelling" (p. 12). Because of the betrayal they have experienced, children who are traumatized are often distrustful of adults (Summit, 1983) and as a result, may be afraid to show their real feelings. To observers who are unfamiliar with the variability and unpredictability of trauma responses, a child's defensive strategies may be mistakenly viewed as evidence of a lack of affect and consequently, as a sign that the child is not telling the truth. Unfortunately, such disbelief by professionals may only strengthen the victim's dissociative strategies (Goodwin, 1985).

Victim Age

Surprisingly, clinicians' credibility ratings do not support our hypothesis that respondents would give as much or more credence to allegations about adolescent victims than they would to those about younger children. The victim's age had the fifth strongest effect on credibility ratings. Clinicians found allegations that a younger child had been sexually abused more credible than those where an adolescent had been so abused. This finding is the reverse of earlier studies in which allegations were significantly more likely to be substantiated where adolescents, rather than young children, were involved (Eckenrode, Powers, Doris, Munsch, & Bolger, 1988; Powers & Eckenrode, 1988).

According to Finkelhor (1993) and Anderson, Martin, Mullen, Romans, and Herbison (1993), preadolescents and early adolescents are at greater risk for sexual abuse than children of other ages. Parents' (N = 1,000) accounts of their children's sexual abuse history (within the year prior to a poll conducted by the Gallup Group; Moore & Schussel, 1995), show adolescents (aged 13-17 years) most vulnerable to sexual abuse (38 per 1,000), followed by children between the ages of 5 to 8 years (29 per 1,000).

Although the onset of sexual abuse may occur in early childhood, it may not be discovered or diagnosed until adolescence or adulthood (Coons, 1986). Thus, adolescents form the largest group of reported cases of sexual victimization (Aiosa-Karpas, Karpas, Pelcovitz, & Kaplan, 1991). Of all reported maltreatment cases, 47% are adolescents (42% of which are substantiated; NCCAN, 1988; Sturkie & Flanzer, 1987). From another report, 13-year-olds to 16-year-olds account for 32% of children who had experienced sexual maltreatment (American Association for Protecting Children, 1986). Clearly, evidence strongly suggests that sexual abuse disclosures by adolescents should be taken seriously.

There is some evidence that children's accurate recall of painful events is developmentally dependent (Steward, Bussey, Goodman, & Saywitz, 1993). However, we found no studies that addressed directly the relationship between the credibility of sexual abuse allegations and age of the victim. Our results are in agreement with Zellman and Bell's (1989) finding that cases involving younger children are more likely to be reported than those in which older children disclose abuse. Finkelhor and Hotaling (1984) speculate that many adults perceive very young children as incapable of purposeful sexual involvement, whereas they view adolescents (15-16 years old) as "capable of engaging in sexual activity with older partners without it automatically being a form of abuse" (p. 115). Similarly, Powers and Eckenrode (1988) suggest that allegations involving younger children may be taken more seriously because they are seen as more vulnerable than older children.

Goodwin (1985), in her discussion of child credibility, proposes that adolescent victims often choose to disclose sexual victimization when they are least likely to be believed, namely, when they have misbehaved. Broussard and Wagner (1988), in their survey of (male and female) undergraduates to determine attribution of responsibility, found respondents more likely to assign responsibility for their abuse to 15-year-olds than to children aged 7 to 11 years. They propose a "blame the victim" mentality that reflects a "stereotype of adolescent molestation victims as provocateurs" (p. 567).

A study of 223 adolescent runaway and homeless youth seeking services (Powers, Eckenrode, & Jaklitsch, 1990) shows that the rate of childhood sexual abuse in this population is significantly higher than in the general population. Because adolescents "tend to deny, retract, or minimize sexual abuse in order to distance themselves from (their abuse)" (p. 95), they are often not recognized as victims. Thus, many incidents of abuse and neglect go unreported and untreated, often culminating in acting-out behaviors that mask the maltreatment and make the abused more vulnerable to revictimization. Drawn into prostitution, drugs, or other types of criminal behavior, the runaways' potential to develop and move toward adulthood is seriously compromised.

Garbarino, Schellenback, and Sebes (1986) cite society's general tendency to regard adolescents with distrust and a lack of empathy. In cases of sexual abuse, these biases may be manifested in a "blame the victim" attitude. According to Summit (1983), "an image persists of nubile adolescents playing dangerous games out of their burgeoning sexual fascination" (p. 178). Consequently, when adolescents make allegations of sexual abuse, they are often suspected of being vindictive.

Victim Behavior

Vignettes in which the victim's behavior changed following the abusive incident received higher credibility scores than those in which there were no obvious changes in behavior. This is consistent with reports of a wide range of behavioral disturbances observed in victimized children and adolescents (Browne & Finkelhor, 1986a; Elwell & Ephross, 1987; Kendall-Tackett, Williams, & Finkelhor, 1993). However, Finkelhor (1993) reports that there are no factors that show a strong enough association to sexual abuse to either validate or invalidate the presence of abuse. No particular symptom has been manifested in a majority of sexually abused children nor have any "specific behavioral markers for sexual abuse" been identified (Green, 1993, p. 899). In his review of research conducted between 1980 and 1990, Green notes the lack of convincing behavioral signs to detect sexual abuse. He states that any of the initial effects observed in children could be in response to the dysfunctional characteristics of incestuous families or to the aftermath of disclosure.

Although many studies have sought to identify behavioral indicators of child sexual abuse, few have used controls, comparisons, or child samples (Aiosa-Karpas et al., 1991; Finkelhor, 1986). Physical findings in cases of sexual abuse are rare, often temporary, and may not be evident by the time the child discloses and is examined by a physician. Psychological problems may not be evident initially or may be subtle and difficult to determine (Gomez-Schwartz, Horowitz, & Saucier, 1985). Thus, controlled, comparative studies of children are needed to identify possible behavioral indicators specific to sexual abuse.

We have located two studies of behavior that appear controlled, at least partially. Kolko, Moser, and Weldy (1988) compared 81 sexually and physically abused, psychiatrically hospitalized children between the ages of 5 to 14 years and found that different types of abuse may have different consequences. Sexually abused children in their sample were more likely to exhibit hypersexualized behavior toward their peers and adults than were children who were physically abused. Dubowitz, Black, Harrington, and Verschoore (1993) compared 132 children, aged 4 to 12 years, suspected of having been sexually abused, with a demographically similar group ($N = 84$) with no history of abuse. In both the initial study and the 4-month follow-up, 43% of the sexually abused children but only 11% of the control group scored in the clinical range of behavior problems according to the Child Behavior Checklist (Achenbach & Edelbrock, 1983).

In the Dubowitz et al. (1993) study, 22% of the parents of the sexually abused children reported them as being excessively sexual, a rate more than 4 times greater than parents of children in the control group. Parents of the sexually abused children were more than 1.5 times more likely (27%) to report that their children demonstrated somatic symptoms and were more than 3 times as likely (14%) to report that their children were enuretic. Although these between-group behaviors were statistically significant, with the possible exception of excessive sexual activity, they are not specific to sexual abuse and are found in children who have experienced other kinds of trauma. Neither of these studies controlled for preexisting problem behaviors or for family variables that may have contributed to the behavioral indicators observed.

It is important to note that a substantial fraction of the children in the sexually abused group did not demonstrate any behavioral problems. Dubowitz et al. (1993) speculate that the absence of symptoms may be related to developmental stages and the child's cognitive and emotional capacity to experience guilt and shame. Alternatively, it is likely that there are children who, despite their sexual victimization, remain symptom free. Because the factors responsible for such an outcome are unknown, rigorous longitudinal studies are surely needed.

Kendall-Tackett et al. (1993), in their comprehensive review of the sexual abuse literature, conclude "that being sexually abused [is] strongly related to some symptoms specific to sexual abuse, such as sexualized behavior, as well as a range of more global symptoms such as depression, aggression, and withdrawal" (p. 167). According to Green (1993), sexualized behavior may reflect the child's adaptive attempts to master the traumatic experience through its re-creation. Phobic withdrawal from sexual activity may be the mirror image of recreation behavior and may reflect the belief that sexuality is associated with danger of further victimization (Cosentino, Meyer-Bahlburg, Alpert, & Gaines, 1993).

Beitchman, Zucker, Hood, DaCosta, and Akman (1991) conclude from their review of the short-term effects of sexual abuse that various types of sexualized behavior are consistently associated with abuse prior to adolescence. Manifestations of hypersexuality (Deblinger, McLeer, Atkins, Ralphe, & Foa, 1989), such as excessive masturbation, inserting fingers or objects into the vagina or anus, and other types of compulsive or provocative (or both) sexualized behavior have been attributed to a process of trauma reenactment and are usually viewed as strongly suggestive that sexual maltreatment has occurred (C. Hartman, personal communication, December 22, 1992).

Studies examining the psychological effects of sexual abuse in children should be read with caution. Many have serious methodological flaws related to lack of attention to controls or comparisons, to differences in types of abuse or abuser characteristics, or length of time since the abuse was initiated or terminated.

For example, two studies that identified depression as a common sequel among children (aged 6-18 years) reported as having been recently sexually abused have limited reliability; neither used a control or comparison group (Koverola, Pound, Heger, & Lytle, 1993; Mennen, 1993). Other sequelae reported in the literature are oppositional behavior, suicidal ideation and attempts (Bryer, Nelson, Miller, & Krol, 1987), drug abuse and other addictions (Kinzl & Biebl, 1992), running away (Rimsza & Berg, 1988), ego deficits, and distorted object relations (Kinzl & Biebl, 1992).

There is some evidence that the effects of sexual abuse are developmentally specific (Gomez-Schwartz et al., 1985; Hussey & Singer, 1993) and, as noted earlier, that children's perception of their abuse may be a function of their cognitive competence and emotional maturity at any given time (Black, Dubowitz, & Harrington, 1994). In a descriptive study, Bender and Blau (1937) reported that behaviors of 16 psychiatrically hospitalized prepubertal children suggested that the negative impact of sexual abuse differed by developmental stage. From a psychoanalytic framework, they observed that children in the "infantile stage" were more likely to demonstrate childish behavior, whereas children in the latency period were more likely to demonstrate impaired academic and social adaptation. Prepubertal children were more likely to present adjustment problems.

Recently, Black et al. (1994) conducted a more rigorously designed study to identify initial effects of childhood sexual abuse. They recruited 44 children, ages 4 to 12, who were being evaluated for suspicion of sexual abuse and compared them with 41 demographically similar children with no history of abuse. Using the Child Behavior Checklist (Achenbach & Edelbrock, 1983); they found no immediate consequences of sexual abuse evident in young preschool children.

Kendall-Tackett et al., (1993) and her colleagues, in a review of 45 case studies of children who had been sexually abused prior to age 18, found that the abused children's symptoms varied by age at assessment (no symptoms were reported for 1/3 of the children). In the preschool group, the most common symptoms were anxiety, nightmares, post-traumatic stress disorder, depression, acting-out, and inappropriate sexual behavior. In school-age children, the most common symptoms were fear, general mental illness, combativeness, nightmares, school difficulties, hyperactivity, and regressive behavior. In the adolescent group, the most common symptoms were depression, withdrawal, suicidal and self-destructive behavior, somatization, delinquency, running away, and substance abuse.

Hussey and Singer (1993), in a study of psychiatrically hospitalized adolescents, reported a higher incidence of use of mood-altering substances among sexually abused adolescents ($N = 87$) compared to nonabused adolescents ($N = 87$). They suggest that drug use may be a type of self-medication, an attempt to cope with difficult feelings related to abuse. They propose that there may be particular psychological mechanisms that, used at earlier developmental phases, may set the stage for subsequent psychopathology (Hussey & Singer, 1993). Clearly, defenses that are adaptive at one developmental stage may become maladaptive when their use persists in later stages.

Perpetrator's History of Substance Abuse

The perpetrator's history of substance abuse had the seventh most powerful effect on credibility ratings. Thus, our expectation that clinicians would be more likely to validate sexual abuse allegations when the perpetrator had a previous history of alcohol abuse than when he did not was upheld.

Ferenczi (1949) called attention to the relationship between sexual abuse and substance abuse among his patients who (during analysis) had disclosed sexual assault of children. He described such patients as "disturbed in their balance and self-control by some misfortune or by the use of intoxicating drugs" (p. 161). Many studies have since found that alcohol abuse contributes to a decrease in, or loss of, the usual inhibitions against acting out sexually aberrant wishes or fantasies (Aarens, Cameron, Roizen, Schnerberk, & Wingard, 1978; Morgan, 1982, cited in Finkelhor, 1984). According to the American Humane Association (Kameen & Thompson, 1983), among 655 cases of father-daughter incest substantiated between 1975 and 1978, substance abuse was present in more than one third. Other researchers have cited the association of substance abuse with sexual abuse (Kameen & Thompson, 1983).

Margolin (1994) identifies substance abuse as one of the perpetrator characteristics representing significant risk. Other contributory factors found among Margolin's sample of aunts and uncles who had sexually abused children were criminal and psychiatric backgrounds, history of sexually deviant behavior, and a history of sexual assault against their own or nonfamily members. Conte (1984) found that a history of substance abuse in a victim's family was associated with the severity of the sequelae to sexual abuse. Torme (as cited in Kameen Thompson, 1983) found, in a sample of 20 cases of incest, that a significant percentage of fathers had histories of violence and chronic alcoholism. In a subsample of 86 adolescent fathers identified as at extreme risk for child maltreatment, Bolton (1987) identified a history of substance abuse and violence. Conversely, Herman (1986), in her study of a psychiatric outpatient population, did not find a statistically significant association between sexual abuse and substance abuse among a subgroup of sex offenders.

The association of substance abuse and child abuse appears to be a serious consideration in placement decisions. Kameen and Thompson (1983), Murphy et al. (1991), and Runyon, Gould, Trost, and Loda (1982) found that parental substance abuse was an influential factor in decisions to remove children from their homes. Gabel, Finn, and Ahmed (1988) also found that parental substance abuse was associated with out-of-home placements of severely disturbed children. Based on a sample of 51 abuse cases reported to child protection services in Scotland, Waterhouse and Carnie (1992) developed an assessment protocol to aid social workers' evaluation of sexual abuse disclosures. Among the criteria used to either substantiate or refute disclosure is the perpetrator's criminal or psychiatric history, including alcohol or drug abuse.

Mian, Martin, LeBaron, and Birtwistle (1994), in a chart review of 125 children referred for suspicion of sexual abuse, compared three groups of 3-year-old to 5-year-old children: those whose incestuous abuse had been validated, those whose extrafamilial abuse had been validated, and those who had not been abused. They found that fathers in the two abused groups (according to their spouses' reports) were more likely than those in the nonabused group to be substance abusers.

Family's Prior Contact With Protective Services

To the extent that a prior history with protective services may reflect family dysfunction, we expected this factor to influence clinical decision making. We were not surprised, then, that respondents found allegations in which the families had such a history more convincing than those with no such history. Relevant to our findings, the Lutzker and Rice (1987) project found relatively high recidivism rates of physical abuse and neglect in families that prior to the study had received child protective services. Moreover, Pierce and Pierce (1985), in their investigation of 205 cases to determine different rates of sexual abuse by gender, found that close to one third of both the male and female samples (28% of 25 males and 31% of 180 females) reported prior substantiated reports by protective services.

Perpetrator Socioeconomic Status

We found no reports suggesting that the SES of the perpetrator is an explanatory factor for child sexual abuse (Araji & Finkelhor, 1986). However, some empirical research has sought to determine the relationship between the SES of the victim's family and sexual abuse. According to Finkelhor (1993), epidemiologic studies fail to demonstrate an association between SES or race and risk for sexual abuse. Sedney and Brooks (1984), in their study of a nonclinical population of 301 women, found that sexual abuse occurs in families from all socioeconomic, racial, and religious environments. They note that these factors, along with the occupational status of the victim's parents, were not associated with the occurrence of either familial or intrafamilial abuse or their frequency. They infer that sexual abuse "is not uncommon in families from a variety of socio-economic, racial, and religious backgrounds" (p. 218).

In agreement, Bagley, Wood, and Young (1994) conclude that "child sexual abuse . . . is found in all types of families, regardless of family structure and social class levels" (p. 694). Finkelhor and Baron's (1986) review of the sexual abuse literature fails to show any relationship between sexual abuse and the SES of the victim's family. Similarly, Laumann et al. (1994), in their national, randomly drawn community sample, found no correlation between a childhood history of being touched inappropriately and age, ethnicity, race, education, or social class.

Despite these findings, a disproportionate number of lower socioeconomic families are seen in public and private agencies (Benson, Swann, O'Toole, & Turbett, 1991). It remains unclear whether this overrepresentation is an artifact of service delivery patterns or is real. According to Hawkins and Tiedeman (1975), "a social control system is more likely to gather in and process members of lower SES and minority groups, as opposed to members of higher SES and majority groups" (p. 64). Moreover, lower income families in crisis are more likely to use public agencies than are higher income families who have the resources to solve their acute problems in the private sector (DeJong & Emmet, 1983).

There is, however, some evidence that supports a relationship between income and sexual abuse in children (up to age 18 years). Moore and Schussel (1995), in their national survey of parents, found that the incidence of sexual abuse among children was 3.5% for families with yearly incomes less than $20,000, 2.8% for families with yearly incomes between $20,000 and $30,000, 0.8% for families with yearly incomes between $30,000 and $50,000, and 0.5% for families with yearly incomes over $50,000. Similarly, in a random sample of 750 young adult males (aged 18-27 years) in Calgary, Canada, Bagley et al. (1994) found a high proportion of those reporting sexual abuse came from disadvantaged families.

In a sample of 492 female college students, Parker and Parker (1991) found that those who reported abuse were more likely to come from lower SES. Father's education and occupation and mother's education were, on average, lower than that of the parents of their nonabused counterparts. Also, in a sample of undergraduates (male and female, $N = 800$), Finkelhor (1980) found that sexually abused children were 1.5 times more likely to come from families with incomes under $10,000 per year than the sample as a whole (33% vs. 19%). In a clinical sample of 112 girls (aged 3-5 years) whose sexual abuse had been substantiated, Mian et al. (1994) found a positive relationship between sexual abuse and SES of the family as measured by income level and education. Perhaps, as Finkelhor (1980) has speculated, children from low-SES families may be exposed to "low income adults [who] are more likely to be child molesters" (p. 272).

Given these contradictory findings, it is not surprising that, in a study of expert and juror knowledge about sexual abuse, Morison and Greene (1992) found that experts were unable to reach consensus on the association between SES and sexual abuse. The reasons for such opposing findings are obscure and suggest the need for rigorous research that controls for sampling bias, varying definitions, and methodology.

In our study, it remains uncertain whether the influence of the factor "SES" reflects a bias based on stereotypic notions of class or an informed judgment. Our vignettes identified only the perpetrator's SES (as defined by professional or nonprofessional status), not the SES of the victim or the victim's family. Although the perpetrators in our vignettes were identified as either "familial" or "nonfamilial," all were known to the victim and the victim's family. Because the literature strongly suggests that most sexual abuse is perpetrated by persons related to or known to victims or their families, it seems reasonable that our respondents would assume that the victim's family background, when not given, was similar to that of the perpetrator.

Some professional groups may be more influenced than others by the social class of the victim.[5] For example, in a vignette study in which the factors of race, SES, and extent of injury were manipulated, Benson, Swann, O'Toole, and Turbett (1991) found that all three factors influenced U.S. physicians' diagnostic and reporting decisions about physical abuse. However, when their study was replicated with a group of nurses in the United States (O'Toole, Turbett, & Nalepka, 1983) and physicians in Northern Ireland (Benson et al., 1991), they found no such tendency. The authors suggest that the discrepancy in the findings in the Northern Ireland study may be due to a more egalitarian selection process for medical training in Northern Ireland. Because the pool of physicians in that country is less class biased than in this country, it is likely that there will be less class disparity between patient and physician. We speculate that the same may be true for nurses in the United States, who, in contrast to other professionals in this country, tend to come from lower socioeconomic backgrounds.

Although ethnicity and the SES of the perpetrator were related to physicians' responses to child physical abuse in the Benson et al. (1991) study, it is important to note that when the level of injury depicted in the vignettes reflected an obvious case of abuse (e.g., cigarette burns on the child's back), the factors of race and SES had no significant effect. Only when the evidence was ambiguous (as in the sexual abuse allegations presented in our vignettes and in most of those encountered in practice) did these factors come into play.

A strong association between physical abuse and neglect and familial social class has been reported in the literature (Gelles & Straus, 1987; Gil, 1973; Helfer, 1987; Moen, Kain, & Elder, 1981, as cited in Garbarino et al., 1986; Pelton, 1985; Wolfe, 1987.) These studies show that children in lower SES households are at greater risk for physical maltreatment and neglect. A similarly strong association was found by Moore and Schussell (1995). Physical abuse rates (in the year prior to their study) were reported at 9.3% for families with yearly incomes less than $20,000, 5.1% for families whose yearly incomes were between $20,000 to $30,000, 3.3% for families whose yearly income was between $30,000 to $50,000, and 2.8% for families whose yearly income was more than $50,000.

Although the relationship between the etiology of physical or sexual abuse and neglect is unclear (Garbarino et al., 1986), our finding of a substantial increase in the risk for sexual abuse among the physically abused suggests commonalities that may be related to factors (in addition to SES) such as substance abuse, family violence, or both. To the extent that these may be associated with SES, sexual abuse may also be associated with SES. More research in this area is needed.

There are several possible, but not mutually exclusive, explanations for our finding that clinicians are influenced by a perpetrator's SES, despite the equivocal reports in the literature. Applying labeling theory to their findings of class prejudice, Benson et al. (1991) propose that individual responses to events will be influenced by prejudicial, stereotypic images, particularly in ambiguous situations.

Our data may also reflect a stereotypic view of sexual offenders as lower class and the assumption that a person's "beliefs, attitudes, and values [about sexual abuse] vary by socioeconomic status" (Davis & Proctor, 1989, p. 259). To the extent that sexual abuse is considered criminal behavior, clinicians may view it as a deviant activity in which high achieving individuals (depicted in the vignettes by SES) are less likely to engage.

A strong association between disadvantaged populations and those incarcerated for illegal activity has been reported in the literature. However, there is evidence that the association is, in part, an artifact of a biased criminal justice system rather than simply of higher prevalence rates among individuals of lower SES (Hampton & Newberger, 1985).

Another possible explanation for our findings may be the truism that individuals are less likely to think badly of those similar to themselves than of those who are dissimilar (Davis & Proctor, 1989, p. 257). Some research suggests that differences between and among individuals may be an even "stronger repellent than similarity is an attractant" (Rosenbaum, 1986, as cited in Davis & Proctor, 1989, p. 258).

Nonsignificant Case Factors

Caretaker and Family Factors

The nonoffending caretaker's history of mental illness did not significantly influence credibility ratings in this study. However, researchers have reported associations between higher risk for sexual abuse and dysfunctional families (Finkelhor, 1986), including parental alcoholism, parental history of abuse (Mian et al., 1994), and mental or physical illness (Friedrich & Reams, 1987; Herman, 1981; Peters, 1976). From their observations of parent-child interactions ($N = 8$), Friedrich and Reams (1987) report that family dynamics, such as a parent's history of sexual abuse, substance use, or mental illness, can influence the outcome of the child's victimization.

Smith and Israel (1987), in their descriptive study of 25 families in which sibling incest had been reported and substantiated, found that families in which such incest occurs are likely to have parents who are physically and emotionally unavailable to their children. Close to three quarters of the mothers and fathers in their sample reported childhood histories of sexual abuse. When they compared 17 sexually abused psychiatric inpatient male and female adolescents between the ages of 13 to 17 years to their (sexually) nonabused controls, Sansonnet-Hayden, Haley, Marriage, and Fine (1987) found that mothers of the sexually abused group were overwhelmingly more likely to have a history of child sexual abuse than mothers of the nonabused group. In a recent study of a national, randomly drawn sample of 2,000 children (aged 10-16 years), Boney-McCoy and Finkelhor (1995) found that prior victimization (not confined to sexual abuse) of a family member made sexual abuse of children significantly more likely.

In a Canadian study comparing two groups of abused girls (aged 3 to 5 years) referred to a large pediatric hospital to nonabused girls of the same age, Mian et al. (1994), found that mothers of children in the two abused groups ($N = 70$) were more likely than those of children in the nonabused group ($N = 42$) to have been sexually abused as children. Friedrich and Reams (1987) interviewed mothers of eight sexually abused children who were in therapy. More than half of the mothers (5) reported a childhood history of sexual abuse.

Elwell and Ephross (1987) studied 20 children (between the ages of 5 and 12 years) from a large urban hospital and from three public protection agencies (17 females and 3 males) shortly after their abuse was reported. They found that 35% of the abused children's parents (primarily mothers) reported a childhood history of sexual abuse, 40% of the abused children's parents (primarily mothers) reported a history of rape, and some reported other forms of family violence.

Child Custody-Visitation Issues

Our hypothesis that family involvement in custody disputes would not influence clinicians' judgments of sexual abuse allegations was validated. Though it has been suggested that professionals should be suspicious of allegations made in the context of custody disputes (Mikkelsen, Gutheil, & Emens, 1992), clinicians in our study were not influenced by this factor. According to Thoennes and Tjaden (1990), the public and the media tend to perceive an epidemic of vindictive mothers who, in the context of custody-visitation disagreements, falsely accuse their husbands of sexually abusing their children. Contrary to this perception, their research shows that a disproportionate number of false allegations are not made during custody-visitation disputes. In their telephone survey of professionals and review of court records ($N = 169$), they found that less than 2% of contested cases involved sexual abuse allegations. They conclude that allegations of sexual abuse when accompanied by custody disputes are no more or less likely to be substantiated than those made in the general population.

In their examination of 439 sexual abuse cases seen at the Kempe National Center between 1983 and 1985, Jones and McGraw (1987) found that "fictitious" cases (as judged by a consensus of professionals) represented a small proportion of their sample ($N = 21$). Although they found that the majority of the so-called fictitious cases ($N = 15$) were those in which there were bitter custody disputes between the mother and her ex-husband, other pathogenic factors, such as the mother-child relationship, psychiatric illness, and previous abuse, may have accounted for or contributed to a false allegation. It is interesting that a different study, cited by Jones and McGraw (1987) and conducted by Jones and Seig (n.d.), showed that sexual abuse allegations made in the context of custody or visitation conflicts were more likely to be designated as reliable than as false.

Perpetrator's History of Violence

Surprisingly, our hypothesis that a perpetrator's history of violence would make it more likely that allegations would be believed was not validated. Several studies have shown associations between alcohol abuse, violence, and child abuse. For example, Bolton (1987) found that, in addition to a history of substance abuse, a father's history of violence and lack of impulse control put children of adolescent parents at further risk for abuse. Tormes (as cited in Kameen & Thompson, 1983) noted that, in addition to histories of alcoholism, incestuous fathers had histories as perpetrators of violence. Elwell and Ephross (1987) reported that parents of some of the 20 sexually abused children in their study reported a history of family violence.

Victim's Gender

Again to our surprise, our expectation that respondents would be more likely to believe that a female rather than a male had been sexually abused was not validated. The gender of the victim was not a significant factor in determining the credibility of the allegations. Whereas it is generally agreed that the prevalence of male sexual abuse is greatly underestimated, the reported rates of sexual abuse for females range from about 1.5 to 4 times that of males (Finkelhor, 1979a; Finkelhor & Baron, 1986; Nasjleti, 1980; NCCAN, 1988). However, our findings (see Chapter 3) and those of Moore and Schussel (1995) suggest about equal rates of sexual abuse for the younger male and female cohorts.

Two Hypothetical Vignettes

Using the empirically determined coefficients, we can calculate the credibility ratings for any possible vignette constructed with our case factors. By varying the combinations of the nine case factors that significantly influenced clinicians' credibility ratings we can construct 2^9, or 512, cases and predict the average credibility of any possible case. The profiles for the most and least credible cases and the predicted average credibility scores for each are presented in the discussion to follow.

To make the predictions, we use the coefficients for each factor noted in Table 5.2 and multiply them by the value of each respective factor. Note that the factor levels are coded "1" or "2" (see Table 5.1). To obtain a predicted average score, the value of each factor (1 or 2) is multiplied by the factor coefficients shown in Table 5.2. The nonsignificant factor coefficients (victim gender, perpetrator age, perpetrator history of violence, nonoffending caretakers childhood history of sexual abuse and psychiatric illness, and child custody) are multiplied by 1.5 (halfway between 1 and 2) to eliminate them. The predicted score is the sum of the factor coefficients multiplied by the factor levels plus the constant, 5.093, shown in Table 5.2.

We applied this procedure to two hypothetical vignettes—one constructed with the most credible and one with the least credible case factors—to obtain a predicted maximum credibility score for the most credible vignette and a minimum score for the least credible vignette.

A Hypothetical Vignette Combining the Most Credible Factors

In a vignette in which all the highest scoring factors are included, the perpetrator is a Caucasian, working-class, nonbiological male family member with a history of substance abuse. He is accused of sexually molesting a minority child (between the ages of 3 to 8 years) of either gender who has expressed negative affect when talking about the abuse and whose behavior had changed following the alleged incident. Furthermore, the victim's family has, in the past, come to the attention of protective services. The most credible vignette, "Tito," then becomes as follows:

> Ms. Adams, a kindergarten teacher, filed a report of suspected sexual abuse for her pupil Tito H. A 5-year-old Hispanic boy, Tito had recently become withdrawn and oppositional at school. Furthermore, Ms. Adams was concerned that Tito's behavior had

become "highly sexualized." When questioned by Ms. Adams, Tito became upset. He cried and told Ms. Adams that Bob, his mother's Caucasian husband, had pulled out his penis and placed Tito's mouth on it. According to Tito, Bob had been drinking. This was not the first time the H. family had come to the attention of protective services. Thus, on being told of the report, Mrs. H. became concerned about retaining custody of Tito. When confronted with Tito's allegations, Bob denied them completely, saying that Tito had made the whole thing up.

Applying the calculation procedure presented earlier (see Table 5.2), we predict that the average credibility score for this vignette would be 5.3 (*fairly confident sexual abuse did occur*) out of a maximum possible score of 6.0 (*very confident sexual abuse did occur*). Among the 16 vignettes included in this study, "Paula" received the highest credibility rating, with a mean score of 4.97.

A Hypothetical Vignette Combining the Least Credible Factors

A vignette follows in which all the lowest scoring case factors are included: the alleged offender is a nonfamilial, minority (black or Hispanic) professional who does not have an alcohol problem. He is accused of sexually abusing a Caucasian male or female adolescent (between ages 13-16) whose affect was either positive or flat when talking about the alleged abuse and whose behavior had not changed following the reported incident. The victim's family did not have prior contact with protective services. Using these factors, the least credible vignette, "Cathy," becomes:

> Dr. D., a black dentist, was accused by Cathy, a 14-year-old Caucasian, of fondling her breasts and genitals while she was sitting in the dentist's chair. Dr. D. has a fine reputation as a respected professional and is known as a teetotaler. As Cathy described the incident to the social worker, she appeared calm and undisturbed by her experience. Cathy's parents expressed surprise at her allegation, noting that they had not noticed any changes in their daughter's behavior that indicated a problem. Dr. D. indignantly denied Cathy's allegations.

Again applying the calculation procedure with the coefficients of Table 5.2, we predicted the clinician's credibility score to be 2.6, (*slightly confident that sexual abuse did not occur*). The lowest possible score would be 1.0 (*very confident that sexual abuse did not occur*). The lowest mean score found among the 16 vignettes included in our study was that of "Jeff," with a mean score of 3.05.

These two extreme cases illustrate the range of average clinician ratings for the 512 sexual abuse allegations. The other 510 possible hypothetical cases would yield predicted credibility scores between 2.6 and 5.3, a range of 2.7 units. Thus, variation in the vignette factors can shift the credibility of an allegation of sexual abuse more than half the total range of five units and more than four within group standard deviations.

Our analyses demonstrate that by selecting and combining a variety of case factors, we can predict the credibility score of a hypothetical case as rated by an average clinician. The regression accounts for 84% of the variance of these group average ratings. Factors we may have inadvertently included in the vignettes or variations in the way different disciplines weight the various factors may be sources of the additional unexplained variation (16%). It should be remembered that these predictions are for so-called average clinicians; individual clinicians will vary considerably around these averages, as will be demonstrated.

Combining Case and Clinician Predictions

Combining the case factors analyzed in the preceding discussion with the respondent factors analyzed in Chapter 4, we can obtain a predicted credibility score that reflects both the case and respondent factors identified in this study. Using the predictive equation shown in Chapter 4 (see Table 4.4), we applied the regression results to predict how a clinician might rate a sexual abuse allegation. We use the same predictive equation for the individual clinician shown in Table 4.4 but replace the constant, 4.04, with the predicted credibility score of the case derived from an analysis of case factors only, using the coefficients in Table 5.2.

From this equation, we predict that our least credulous clinician, George, when evaluating the least credible allegation, will be *fairly confident sexual abuse did not occur* (2.22). Our most credulous clinician, Susan, evaluating the same allegation, will be very close to a neutral score of 3.5 (score 3.41). Thus, of the 512 possible cases, only the least credible will be rated slightly below neutrality by Susan. The other 511 possible cases will be rated as credible by this most credulous clinician.

Evaluating the most credible allegation, George, our least credulous clinician, would be *fairly confident it did occur* (4.84), whereas we expect that Susan, evaluating the same allegation, would be *very confident it did occur* (6.03).[6] Note that the extreme range of these results, from the least credulous clinician evaluating the least credible vignette or allegation to the most credulous clinician evaluating the most credible vignette or allegation, spans about 80% of the entire scale.

Summary and Conclusions

Of 15 case factors, 9 significantly affected clinicians' evaluation of the credibility of the 16 sexual abuse allegations. The factor of race accounted for two of the three most powerful effects on credibility ratings. In vignettes where the perpetrator was Caucasian and related to the victim who was a young (between the ages of 3 to 8) minority member, respondents demonstrated the greatest confidence that sexual abuse had occurred. Respondents were also influenced toward greater credibility by the victim's expression of negative affect when describing the alleged abuse and by the victim's behavior change following the event. Furthermore, belief in the allegations was greater where the victim's family had received previous protective service intervention and where the perpetrator was a working-class family member who had a history of alcohol abuse.

Of the 15 case factors, 6 had no significant effect on credibility ratings: the perpetrator's age and history of violence, the nonoffending caretaker's history of sexual abuse or psychiatric illness, the victim's gender, and child custody issues.

We have demonstrated that credibility ratings can range from *fairly confident sexual abuse did not occur* to *very confident it did occur* by selection of the most and least credible factors and respondents.

Thus, our findings empirically demonstrate that interpretations of sexual abuse allegations can be highly subjective. Despite the high percentage (72%) of respondents in our study who reported direct experience working with child or adolescent sexual abuse or both, several case factors beyond the boundaries of clinical relevance significantly influenced credibility ratings—some in unexpected directions.

Notes

1. Because the fractional factorial design of this study allows the possible confounding of interactions with main effects, the study should be replicated with a new set of 16 vignettes in which the race of the perpetrator is reversed.

2. Our discussion does not refer to deliberate social programs designed to improve the educational or occupational status of minorities and women.

3. Although we did not ask respondents in the initial study to identify their race, the racial distribution of the four disciplines nationally makes it highly likely that the majority of respondents were Caucasians. We did, however, analyze the racial composition of the respondents to our follow-up study. Of the 98% who identified their race, 91% were Caucasian, 2% were African American, 4% were Hispanic, and 3% were Asian.

4. For purposes of analysis, we defined familial sexual abuse as sexual maltreatment by a biological father or by a male who lived in the home of the alleged victim (e.g., uncle, stepfather, or boyfriend).

5. Pediatricians in our study were more influenced than the other disciplines by the SES of the perpetrator.

6. The maximum possible score is 6.0; a predicted score of 6.03 merely reflects the error band of the equation.

PART IV

Effects of Childhood
Abuse on Personal
Relationships and
Professional Behavior

6

Effects of
Childhood Abuse
on Adult Mental
Health

Overview

We compared the mental status of the abused and nonabused respondents with the Brief Symptom Inventory (BSI; Derogatis, 1983) and the Mississippi Civilian Post Traumatic Stress Disorder Scale (MCPTSD; Keane, 1988).

By self-report, the sexually abused

scored significantly higher than their nonabused peers on eight of the nine BSI scales and on the Global Severity Index (GSI).[1]
scored significantly higher than their nonabused peers on the MCPTSD scale.

were more likely, if their first abuse had occurred prior to age 12 years, to score significantly higher on the BSI Somatization scale than their peers whose abuse had initially occurred later.
females were significantly more likely than the nonabused to meet the criteria for a positive diagnosis.

By self-report, the physically abused

scored significantly higher than their nonabused peers on four of the nine BSI scales and on the GSI.
scored significantly higher than their nonabused peers on the MCPTSD scale.
were more likely, if their first abuse had occurred prior to age 12, to score significantly higher on the Obsessive Compulsive, Depression, Hostility, Phobic Anxiety, and Psychotism Scales of the BSI and the GSI than their peers whose abuse had initially occurred later.
males were 2 times as likely as their nonabused peers to meet the criteria for a positive diagnosis.
who suffered multiple abuse were significantly more likely than their peers who had experienced abuse once only to score higher on the BSI's Somatization and Depression Scales.

By self-report, respondents who experienced both sexual and physical abuse

suffered significantly more damaging psychological effects than those who had been sexually or physically abused only.

Introduction

Empirical research suggests that a substantial fraction of adults abused as children manifest serious initial and long-term mental health problems (Beitchman, Zucker, Hood, DaCosta, & Ackman, 1991; Browne & Finkelhor, 1986a, 1986b). Unfortunately, much of the research to determine the damaging psychological effects specific to sexual and physical abuse is contradictory. Outcome studies suffer from the characteristic flaws of sexual abuse research, namely, definitional problems; sampling bias; lack of, or inappropriate, controls or comparisons; and use of nonstandardized instruments.

Table 6.1 Cronbach Alpha Reliabilities and Means and Standard Deviations for BSI Form of the SCL-90-R Scales

Code	Scale Name	Cronbach Alpha	Male Mean Score (SD) N = 169	T^a	Female Mean Score (SD) N = 220	T^b
SOM	Somatization	.75	.18 (.30)	54	.18 (.32)	51
OC	Obsessive-compulsive	.84	.58 (.53)	57	.57 (.53)	55
IS	Interpersonal sensitivity	.83	.52 (.56)	60	.57 (.59)	57
DEP	Depression	.88	.41 (.48)	59	.42 (.51)	56
ANX	Anxiety	.84	.39 (.39)	57	.44 (.51)	54
HOS	Hostility	.73	.38 (.38)	55	.32 (.33)	53
PHOB	Phobic anxiety	.63	.13 (.26)	56	.14 (.27)	53
PI	Paranoid ideation	.80	.40 (.54)	55	.37 (.44)	54
PSY	Psychotism	.56	.23 (.36)	59	.20 (.33)	57
GSI	Global severity index	.96	.36 (.33)	57	.35 (.33)	54

a. T scores from adult nonpatient norms, Norm B Males (Robins et al., 1982; see text).
b. T scores from adult nonpatient norms, Norm B Females.

We attempted to address some of these problems in our follow-up survey to determine the impact of childhood abuse on the mental status of the respondents.[2] First, the large sample permitted statistically significant comparison of abused and nonabused respondents. We used explicit definitions for child sexual abuse and physical abuse (Giovannoni & Becerra, 1979; Kempe & Helfer, 1974), an age ceiling for abuse (18 years), and standardized instruments with proven reliability and validity (the short version of the Symptom Checklist-90-R [BSI]; Derogatis, 1983), and the MCPTSD (Keane, 1988).

The results we obtained (based on 389 respondents) are summarized by the Cronbach Alpha reliability coefficients (Cronbach, 1951; see Table 6.1), and the means and standard deviations for the subscales of the BSI and the GSI. Subscale alphas range from a low of .56 for Psychotism (PSY) to a high of .88 for Depression (DEP).[3] The GSI showed an alpha of .96. By t test, we found no statistical difference between the male and female respondents.

The T-score equivalents of the mean raw scores, according to the BSI scoring manual (Robins, Helzer, Ratcliff, & Seyfried, 1982), are given in Table 6.1 (T scores are constructed to have a mean of 50 and a standard deviation of 10 for the norm group, in this case, adult nonpatients). For our sample of professionals, the T-score means fall into the 54 to 60 range for males and the 51 to 57 range for females. Although the sample mean scores are above the norm (50), the difference is less than one standard deviation above the BSI norm group means. Therefore, as a group, our respondents' mental status is relatively similar to the so-called norm.

Caseness

According to Derogatis's operational definition of *caseness* (or positive diagnosis; as cited in Robins et al., 1982), an individual meets the criteria for a positive diagnosis when the T score for the GSI is equal to or greater than 63 or when a T score[4] for any two subscales is equal to or greater than 63.

To determine if we could predict a positive diagnosis from respondent gender, physical abuse, and sexual abuse history, we conducted an analysis of variance. We found significant effects ($p <$ .05) for gender (32% of males and 21% of females qualified as cases) and physical abuse (24% of those not physically abused and 45% of those physically abused qualified as cases) but not for sexual abuse ($p = .23$). According to our data, a childhood history of sexual abuse *only* does not significantly increase the likelihood of meeting the criteria for a positive diagnosis.

Men were more likely to meet the criteria for caseness than were women. For males, having a childhood history of physical abuse doubled the probability of having a positive diagnosis (29% to 59%). For females, the probability of having a positive diagnosis increased approximately 1.5 times (21% to 31%). However, the interaction between gender and physical abuse was not significant ($p = .14$).

We considered that these findings might be related to the relatively longer duration of physical abuse experienced by our respondents (those physically abused were abused, on average, 2 to 3 times longer than those sexually abused) and to a definition of physical abuse that was more restrictive than that of sexual abuse (see Chapter 2). Accordingly, respondents reporting a childhood history of physical abuse had, most likely, experienced the most severe, prolonged physical maltreatment.[5]

To make our definition of sexual abuse more compatible with that of physical abuse, we constructed a new variable, "severe sexual abuse" to include intrusive types of sexual activity only: oral sex, penetration by fingers, attempted penile penetration, and penile penetration.[6] Again, following the Robins et al. (1982) definition of caseness, we conducted an analysis of variance in which the dependent variable was caseness and the independent variables were history of physical abuse, history of severe sexual abuse, and gender.

As in our findings with the original broad definition of sexual abuse, we could predict caseness by physical abuse ($p = .014$) and gender ($p = .025$) but not by severe sexual abuse ($p = .267$). Of the 329 respondents who reported neither physical or sexual abuse, about 24% met the criteria for caseness. Of the 27 people who had been severely sexually abused only, about 26% met the criteria for caseness. In contrast, of 27 people who had been physically abused only, about 37% met the caseness criteria.

With the more restrictive definition of sexual abuse, we did find a significant interaction between sexual abuse and physical abuse ($p = .030$). Of the six respondents who reported both physical abuse and severe sexual abuse, five (83%) qualified as cases. Thus, having experienced both types of severe abuse makes it more than 2 to 3 times more likely that respondents would meet the criteria for caseness than either physical or sexual abuse separately.

Regardless of gender, the effects of physical abuse on mental status, as measured by the BSI, are far more severe than those of sexual abuse. Moreover, the effects of having been both physically and sexually abused increases the risk significantly. Having a history of both physical and sexual abuse as a child predicts the greatest risk for serious mental health consequences.

It is interesting that men who had been physically abused as children were far more likely to meet the criteria for a positive diagnosis than were women physically abused as children. Because most boys are physically abused by their fathers and most girls by their mothers, boys are likely to be subjected to the more severe, injurious types of abuse (Rosenthal, 1988). Thus, our male respondents may have been particularly vulnerable to the more damaging mental health consequences of abuse.

Psychological Symptoms

Respondents who had suffered sexual abuse or physical abuse as children share certain psychological symptomatology (albeit mod-

Table 6.2 Correlation of BSI Scales and Sexual Abuse

Code	Scale Name	Correlation With Sexual Abuse	Means and (SDs) Not Abused	Abused	t Ratio	Signifi- cance
SOM	Somatization	.11[a]	.16 (.29)	.24 (.38)	2.12	.0349
OC	Obsessive-Compulsive	.11[a]	.54 (.49)	.68 (.62)	2.08	.0384
IS	Interpersonal Sensitivity	.19[b]	.49 (.50)	.75 (.75)	3.89	.0001
DEP	Depression	.19[b]	.36 (.42)	.59 (.66)	3.89	.0001
ANX	Anxiety	.13[b]	.39 (.42)	.53 (.57)	2.64	.0087
HOS	Hostility	.06	.34 (.32)	.39 (.46)	1.18	.2372
PHOB	Phobic Anxiety	.17[b]	.11 (.22)	.22 (.37)	3.35	.0009
PI	Paranoid Ideation	.15[b]	.34 (.44)	.51 (.62)	2.93	.0036
PSY	Psychotism	.20[b]	.18 (.29)	.34 (.48)	4.06	.0001
GSI	Global Severity Index	.18[b]	.32 (.28)	.46 (.43)	3.65	.0003

a. Significant at confidence level of .05 or less.
b. Significant at confidence level of .01 or less.

erate) that significantly sets them apart from their nonabused peers. Physically or sexually abused respondents reported symptoms related to reality testing, depression, anxiety, and somatization. Both showed a greater level and depth of distress as measured by the GSI than their nonabused peers ($p < .0003$ for sexual abuse; $p < .0129$ for physical abuse).

The correlation between sexual abuse and the BSI subscales is shown in Table 6.2. With the exception of Hostility, all the BSI scales are significantly correlated to childhood sexual abuse.[7] These correlations were, however, rather small, ranging from .11 for Somatization (SOM) and Obsessive-Compulsive (OC) to a high of .20 for PSY. The three highest correlations with sexual abuse history were PSY (.20), Interpersonal Sensitivity (IS; .19), and DEP (.19; see Table 6.2). The correlation between sexual abuse and the MCPTSD scale was a statistically significant +.19 ($p < .001$).

Analysis of respondents who reported a history of physical abuse (again coding *not physically abused* as 0 and *physically abused* as 1) showed correlations between physical abuse and the BSI scales similar to those for sexual abuse for the DEP, SOM, and Anxiety (ANX) subscales and the GSI. Although both sexual and physical abuse were correlated with the PSY subscale, the correlation was much stronger for sexual abuse. The IS and OC scales that were

Table 6.3   BSI Scales Correlated With Physical Abuse

Code	Scale Name	Correlation With Physical Abuse	Not Abused	Abused	t ratio	Significance
SOM	Somatization	.11[a]	.17 (.30)	.29 (.43)	2.18	.0296
OC	Obsessive-Compulsive	.05	(.52) .57	.67 (.56)	1.05	.2939
IS	Interpersonal Sensitivity	.05	.54 (.57)	.64 (.63)	1.00	.3171
DEP	Depression	.18[b]	.38 (.45)	.71 (.77)	3.71	.0002
ANX	Anxiety	.15[b]	.40 (.43)	.65 (.70)	2.98	.0030
HOS	Hostility	.05	.34 (.34)	.41 (.51)	0.95	.3410
PHOB	Phobic Anxiety	.06	.13 (.27)	.19 (.25)	1.17	.2427
PI	Paranoid Ideation	.10	.37 (.48)	.54 (.58)	1.94	.0535
PSY	Psychotism	.10[a]	.20 (.34)	.33 (.40)	1.99	.0477
GSI	Global Severity Index	.13[b]	.34 (.31)	.49 (.44)	2.50	.0129

a. Significant at confidence level of .05 or less.
b. Significant at confidence level of .01 or less.

significantly correlated with sexual abuse did not significantly correlate with physical abuse (see Table 6.3). The correlation of a childhood history of physical abuse and MCPTSD was +.15 ($p < .001$), somewhat weaker than for sexual abuse.

Because the BSI scales were highly intercorrelated, we conducted a multivariate analysis of variance with sexual abuse and physical abuse histories as the independent factors and with the nine BSI symptoms and the GSI index as dependent variables. The results indicate a nonsignificant interaction of physical and sexual abuse ($p = .063$) and a statistically significant independent effect for physical abuse history ($p = .042$). A history of sexual abuse was not significant ($p = .086$).

There were no significant univariate effects for the interaction of physical and sexual abuse. However, the Roy-Bargman step-down F tests (Roy & Bargman, 1958) indicated a significant interactive effect for Phobic Anxiety (PHOB; $p = .002$). The univariate effects for physical abuse history were significant for DEP ($p = .009$) and ANX ($p = .033$). The Roy-Bargman step-down F tests showed only DEP ($p < .001$) significant for physical abuse.

The univariate effects for sexual abuse history were significant for SOM ($p = .022$), IS ($p = .021$), DEP ($p = .011$), ANX ($p = .015$), PSY ($p = .023$) and the GSI index ($p = .022$). However, the Roy-Bargman step-down *F* tests showed only SOM significantly affected by a history of childhood sexual abuse ($p = .022$).

These results indicate some effect of childhood physical abuse on adult symptomatology, especially DEP and ANX. The indication for sexual abuse history is less clear. When controlling for physical abuse and examining all the possible effects together, there is not quite a statistically significant effect. However, in the univariate and step-down analysis, we found some indication of a statistically significant effect of sexual abuse history, especially on SOM.

Thus, many of the psychological effects of physical and sexual abuse evidenced by our respondents are similar. However, there are some differences in symptomatology between the two abused groups. Those who reported a history of childhood sexual abuse were more likely than their physically abused peers to have symptoms related to interpersonal relationships, phobias, obsessive-compulsiveness, and paranoid ideation. Our findings and those of Briere and Runtz (1990) contrast with those of Wind and Silvern (1992) who, in their sample of 259 working women, found "a highly generalized response to abuse regardless of its specific sexual or physical nature" (p. 276).

Other researchers have used the SCL-90-R to measure mental health status among adults abused as children. For example, Murphy et al. (1988) compared psychological functioning in 391 women (drawn from a larger random community sample) who had been sexually or physically victimized as children (on average, 37 years previously) with women who had no such history. Like us, they found significant differences in symptomatology among the groups. Problems with interpersonal sensitivity, phobias, and paranoia, differentiate the sexually abused group from their physically abused and nonabused peers; problems with somatization set the physically abused group apart from their sexually abused and nonabused peers. Chu and Dill (1990), in their sample of 98 women in a psychiatric hospital, also found no correlation between SCL-90-R scores and sexual abuse. They do, however, report a correlation between physical abuse and the subscales of ANX, PSY, IS, HOS, PI, and the GSI.

When we compared respondents whose initial sexual abuse had occurred prior to age 12 with those who had been abused at age 12 or older, we found that only the SOM scale was significantly higher for those abused at the younger ages. None of the other eight subscales of the BSI, nor the MCPTSD scale, showed a statistically significant difference by age at onset of abuse.

A similar comparative analysis of those whose physical abuse had initially occurred prior to or after age 12 revealed significant differences. Those abused at younger ages scored higher on the OC, DEP, HOS, PA, and PSY symptom dimensions and on the GSI. The remaining four subscales and the MCPTSD scale showed no significant differences with age at initial abuse. Note that those abused initially at a younger age were probably abused for longer periods. Thus, the greater severity of psychological effects may also be related to longer duration as well as age at onset.

Although Murphy et al. (1988) found specific psychological effects of sexual abuse related to age, their results differ from ours. Compared to women who had never been sexually assaulted, women who reported sexual victimization prior to age 12 were more likely to score higher on the ANX and GSI scales. In contrast to our results, women who reported sexual victimization between the ages of 12 and 17 years (Murphy et al., 1988) reported more obsessive-compulsive symptoms, greater interpersonal sensitivity, more anxiety, and greater levels of hostility and paranoid ideation. In addition, Murphy et al. found that the SCL-90-R discriminated, on 11 of the scales, between women who had experienced single versus multiple abuse.

Post-Traumatic Stress Disorder (PTSD)

As noted earlier, we found statistically significant associations between both childhood sexual abuse and childhood physical abuse and MCPTSD scores (+.19 and +.15, respectively). Gelinas (1983) was the first to make the association between PTSD and the damaging effects of child sexual abuse. This link has since been further explored (Boney-McCoy & Finkelhor, 1995; Cameron, 1994; Coons, Bowman, Pellow, & Schneider, 1989; Deblinger, McLeer, Atkins, Ralphe, & Foa, 1989; Jones & Krugman, 1986; Kendall-Tackett, Williams, & Finkelhor, 1993; Lindberg & Distad, 1985).

The diagnosis of PTSD was first included in the American Psychiatric Association's (1980) *Diagnostic and Statistical Manual of Mental Disorders*, 3rd edition (*DSM-III*), as a disorder that could develop from any "out-of-the-ordinary" life distressing event. Initially conceived as combat related, subsequent study has revealed that the diagnosis can be a consequence of natural disasters and abuse-related trauma. In sexually abused children, PTSD may occur immediately or be delayed by months or years following the abuse (Heiman, 1992).

Adult survivors of sexual abuse, like Vietnam veterans, are often treated with suspicion by the public and misdiagnosed by the mental health community. In an interesting longitudinal study that draws a parallel between Vietnam veterans suffering from PTSD and adult survivors of childhood sexual abuse, Cameron (1994) surveyed 72 women who had entered therapy to deal with the long-term effects of childhood sexual abuse. She found that the majority were experiencing PTSD symptoms (according to *DSM-III-R* criteria) 20 to 50 years after the initial incident. Reexperiencing the trauma was common; 93% of the total sample reported flashbacks, 75% intrusive thoughts, and 71% dreams in which they felt hopeless, helpless, and terrified. Being overwhelmed by feelings similar to those they had experienced as children were reported by 84%; 86% reported having been depressed, and 65% had thought about suicide.

Cameron believes that differences between the Vietnam and abuse experiences make the latter even more difficult to treat. She notes that the women in her sample were traumatized by caregivers rather than by the chance of war; their trauma, in many cases, was of longer duration. Contrary to the publicly exposed trauma of combat, many adult survivors were, as children, forced or coerced to endure their abuse in secret. Psychologically isolated, the development of their sense of reality, family, and self was often distorted.

In a review of records of 87 psychiatric child patients to compare rates of PTSD in sexually abused (SA), physically abused (PA), and nonabused (NA) patients (Deblinger et al., 1989), no significant differences in PTSD were found across the three groups (20.7% SA; 6.9% PA; 10.3% NA), but significant differences in the PTSD subcategory of reexperiencing phenomena and a tendency in the avoidance-dissociative subcategory were found. Children in the SA group were more likely than their peers in the NA group to demonstrate sexually inappropriate behaviors and more likely than their peers in both the PA and NA groups to demonstrate sexually abusive behaviors. Although differences did not quite reach the 5% significance level, both the sexually and physically abused groups were more likely than the nonabused group to score higher in the avoidance-dissociative subcategory of PTSD ($p = .06$ SA; $p = .07$ PA).

In a randomly drawn national sample of about 3,000 professional women, Elliott and Briere (1992) examined the long-term effects of an early history of sexual abuse as measured by the Trauma Symptom Checklist-40 (TSC-40), an expanded version of the TSC-33 (Briere & Runtz, 1989). Comparing those who reported childhood abuse (to age 16) to those who reported no abuse, they, also, were able to discriminate between the abused and nonabused group. The sexually abused group scored higher than the nonabused group on anxiety (4.74 vs. 3.80), depression (6.98 vs. 5.74), and post-traumatic symptoms (26.02 vs. 20.91).

Mediating Variables

Increased statistical sophistication, along with awareness of the multidimensional aspects of childhood abuse and its long-term consequences, has generated interest in the contextual correlates of abuse (Alexander, 1993; Bagley & Ramsay, 1986; Briere & Runtz, 1988; Conte & Schuerman, 1987; Green, 1993).

> The extent to which a given individual manifests abuse-related symptomatology and distress is a function of an undetermined number of abuse-specific variables, as well as individual and environmental factors that existed prior, or occurred subsequent to, the incidents of sexual abuse. (Briere & Elliott, 1994, p. 64)

As early as 1979, Finkelhor identified factors that could modify the effects of sexual abuse: age at abuse, age and gender of the offender, and extent to which force accompanied the abuse. Work done since suggests that additional variables related to the abuse, the abused, the abuser, and family dynamics may alleviate or exacerbate the effects of victimization (Bryer, Nelson, Miller, & Krol, 1987; Gold, 1986; Okami, 1991; Parker & Parker, 1991).

Age, Duration, and Frequency

We found no significant relationship between age at onset (other than the Somatization scale) or duration of sexual abuse and mental health status as measured by the BSI and the MCPTSD scales. We did, however, find that respondents who suffered longer periods of abuse were significantly less likely to be in a current sexual relationship (correlation = -.26; p < .05) and that those who reported the most severe sexual abuse[8] were least likely to be satisfied with their current sexual relationships (r = -.17; p < .05).

Although we found no significant relationship for physical abuse between age at onset and the BSI subscales, we did find a strong correlation between the duration of physical abuse and the MCPTSD scale (r = .43; p < .05) and BSI subscales of OC and IS (correlations ranged from .16 to .53) with the median correlation among the 10 symptoms .41 (p < .05).

Tsai, Feldman-Summers, and Edgar (1979) recruited three groups of 30 women each: those who sought therapy related to childhood abuse, those with a childhood history of abuse but never in treatment, and those with no history of child abuse. Measured by the Minnesota Multiphasic Personality Inventory (MMPI; Carson, 1969), both age at which abuse had last occurred and duration of abuse appeared to have a mediating effect on later psychological adjustment. Women in the clinical group who had last been sexually abused at age 12 or older reported more negative feelings about the event than those whose last abuse had occurred at earlier ages and those in the nonclinical or control group. Abuse of long duration suggested more serious outcomes, because abused women seeking treatment reported longer duration of abuse than those who had never sought treatment.

Courtois (1979) interviewed 31 women (aged 21-50) recruited through advertisements, agency, and private practice referrals who had experienced incestuous relationships. Her findings differ from those reported by Tsai et al. (1979). Courtois found that younger, rather than older, age of initial abuse was related to greater psychological problems. Compared to those who had experienced their first abuse after puberty, women in the Courtois study who had experienced abuse prior to puberty reported a more severe sense of self and harsher perceptions of their long-term male relationships.

Okami (1991), in an exploratory study, found a relationship between age at onset of abuse and severity of outcome. He compared two adult samples: one nonclinical (N = 63) and the other clinical (N = 7). Both groups had experienced similarly severe sexual abuse as children (two thirds reported vaginal or anal intercourse or oral sex; one third, touching, kissing, or genital "apposition").

It is surprising that 67% of the nonclinical group reported that the contact had been positive,[9] although all in the clinical group rated the encounters as negative. Consistent with Courtois's (1979) findings, Okami (1991) found that those in the nonclinical group who viewed their experience as positive placed their first sexual encounter at a later age (11 years) than those who viewed it as negative (9.5 years).

Not surprisingly, frequency of abuse has been identified as a contextual variable that may affect psychological adjustment. In a study of 377 women in a large urban Canadian community, Bagley and Ramsey (1986) found that, compared to women who reported a single incident of sexual abuse, those who reported multiple incidents were about 8 times more likely to have made a suicidal gesture (31% vs. 4.1%) and about 6 times more likely to have attempted suicide during their lifetime (10% vs. 1.6%).

However, we did not find a significant difference (by t test) between respondents who as children had experienced multiple sexual abuse and those who had experienced abuse only once. Comparison of the multiply physically abused with those who had been abused once only revealed a statistically significantly higher score on the SOM (.29 vs. .04) and DEP scales (.48 vs. .00). None of the other BSI scales or the MCPTSD scale showed significant differences.

Using data obtained from the Hopkins Symptom Check List (HSCL; Derogatis et al., 1973) and a dissociation scale, Briere and Runtz (1988) sought correlations between the age at onset of sexual abuse, age of the abuser, use of force, presence or absence of intercourse, relationship of the abuser to the victim, the number of abusers, duration and frequency of abuse, and symptomatology. Among the 14.7% of the 278 college women in their sample who had been abused, those who experienced a longer duration of abuse, had been violated by older perpetrators, or had experienced parental incest showed significantly higher levels of anxiety, dissociation, and somatization.

In a study of a group of low-income single mothers ($N = 206$) recruited from public health clinics, Hall, Sachs, Rayens, and Lutenbacher (1993) investigated the relationship between a history of childhood abuse (prior to age 18) and depressive symptoms. They found that the degree of violence associated with sexual abuse was related to the level of long-term damage. Of the 70% who reported childhood abuse, those who had experienced sexual abuse accompanied by violence and physical abuse scored higher on depression (Center for Epidemiologic Studies—Depression Scale; Radloff, 1977) than those whose abuse had not been violent.

Wind and Silvern (1992) investigated the associations between different types of abuse and symptomatology among a group of women employed at a state university (N = 259). They found that severe physical maltreatment and incest may have similar long-term effects, as measured by the Beck Depression Inventory (BDI; Beck, 1978) and a negative experience scale (created by the authors) that scores the frequency of dangerous events occurring after age 18. The psychological relationship of the perpetrator to the victim, the frequency and duration of physical maltreatment, and incest were all significantly related to the subjects' symptomatology according to the BDI (Beck, 1978), the TSC-33 (Briere & Runtz, 1989), and the Coopersmith Self-Esteem Inventory (CSEI; Coopersmith, 1981).

The more severe the physical maltreatment, the more likely were respondents to score higher on the BDI ($p < .006$), to report more trauma-related symptoms (TSC; $p < .000$), lower self-esteem (CSEI; $p < .016$), and more negative experiences as adults ($p < .000$). They found no significant associations between single versus multiple perpetrators, age at onset of sexual abuse, and symptomatology. They did, however, find significant relationships between rates and duration of abuse, familial abuse, severity of abuse and use of force, and symptomatology.

Although results of these studies indicate no clear pattern between age at onset of abuse and type of abuse and mental status, most suggest that childhood abuse can have long-lasting, damaging psychological sequelae. Currently, the factors that contribute to negative (or positive) outcomes are unclear. Future research with much larger samples to allow detection of significant effects and the use of standardized definitions and instruments are necessary to establish the associations between these variables and the psychological outcome of childhood abuse.

Disclosure

Disclosure has been identified as a factor that can influence the outcome of childhood sexual abuse. In our follow-up study, 64% of the 88 respondents who reported a childhood history of sexual abuse disclosed their abuse to someone. Of the 33 respondents who reported a childhood history of physical abuse, 61% had disclosed, whereas 53% of those who witnessed sexual abuse and 57% of those who witnessed physical abuse disclosed.

Of the 88 sexually abused respondents who disclosed, 33 (37%) disclosed within hours, days, or months. Most of these early disclosures[10] were to their mothers (42%; N = 14); 27% (N = 9) were to their fathers. Five disclosures were to siblings and four to other relatives. Only one of the early disclosures was to the police.

More often, disclosures occurred years later (61%; N = 54).[11] Of these 54, 23 (43%) were to therapists or therapeutic groups (all respondents were clinical social workers, psychologists, psychiatrists, or pediatricians); 11 (20%) were to friends; 8 to spouses, lovers, or girl or boy friends; 5 were to parents; and 5 to other relatives. It is interesting that two respondents disclosed their own childhood sexual abuse to their clients in the course of treatment.

Our findings are consistent with those of Finkelhor's (1980) survey of college students (N = 796). Of the 19% of women and 9% of men who had experienced sexual abuse during their childhood, 63% had disclosed. However, we found greater frequencies of disclosure than those reported by Laumann et al. (1994) in their national study of the social organization of sexuality and those of the *Los Angeles Times* Poll conducted in 1985 (Finkelhor, Hotaling, Lewis, & Smith, 1989). According to Laumann et al., only 22% of those who reported a childhood history of sexual abuse had ever disclosed their abuse. The Los Angeles poll data show that, of the 27% of the women and 16% of the men who reported a childhood history of sexual abuse (N = 2,630), less than half had disclosed their abuse to anyone within the year following the event (43% of the males; 41% of the females). Bagley, Wood, and Young (1994), in their study of the behavioral sequelae of child sexual abuse among a stratified random community sample of 750 males, found that the majority of those who reported unwanted sexual acts prior to age 17 (16% of the entire sample) had never reported their abuse to anyone. In a study of psychological functioning in a community sample of female sexual abuse survivors (N = 391) interviewed by telephone (Murphy et al., 1988), only 7% of those who had experienced any type of sexual assault had disclosed to anyone; of those who had disclosed, only 4% had done so to the criminal justice system. Finkelhor (1994), in his international study of child sexual abuse, found that no more than 50% of those abused had disclosed their abuse.

Rates of disclosure to authorities are consistently low. In an analysis of 365 intakes of adults molested as children, Kendall-Tackett and Simon (1987) found that 18% had reported their abuse to the legal authorities. Janus and Janus (1993), in their national telephone survey of sexual behavior in the United States (N = 2,689), found that of the 17% who reported a childhood history of sexual abuse, only 12% of the abused had reported it to authorities. Anderson, Martin, Mullen, Romans, and Herbison (1993), in their survey of a community sample of approximately 500 women in New Zealand, found that only 7% of those abused had ever reported the incident to social services or police; intrafamilial abuse was the least likely to be reported. Thus, it appears that in most reported populations, the majority of sexual abuse victims keep their abuse a secret (Jehu, 1989) and that those who do disclose, rarely disclose to authorities.

Underreporting of abuse has been attributed to factors such as race and class bias (Newberger, Hampton, Marx, & White, 1986) and the reluctance of victims, offenders, and nonoffending caretakers to disclose (Faller, 1990). According to Faller (1990), many victims believe they have little to gain and everything to lose by disclosing sexual victimization. Realistically, they anticipate reprisals, stigma, and censure.

When victims do disclose, offenders believe they have everything to gain by denying the allegations, because the aftermath may bring catastrophic consequences. In addition, nonoffending caretakers (usually women) are often strongly motivated to deny, disbelieve, or repudiate an allegation (particularly in cases of intrafamilial abuse). Their anticipation that the abuse will be viewed as a reflection of poor parenting is often validated, because some professionals (and nonprofessionals) consider nonoffending caretakers responsible for their children's abuse (Gardner, 1994). Fear about losing financial and emotional security and worry about the potential intrusiveness of protective services (Faller, 1990) is often realistic.

In contrast to Anderson et al. (1993), we found no significant differences in frequency of disclosure as a function of the victim's relationship to the perpetrator. Although respondents sexually abused by nonfamily members were somewhat more likely to disclose than those abused by family members, the differences were not significant. Not surprisingly, we did find that respondents abused by a nonfamily member were more likely to disclose immediately. Of those who were abused by nonfamily members, 38% disclosed within hours of the incident, whereas only 12% of those who had been abused by family members did so ($p < .05$).

Disclosure of their abuse did not affect the mental status of our respondents. The disclosure variables for both types of abuse (sexual and physical) did not add substantially to the relationship of abuse severity predicting MCPTSD scores. When we examined whether disclosure had any effect beyond the existence of the abuse itself, we found that the disclosure variables did not add a statistically significant predictive power to the severity of the abuse. We found no significant relationship of disclosure to caseness (Derogatis, 1983) beyond having been abused (physical or sexual). Similarly, Parker and Parker (1991), in their sample of 135 college women sexually abused as children, found no significant differences between disclosure and levels of self-esteem or perceived competence (Texas Social Behavior Inventory [TSBI]; Helmreich & Strapp, 1974).

Trust and Betrayal

In an interesting study to determine the effect of religious beliefs on the outcome of childhood sexual abuse, Elliott (1994) surveyed a random sample of 1,630 professional women, most of whom held graduate degrees. Although she found that religious orientation alone did not affect the prevalence rate of sexual abuse, she did find intrafamilial abuse particularly traumatic for girls in conservative Christian families. Intensity of symptoms among this group was far greater than that of incest survivors of "other" religious affiliations. According to Elliott, "the trauma associated with incest and a simultaneous failure of Christian ideology to protect her" (pp. 106-107) results in "double traumatization and betrayal" (p. 106).

Elliott's findings are consistent with Browne and Finkelhor's (1986b) hypothesis that the degree of betrayal experienced by the child victim and the power differential within the victim-victimizer relationship affects the outcome of the abuse. Similarly, Silver, Boon, & Stones (1983), in their volunteer sample of adult female incest survivors ($N = 77$), found that victimization by a trusted person in an unequal relationship is extremely difficult to integrate into a child's existing meaning system. In contrast, Bryer et al. (1987), in a study of 66 women admitted to a psychiatric hospital, found no difference in severity of symptoms between patients who had experienced incest and those who had experienced other types of abuse. Of course, on admission, these patients had been screened for severity of symptoms.

Not surprisingly, quality of parenting may influence the consequences of childhood abuse. Parker and Parker (1991) reviewed
questionnaire data from 135 female college students who had been
sexually abused as children and they found no significant differences
associated with any of five abuse variables: (a) relationship to perpetrator, (b) nature of the abuse, (c) age at onset, (d) duration of abuse,
and (e) number of different abusive incidents. "It was only when
abuse was combined with poor parenting [that they found] higher
levels of maladjustment" (p. 194). Parker and Parker conclude that
"abuse itself makes little difference among those who have experienced good parenting" (as defined by the subjects; p. 194). Consistent
with these results, Gold (1986) found, among her sample of 103
women who had a childhood history of sexual abuse, that the level
of the mother's support in response to the abuse was positively
related to levels of adult psychosexual functioning. However, *good
parenting* and *maternal support* are complex constructs that require
operational definitions if they are to have usable meanings.

Attribution

The role of cognition in determining an abuse victim's subsequent psychological functioning has been the focus of attention for
many researchers. It appears that "the reported coping difficulties of
some victims . . . may be due to the attribution that they make for bad
events" (Gold, 1986, p. 474). In a sample of convenience, comparing
103 women who reported a history of childhood sexual abuse to 88
women who reported no such history, Gold found a strong correlation between the subjects' worldview and psychosexual functioning.
Based on data obtained from the Attributional Style Questionnaire
(Peterson et al., 1982), women who were abused were more likely
than their nonabused peers to report negative attributions, to perceive themselves as responsible for bad experiences, and to view
positive incidents as beyond their control.

Similarly, Silver et al. (1983), in their volunteer sample of women
survivors of incest ($N = 77$), found that a child's interpretation of an
abusive event influenced subsequent psychological functioning. The
ability to integrate the incestuous experience was related to better
adaptation, according to the SCL-90 (Derogatis, Rickels, & Rock,
1976), the Social Adjustment Scale (SAS; Weissman & Bothwell,

1976), and the 10-item Rosenberg Self-Esteem Scale (Rosenberg, 1965). Women who had yet to assign meaning to the sexual abuse (80%) showed greater emotional distress (SCL-90), disturbed social functioning (SAS), lower self-esteem (Rosenberg, 1965), and less resolution of the trauma than those (only 20%) who had integrated it into their view of themselves and the world.

To examine the association between trauma-related beliefs and psychological status, Hazzard used the Trauma-Related Beliefs Questionnaire (TRBQ; Hazzard, 1993), three subscales of the SCL-90-R (IS, DEP, ANX), and the GSI. The TRBQ is a 56-item scale designed to measure beliefs that are compatible with Finkelhor and Browne's (1985) model of four traumagenic dynamics (self-blame/stigmatization, betrayal, traumatic sexualization, and powerlessness). Data obtained from 59 female sexual abuse survivors recruited by referral and advertisement suggest that cognitive styles can affect the outcome of abuse. Women who endorsed a self-blaming attitude felt betrayed, powerless, and vulnerable. Furthermore, they were more likely to report problems with their sexual and interpersonal relationships and to be depressed, anxious, or both than were their peers whose self-attributions were positive.

Overlapping Abuse

Not surprisingly, being both physically and sexually abused as a child has significantly more damaging long-term effects than either sexual or physical abuse alone. In our follow-up study, we found additive effects for both physical and sexual abuse as measured by five of the BSI scales: SOM ($p = .0073$), DEP ($p < .0001$), ANX ($p < .0004$), GSI ($p = .0013$), and PST ($p = .0011$), and the MCPTSD scales ($p < .0001$).

We also found a significant interaction between physical and sexual abuse for positive diagnosis (caseness) as measured by the BSI. Those who were both physically and sexually abused were far more likely (83%) than those who had been physically or sexually abused only to qualify as cases.

There are many similar findings. In a study to determine the psychological consequences of childhood sexual or physical abuse, Bryer et al. (1987) interviewed 66 females recruited from 124 consecutive admissions to a private psychiatric hospital and found that the severity of psychiatric symptoms on all subscales of the SCL-90-R and the GSI were positively correlated with the patients' childhood history of physical or sexual abuse ($p < .001$). As in our work, the severity of symptoms was significantly greater when patients had experienced both types of abuse.

Chu and Dill (1990) surveyed 98 female psychiatric inpatients to determine the frequency of dissociative phenomena among those who reported a history of sexual abuse. They found that scores on the Dissociative Experiences Scale (Bernstein & Putnam, 1986) were about threefold greater for subjects who reported histories of both childhood physical and sexual abuse than those who reported only one type of abuse or no abuse.

In another study to determine the relationship between dissociation and a childhood history of abuse (Swett & Halpert, 1993), 88 women admitted to an inpatient psychiatric facility were evaluated. Again, subjects exposed to both physical and sexual abuse were likely to report more severe symptomatology, as reflected in significantly higher levels of dissociation, than those who had been sexually abused or those who reported no such history. In agreement, Wind & Silvern (1992), in their study of 259 women workers at a state university, found that the long-term effects of childhood maltreatment were most damaging when abuse had been incestuous and when physical and sexual maltreatment co-occurred.

Summary and Conclusions

Clearly, childhood abuse does not incapacitate everyone or prevent the achievement of high professional status. However, the relationships among physical and sexual abuse and mental health status reported in this chapter demonstrate that, among a representative sample of practicing professionals, there can be major psychological effects of childhood abuse.

We found a strong association between a childhood history of physical abuse and positive diagnosis, using the Robins et al. (1982) definition. Men were more likely than women to qualify as cases. Although a positive diagnosis was not related to a childhood history of sexual abuse, it was significantly related to a childhood history of physical abuse. Respondents who had been both physically and sexually abused were far more likely (83%) than their peers who had a history of physical or sexual abuse only to meet the criteria for caseness.

In this study, a history of childhood sexual abuse was significantly related to symptomatology, as measured by the MCPTSD scale and to all the BSI subscales except Hostility. However, these correlations are relatively small and not clinically significant (about .10 to .20). A history of childhood physical abuse correlated with four of the BSI subscales and with the MCPTSD scale. Again, these relationships were significant but relatively small.

Thus, although our data support the conclusion that a childhood history of sexual or physical abuse is significantly related to adult symptomatology as measured by the BSI subscales and the MCPTSD scale, its effects for most victims are not great enough to allow a prediction of a history of child sexual abuse.

We found some statistically significant, but clinically irrelevant, predictive power when we attempted to identify respondents who had been physically or sexually abused as children based on their adult symptomatology. In all cases, predicting that respondents had not been abused produced about the same accuracy as that obtained by using the discriminant functions based on psychological symptom scores. Our results are similar to those of Laumann et al. (1994) who also created a severity scale of abuse and found no significant differences in symptomatology or behaviors. Clearly, adult psychological symptoms may be related to factors other than childhood abuse. Bagley and Ramsey (1986) propose, quite reasonably, that "although often of major importance, [childhood abuse] is but one of a number of disruptive events influencing later mental health" (p. 43).

The standardized instruments used in this study do not show much discrimination and, as a result, have poor predictive power. Other measures of symptomatology (for example, dissociation) may prove more sensitive to the psychological symptoms generated by childhood abuse (Briere & Runtz, 1990; Chu & Dill, 1990). Variables other than those included in our analyses (for example, sexually abusive and sexually inappropriate behaviors and negative adult experiences, such as sexual and physical assault) may produce more significant results. Alternatively, it may be that, in this population, for reasons as yet unknown, a substantial number of those abused do not suffer long-term psychological effects related to childhood physical or sexual abuse. These are critical areas for further research.

Our data suggest that adult mental health for both men and women may be a function of having been either physically abused only or both physically and sexually abused. We speculate that the more damaging psychological sequelae found among those physically abused may be related to their having experienced the most extreme and prolonged maltreatment.

For the most part, respondents who reported a childhood history of sexual abuse appear to be among the so-called fortunate abused, perhaps by virtue of the shorter duration of their abuse and lower rate of incest (see Chapter 3). We propose that the extrafamilial victimization experienced by the majority of our respondents would have elicited more parental support and, consequently, would have caused significantly less family disturbance than would the intrafamilial abuse so often found in clinical populations.

Factors additional to those identified in this study may also ameliorate or aggravate the more damaging effects of childhood abuse in this population (see the growing literature on negative and positive attribution of traumatic events, e.g., Gold, 1986; Peterson et al., 1982; Wolfe, Gentile, & Wolfe, 1989). Parental support (Gold, 1986; Parker & Parker, 1991) is clearly an important factor. The idea that cognition can alter emotions can be found in the writings of the Greek Stoics (Beck, 1990). Subsequently, Beck and his associates based their cognitive theory and therapy of depression on these assumptions. Thus, the outcome of abuse may be more dependent on the child's perception of the event than on its objective reality. Clearly, more research is needed to identify specific factors and the complex interactions that facilitate the capacity to respond resiliently to childhood abuse.

Notes

1. The GSI score represents the global index of the level of an individual's psychological distress.

2. All data reported in this chapter were obtained in the follow-up study.

3. Alpha coefficients greater than .80 are considered satisfactory for research. Those greater than .93 are satisfactory for clinical predictions (DeVellis, 1991).

4. Recall that the T score is a standardized score with a mean of 50 and a standard deviation of 10.

5. The restrictive definition of physical abuse may also account for the very low prevalence rate for physical abuse reported by our respondents.

6. "Severe sexual abuse" was rated "1"; other less severe types of sexual activity were scored "0."

7. We used a code of "0" for "not sexually abused" and "1" for "sexually abused."

8. We constructed a scale for the "Severity" dimension, which included an index of the duration of sexual abuse; whether the perpetrator was a family member; and whether the abuse included the activities of oral sex, penile penetration, attempted penile penetration, or digital penetration. Based on our analyses, the effects of severity of child sexual abuse only slightly improved the correlations and multiple regressions predicting respondents' psychological symptoms. The increases are not sufficient to produce a significantly different prediction.

9. Okami acknowledges that his sample, recruited by advertisement, specifically sought adults who had experienced some positive reactions to childhood sexual encounters, either with adults or with older children.

10. For this analysis, we coded the number of disclosures (not the number of people who disclosed). Thus, if one person disclosed to two people, we counted it as two disclosures.

11. The discrepancy between the number of sexually abused and number of disclosures is a result of missing data.

7

Personal Relationships and Professional Practice

Overview

The initial and follow-up surveys examined the effects of a history of childhood sexual and physical abuse on the personal and professional lives of clinical social workers, pediatricians, psychiatrists, and psychologists.

Respondents who reported a history of childhood sexual abuse were *less* likely than those who had not been sexually abused

to be married (66% vs. 76%); (significant only for men, 71% to 86%).

to have raised children (64% vs. 79%).

to be satisfied with their current sexual relationships.

Respondents who reported a childhood history of sexual abuse were *more* likely than those who had not been sexually abused

to be in nonmarital, significant relationships (8% vs. 2%).

to be a member of a family violence team (9% vs. 4%).

to devote more time working directly with sexual abuse cases (12% vs. 8%).

to have abused another person (24% vs. 5% for males; NS for females).

to have engaged in sexual activity with their clients (8% vs. 2%; males only).

Respondents who reported a childhood history of physical abuse were *more* likely than those who had not been physically abused

to be members of a family violence team (14% vs. 4%).

to have abused another person (65% vs. 3% for men; 19% vs. 2% for women).

Respondents who reported a history of both childhood physical and sexual abuse were

3 times more likely to be members of a sexual abuse team (22%) than were their peers who reported no abuse history (6%) or had been sexually or physically abused only (6% and 7%, respectively).

7 times more likely to be members of a family violence team (22%) than respondents who reported no abuse history (3%), 3 times more likely than those who reported physical abuse only (7%) or sexual abuse only (6%).

These astonishing ratios are clearly of great importance to clinical practice.

Introduction

In this chapter, we present the effects of childhood abuse on adult personal and professional functioning. The data on the effects of a personal history of abuse on marital status and child rearing were obtained from the initial survey. The data on the effects of a childhood history of abuse on the abuse of others and on sexual and professional behavior were obtained from the follow-up study.

Personal Relationships

Marital Status

Respondents who reported histories of sexual abuse were less likely to be married (66% of 110) than their peers who had not been sexually abused (76% of 543). The marital status distribution is significantly different at the $p < .05$ level. (There were no significant differences in marital status for the effect of physical abuse.)

The marital effects, however, differed strikingly by gender (see Figure 7-1). Women who had been sexually abused were not significantly more likely to be unmarried (38% of 72) than women who had not been so abused (32% of 293). Yet, men who had been sexually abused were twice as likely to be unmarried (29% of 38) as men who had not been abused (14% of 249). The difference is statistically significant at the $p < .05$ level.

We conducted an analysis to compare marital status of respondents who had been both physically and sexually abused to those who had been sexually abused only. The results for both men and women were unchanged; the existence of both types of abuse did not affect marital status.

Significant Relationships

Men and women in the sexually abused group were 4 times more likely to be in nonmarital, significant relationships (8% of 110) than were those who were not sexually abused (2% of 542). This strong effect did not differ by gender or by either a history of physical abuse only or by a history of both physical and sexual abuse (overlapping). These high rates of sexually abused respondents who reported nonmarital but significant relationships may be a reflection of sexual preference. This is an important area for further research.

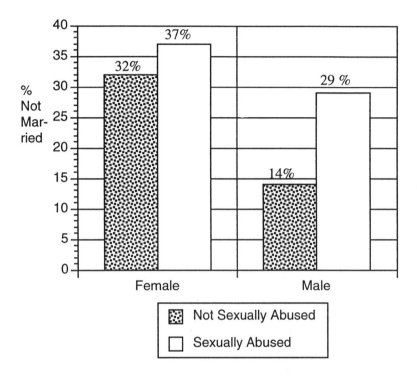

Figure 7.1. Percentage Not Married by Sexual Abuse Category
NOTE: Findings are from the initial survey.

Child Rearing

We found a strong association between reports of childhood sexual abuse and childlessness. Among male and female respondents who had not been sexually abused, 21% of 541 reported that they had not raised children. For the sexually abused, 36% of 110 reported childlessness. For those who had been both physically and sexually abused, 44% of 18 had not raised children. This relationship (using a χ^2, 1 df test) was highly significant at the .0006 level.

For women, the effect was extremely strong. Of the 292 women who had not been sexually abused, 24% reported that they had never raised children, whereas 44% of the 72 sexually abused women had never raised children. This difference is statistically significant at the .0005 level by chi square analysis. Thus, childlessness was almost double among women who had been sexually abused compared to nonabused women. The presence of both physical and sexual abuse did not increase the effects of sexual abuse alone on childlessness (45% of 11 women). For men, there were no significant effects of abuse history on child rearing ($p = .62$).

Our findings of major gender-specific associations between sexual abuse and marital and child rearing status are consistent with the literature on childhood incest that reports the unmarried rate of victims at about 40% (Courtois, 1979; Meiselman, 1978). Furthermore, many individuals who have been sexually abused as children have reported difficulty establishing and maintaining intimate, trusting relationships as adults (Browne & Finkelhor, 1986b; Finkelhor, Hotaling, Lewis, & Smith, 1989; Fish-Murray, Koby, & van der Kolk, 1987; Herman, 1986; Lister, 1982; van der Kolk, 1987).

In our study, respondents who reported childhood sexual abuse histories were less likely to commit to major relational responsibilities than were their nonabused cohorts. For men, this was reflected in a reluctance to commit to marriage; for women, in a reluctance to raise children (see Figure 7.2).

Consistent with our data, Janus and Janus (1993) found that women who reported a childhood history of sexual abuse were 1.5 times more likely to be employed full-time outside the home ("career women") than those who did not report such a history ("homemakers"). Although Janus and Janus do not include data on the marital or child-rearing status of the career group, we speculate that they would be less likely to be raising children than would those in the homemaker group.

Traditionally, marriage has meant a major financial commitment for males; for women, the major commitment has been to raise children. Whereas willing to marry, the sexually abused women in our initial survey were less likely to commit to the emotional and physical responsibilities required by child rearing. This reduction in obligation may have enabled them, more than their peers with children, to pursue careers and consequently, to be disproportionately represented among the older female cohorts in this study.

A different possibility for the reduced rates of child rearing among women who had been sexually abused as children is the

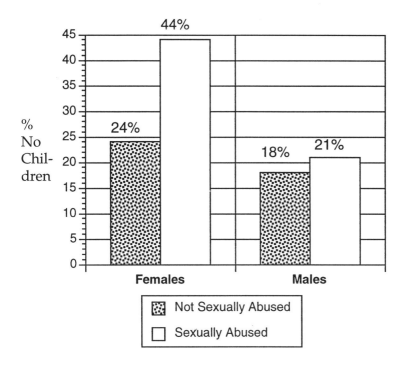

Figure 7.2. Childlessness by Sexual Abuse Category
NOTE: Findings are from the initial survey.

potentially long-term infertility effects of untreated sexually transmitted diseases that may have been contracted during the sexual
abuse. These are areas that need further investigation.

These findings should be interpreted with caution. Although
the initial study shows a significant relationship between a childhood
history of sexual abuse, marital status, and child rearing, we found
no significant relationship in the follow-up study where we asked
for greater detail.[1] In the latter, the relationship between sexual
abuse, marital status, and child rearing was not statistically significant by gender or for the sample as a whole. These are important
areas for future study.

Sexual Satisfaction

In the follow-up survey, we asked two questions about our respondents' sexual relationships. The first was a screening question: "Are you currently in a sexual relationship?" Next, we asked respondents to evaluate, on a 9-point rating scale, how satisfied they were with their current sexual relationships: 8 = *could not be better*, 7 = *excellent*, 6 = *good*, 5 = *above average*, 4 = *adequate*, 3 = *somewhat inadequate*, 2 = *poor*, 1 = *highly inadequate*, and 0 = *could not be worse.*

We examined the effect of a reported history of childhood abuse on ratings of current sexual satisfaction by gender. We found a strong relationship between having been sexually abused as a child and the respondents' current level of sexual satisfaction. Respondents who had not been sexually abused, on average, expressed significantly higher satisfaction with their current sexual relationships than did those with a childhood history of sexual abuse. A two-way analysis of variance examining gender and history of sexual abuse showed both factors significantly affecting the respondents' current sexual satisfaction (for gender, the $F_{(1,331)}$ = 8.3; p .01, and for history of sexual abuse, $F_{(1,331)}$ = 5.27; $p < .05$). There was no statistically significant interaction.

The average sexual satisfaction score of the nonabused was 5.35; the average score of the sexually abused was 4.79. (Note, the scale on sexual satisfaction ranged from 0 to 8, with a score of 5 meaning *above average.*) The standard deviations were about 2.0, making this difference between the abused and not abused about one fourth of a within-group standard deviation.

Sexual satisfaction also differed by gender. In general, women (whether or not they had been sexually abused) demonstrated significantly more satisfaction (mean, 5.49) than did men (mean, 4.94). Again, the difference was about one fourth of a within-group standard deviation.

An analysis of physical abuse and combined sexual and physical abuse showed no significant relationship of sexual satisfaction beyond the effects of gender and sexual abuse history. There was no interaction between gender and sexual abuse history on sexual satisfaction.

An association between childhood sexual abuse and sexual dysfunction has been reported (Elliott & Briere, 1992; Finkelhor et al., 1989; Green, 1993). Data from the Laumann et al. (1994) national survey of a community sample support an association between childhood sexual contact, subsequent sexual assault, and the quality of adult sexuality. Having been "sexually touched" as a child appears to have made this group more vulnerable to adult sexual victimization. Both men and women in the "touched" group were more likely than those in the "nontouched" group to have been forced to have sex (10% vs. 1% for men; 47% vs. 16% for women).[2]

In the Laumann et al. (1994) study, both men and women with a history of sexual contact as children were more likely than those with no such history to report that their sexual experiences had been affected by emotional problems. Both genders in the touched group reported experiencing performance anxiety and an inability to come to climax. Women in the touched group were more likely than women in the nontouched group to have had problems with vaginal dryness. They were also more likely than men in the touched and nontouched groups to report a lack of interest in sex. Men in the touched group were more likely than those in the nontouched group to have experienced difficulty with erections.

Although not necessarily pathological, those in the touched group reported a greater number of sexual relationships. They were significantly more likely than the nontouched group to have engaged in oral, anal, and group sex; to have masturbated; and to have a homosexual-bisexual identification. Although these findings were all significant at the .05 level, Laumann et al. (1994) caution that there is "no evidence that a majority of those with childhood sexual encounters have problems in their adult sexual lives. The differences, although consistent, are modest" (p. 346). Further analysis of these data and more research in this area is warranted.

Tsai, Feldman-Summers, and Edgar (1979) sought to determine specific factors to explain different sexual adjustments in adults. They compared three groups of 30 women each and found that abused women seeking treatment were significantly less well adjusted sexually than the women who were abused but had never sought treatment or a control group of women who had never been sexually abused. The clinical group reported having fewer orgasms during intercourse, more sex partners, less sexual satisfaction, and a perception of poorer quality of their close relationships with men.

Gold (1986) studied long-term psychosocial consequences of childhood sexual abuse (i.e., comparing 103 abused women with 88 who were not abused). Those who had been sexually abused as

Table 7.1 Correlations of Sexual Abuse Factors to Sexual Functioning

Sexual Abuse Factor	Having a Sexual Relationship		Satisfaction With Sexual Relationship		Gay, Lesbian, or Bisexual	
	Women	Men	Women	Men	Women	Men
Sexually abused				-.13		
Time sexually abused[a] (days, months, years)			-.29	-.41*	-.10	
Age at first abuse[a]	+.18	-.43		+.06	-.21	+.19
Age at last abuse[a]		-.53			-.14	+.14
Times abused[a]	-.24	-.37*	-.22	-.21		+.44*
Years abused[a]	-.21	-.36*	-.17	-.19	+.10	
Fondling private parts			-.11	-.18*		
Oral sex			-.16*			
Penetration by fingers						+.20**
Other sex acts	-.12				+.13*	
Abused by male stranger	-.15*					
Abused by female acquaintance	-.14*					
Abused by male family member		-.10	-.14	-.19*		
Coercion or violence	-.19**			-.18*	+.15*	

NOTE: Those variables noted with an "a" are based on only those respondents who were sexually abused. In this table, correlations less than .10 are omitted.
*$p < .05$. **$p < .01$.

children were more likely than the nonabused group to report greater sexual distress and dissatisfaction with their current sexual relationships.

Sexual dysfunction may be associated with childhood sexual abuse in general and with certain abuse characteristics, such as duration and type of abuse and coercion (Green, 1993). Accordingly, in our follow-up survey, we examined the effects of duration, relationship of the perpetrator to the victim, and type of sexual abuse on three indicators of sexual functioning by gender: (a) whether the respondents were currently involved in a sexual relationship; (b) if they were, how satisfied they were with the relationship; and (c) sexual orientation. The results are presented in Table 7.1.

Men who experienced long-term multiple incidents of sexual abuse (see Chapters 3 and 6) were least likely to report being involved in a sexual relationship at the time of the study. Those engaged in a sexual relationship, compared to their peers who were not abused, reported significantly lower sexual satisfaction. They were least satisfied when sexual abuse had involved the fondling of their private parts or oral sex. The presence of coercion or violence or abuse by a male family member was also related to lower satisfaction.

Women who had been abused by a male stranger or a female acquaintance or who had been coerced were less likely to be currently involved in a sexual relationship than the nonabused. In contrast to the men, none of the factors identifying type of abuse significantly affected the women's satisfaction with their current sexual relationship.

Abusing Another Person

In the follow-up study, we asked our respondents about personal and professional boundary violations. We prefaced these questions with the following statement:

> As a professional, you are familiar with theories that propose that individuals who were abused as children are at higher risk to become abusers than those who were never abused. The following questions address this issue. We appreciate your response to these very personal questions.

The question about personal boundary violations was, "Have you ever sexually or physically abused another person?"

Among the 389 respondents to the follow-up survey, we found a relationship between a childhood history of sexual abuse and the physical or sexual abuse of another for both genders. Men who reported a childhood history of sexual abuse were almost 5 times more likely (24% to 5%) to have abused another person than men without such history. This effect was highly significant (χ^2 test $p <$ .001). For women, the effect was in the same direction (7.3% to 1.8%), but was less significant (χ^2 test $p < .05$).

Both men and women who reported a childhood history of physical abuse (about 7% of the total sample) were far more likely than those who had not to have abused another person. Among the 16 female respondents who reported a childhood history of physical abuse, 19% ($N = 3$) reported that they had physically or sexually abused another, whereas only 2% of the 204 women ($N = 4$) who had not been physically abused reported that they had done so (χ^2 $p < .001$).

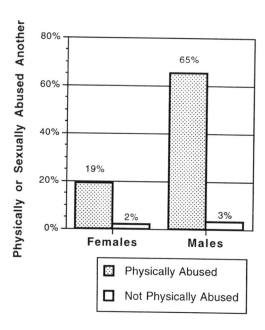

Figure 7.3. Relationship Between History of Physical Abuse and Physically or Sexually Abusing Another Person
NOTE: This reflects follow-up survey data.

Among the 17 men who reported a childhood history of physical abuse, 11 (65%) reported that they had physically or sexually abused another (see Figure 7.3), whereas only 3% of the nonphysically abused respondents reported that they had physically or sexually abused another person (χ^2 $p < .00001$).

To determine the power of the relationship between childhood physical abuse and physical or sexual abuse of another person, we analyzed the positive predictive power (PPP) and negative predictive power (NPP) (Elwood, 1992) for predicting whether a man who was physically abused as a child would, as an adult, physically or sexually abuse another person (see Table 7.2). When we predicted that all men who reported having been physically abused as a child would reveal that they had physically or sexually abused another person, we were correct 65% of the time. The negative predictive power was 97% (i.e., if a man had not been physically abused as a

Table 7.2 For Males: Predictive Power of a Childhood History of Physical Abuse Predicting Abusing Another as an Adult

		Group to be predicted: Abuse another as an adult					
Test		Yes		No		Total	
Physically abused as a child	Yes	11	a	6	b	17	(a + b)
Not physically abused as a child	No	4	c	148	d	152	(c + d)
		15	(a + c)	154	(b + d)	169	N

Positive predictive power (PPP) = a/(a + b) = 11/17 = 65%
Negative predictive power (NPP) = d/(c + d) = 148/152 = 97%
Prevalence = (a + c)/N = 15/169 = 9%
Sensitivity = a/(a + c) = 11/15 = 73%
Specificity = d/(b + d) = 148/154 = 96%

child, we could predict correctly 97% of the time that he would not have physically or sexually abused another).

We also sought to determine if we could predict whether the abuse of another person would allow inference of a history of childhood physical abuse (see Table 7.2). For males, the positive predictive power was 11/15 = 73%; the negative predictive power was 148/154 = 96%. Thus, a man with a past or current history (or both) of abusing others is highly likely (73%) to have had a childhood history of physical abuse. On the other hand, a person who has no history of abusing someone as an adult, will, most likely, not have a childhood history of physical abuse (96%). A series of cross-tabulation analyses revealed that having a childhood history of both physical and sexual abuse did not significantly add to the effect of abusing another person.

We examined the effect of childhood sexual abuse on abusing another person as an adult (see Table 7.3). Although we found the effect was highly significant ($p < .001$) for both genders combined, the PPP was 12/88 or only 14%, whereas the NPP was 291/301 or 97%. Thus, we can predict that a person who was not sexually abused as a child will be unlikely, as an adult, to abuse another. However, if we predict that everybody who was sexually abused as a child will subsequently abuse another, we would be correct only 14% of the time (and incorrect 86% of the time).

Table 7.3 For Both Males and Females: Predictive Power of a Childhood History of Sexual Abuse Predicting Abusing Another as an Adult

Test	Group to be predicted: Abuse another as an adult						
		Yes		No		Total	
Sexually abused as a child	Yes	12	a	76	b	88	(a + b)
Not sexually abused as a child	No	10	c	291	d	301	(c + d)
		22	(a + c)	367	(b + d)	389	N

Positive predictive power (PPP) = a/(a + b) = 12/88 = 14%
Negative predictive power (NPP) = d /(c + d) = 291/301 = 97%
Prevalence = (a + c)/N = 22/389 = 6%
Sensitivity = a/(a + c) = 12/22 = 55%
Specificity = d/(b + d) = 291/367 = 79%

Despite the increased interest in the concept of *intergenerational transmission of abuse* (Bagley, Wood, & Young, 1994; Freeman-Longo, 1986; Green, 1993; Hanson, Lipovsky, & Saunders, 1994; Sansonnet-Hayden, Haley, Marriage, & Fine, 1987; Smith & Israel, 1987; Summit, 1983), most studies of the abuse-to-abuser process are retrospective and therefore subject to many limitations. They are vulnerable to memory distortion and changes in how society defines abuse. Furthermore, much of the research has been conducted with offenders who may have a self-serving interest in being viewed as victims.

Bagley and Sewchuk-Dann (1991) compared 65 young sexual offenders in a Canadian residential treatment center with 220 controls from the same institution who had no history of sexual assault. They found that the sexually assaultive group were more likely to have been subjected to emotional, physical, or sexual abuse in their families of origin. More than half the sexually assaultive group, compared to 10% of the controls, had experienced sexual abuse of long duration. In another study of a randomly drawn community sample of males (N = 750) between the ages of 18 and 27, Bagley et al. (1994) found that those who had experienced multiple sexual and emotional abuse were more likely to have engaged in sexual contact with children of both genders and with male adolescents.

Hanson et al. (1994) interviewed 74 male incest offenders (and their therapists) and found that 25% of the perpetrators had reported histories of childhood sexual abuse. In a descriptive study of 25 families in which sibling incest had been substantiated, Smith and Israel (1987) found that 52% of the perpetrators had themselves been abused (either within or outside their families).

Mian, Marton, LeBaron, and Birtwistle (1994) sought to determine familial risk factors for abuse of young females in Canada. A comparison of families who had experienced intrafamilial abuse (N = 42) with those who had experienced extrafamilial (N = 28) abuse and those who had not been abused (N = 42) showed that fathers in both abused groups, who themselves had been physically victimized as children, were more likely to physically abuse another person than those who had no abuse history.

Kaufman and Zigler (1987) challenge the unqualified acceptance of intergenerational transmission of child abuse. From their review of three prospective studies (Egeland & Jacobvitz, 1984; Hunter & Kilstrom, 1979; Straus, 1979), Kaufman and Zigler estimate the rate of transmission of abuse at about 30%. Accordingly, they note that the majority of abusers report no child abuse history, and a substantial number of parents who have child abuse histories do not abuse their children. They conclude that the cycle of abuse cannot be attributed solely to a childhood history of abuse. Its influence on subsequent abusive behavior cannot be separated from poverty-related factors, such as stress and lack of social support. In agreement, Pelton (1985) speculates that the social, cultural, and economic factors that contribute to child physical abuse are re-created in each generation, thereby perpetuating the transmission of abuse.

It is interesting that in a controlled, prospective study of substantiated cases of child physical and sexual abuse and neglect (N = 908) to determine whether being abused or neglected as a child was associated with subsequent adult arrests for violent crimes (including child abuse and neglect), Widom (1989a, 1989b) found no evidence for an abuse-to-abuser transmission. Although her data show that having been abused or neglected as a child increases the risk (for both males and females) of being arrested for adult criminal behavior (29% vs. 21%), she found no such association between an early history of physical or sexual abuse, neglect, or both (to age 11) and later arrests for child abuse and neglect. Cohorts in the control group (667) were as likely to be arrested for child abuse and neglect as were those in the experimental group (1.1% vs. 1.0%).

The discrepancies between the Widom studies and ours may be indicative of differences in the populations. Unlike our sample of so-called fortunate abused, Widom's population represents the most extreme reported cases of maltreatment and neglect, most of which came from lower SES backgrounds; unreported, unsubstantiated cases of child abuse and neglect are not included nor are cases of undocumented criminal activity. Furthermore, at the time of the Widom study, subjects were relatively young (between the ages of 20 and 30). Perhaps, with increased age and onset of parenting, an association between a childhood history of abuse and neglect would be more likely.

Although many studies have linked adult violent and abusive behavior to earlier maltreatment, to our knowledge, our data are the first to demonstrate that, in a nonclinical sample, having been physically abused as a child is strongly associated with later abusive behavior, thereby providing a post-hoc longitudinal view of the connection between victim and victimizer. These prospective and retrospective predictions have important clinical implications. Clients (both male and female) who report a childhood history of either physical or sexual abuse are at greater risk to subsequently abuse others. The reverse is also true; there is a strong likelihood that clients who are physical or sexual abusers have a childhood history of abuse.

Responsible practice requires that the "contribution of . . . victimization" (Sansonnet-Hayden et al., 1987, p. 756) to abusive and dysfunctional relationships not be ignored. To minimize the opportunity for ongoing abuse and to reduce potentially damaging consequences, many researchers recommend that clinicians ask clients directly about a history of childhood abuse and domestic violence (Brekke, 1987; Bryer, Nelson, Miller, & Krol, 1987; Gelinas, 1983; Lanktree, Briere, & Zaidi, 1991; Ogata et al., 1990). Consistent with that practice, we recommend that when adult clients acknowledge a childhood history of abuse, straightforward inquiry about the possibility of past or current (or both) abusive relationships is clinically indicated. By not questioning the client directly, the clinician unwittingly colludes with the client's need for secrecy while reinforcing his or her feelings of guilt and shame.

Clearly, inquiries about and responses to such sensitive and emotionally charged issues should be made in the context of an empathic relationship. Limitations on client-therapist confidentiality and legal requirements for reporting must be made explicit before such questioning takes place.

There are no definitive theories to explain why individuals who were abused as children subsequently become abusers. However, there have been various attempts, mostly psychodynamically based, to explain the complex interaction of factors that contribute to the victim-to-victimizer process. Bagley et al. (1994) speculate that the phenomenon may be a manifestation of the victim's identification with the aggressor, "fixated arousal patterns" (p. 683), a sexual addiction, or a lack of empathy due to arrested development. They suggest that such behavior is learned and is manifested in transgenerational patterns of deviance and antisocial behavior.

From his work at a sex offender unit, Freeman-Longo (1986) speculates that sex offenders who were sexually abused as children may be reenacting their abuse or expressing displaced rage. Like Bagley et al., Freeman-Longo views sexual assaults as a manifestation of a lack of empathy that allows offenders to deny the damage inflicted by their behavior.

Grevan (1991) builds a strong case that religion is a contributing factor to the physical abuse of children. According to Grevan, such abuse is rationalized and condoned as a way of ensuring a child's salvation. DeJonge (1995) also writes about the role of religion and the "underlying attitudes toward children" (p. 30) that justify their shaming and humiliation. In an attempt to understand the dynamics of the transmission of child abuse, deJonge proposes that the experience of child abuse precludes the formation of stable parent-child attachments. Thus, parents who have experienced the pain and degradation of maltreatment are bereft of the capacity to empathize with either their own or their children's suffering. Consequently, unmodified, unexpressed rage toward their abusive parents is projected onto their own children, thereby perpetuating the abuse cycle. Although a failure in parent-child attachment may contribute to the intergenerational transmission of abuse, other factors, such as the personal attributes of the child and parent, how the child deals with stress, and environment, such as poverty and extent of social supports must be considered (Justice & Justice, 1990).

Clearly, we need research to determine what differentiates victims of abuse who go on to become victimizers from those who do not (Freeman-Longo, 1986). Longitudinal, prospective studies of families that follow parenting over time (National Research Council, 1993) can begin to address the question, "Under what conditions is the transmission of abuse most (or least) likely to occur?" (Kaufman & Zigler, 1987).

Professional Behavior

In this section, we present the effects of childhood abuse on professional practice and boundaries. We speculated that clinicians who reported a history of childhood sexual abuse would be more likely than their peers with no such history to be working in the area of child abuse. Accordingly, in both studies we looked for an association between respondents' history of childhood abuse and (a) being a member of a family violence or sexual abuse team and (b) the fraction of time respondents spent in direct service to sexually abused clients. Again, where we found no between-study differences, we report data from the initial study only.

Work Setting and Field of Practice

Sexually abused respondents were twice as likely as those not sexually abused to be members of family violence teams (9% vs. 4%) and to devote more time working directly with sexual abuse cases (12% vs. 8%). Those who reported histories of physical abuse were 3 times as likely to be members of a family violence team (14% vs. 4%) as those who did not report such abuse.

When we compared respondents who were members of sexual abuse teams by a childhood history of sexual abuse only and physical abuse only, we found no significant differences. However, when we compared those who were members of sexual abuse teams by a childhood history of both physical and sexual abuse, we found they were 3 times more likely (22%) to be so involved than those who had not been abused either physically or sexually (6%), those who had been physically abused only (7%), or those who had been sexually abused only (6%).

We found a similar but even more powerful relationship for membership on family violence teams. Those who reported a childhood history of both physical and sexual abuse were 7 times more likely to be members of family violence teams (22%) than respondents who reported no abuse history (3%) and 3 times more likely than those who reported physical abuse only (7%) or sexual abuse only (6%). The eta[3] for predicting sexual abuse team membership from abuse history was .10 (p = .06); the eta for predicting family violence team membership from abuse history was .16 ($p < .001$). These findings strongly suggest that clinicians who have a childhood history of both types of abuse are significantly more likely than their peers who have experienced no abuse (or only one type of abuse) to be attracted to working with abused populations. Consequently, clinicians who have experienced both types of abuse may be over-represented on sexual abuse and family violence teams, in effect, potentially producing a tendency toward greater belief that allegations of abuse have occurred. As noted in Chapter 4, more research is needed to determine whether this tendency is a reflection of empathy, or bias as a result of overidentification.

Sexual Boundary Violations

We asked each respondent, "Have you ever engaged in sexual activities with your clients-patients?" Close to 4% ($N = 14$) of the total sample ($N = 393$) answered in the affirmative. Respondents with a history of childhood sexual abuse were 3 times more likely to have engaged in sexual activities with clients than their peers with no history of sexual abuse (8% vs. 2.3%; $p < .05$).[4] This association was much stronger for males than females.

Consistent with our findings, most reports of client-therapist sexual boundary violations involve male therapists[5] (Holroyd & Brodsky, 1977). Sexual activity with clients is, apparently, a rare event among female clinicians. Only one (2%) of the women in our study who had been sexually abused as a child reported sex with a client (she reported a childhood history of both physical and sexual abuse). None of the women who had not been abused reported such activity. Conversely, 5% of the male professionals who had not been sexually abused as children reported sex with a client. This value more than tripled to 18% for male professionals who reported a childhood history of sexual abuse. The relationship between a personal history of sexual abuse and subsequent sex with clients or patients was statistically significant only for the males (see Figure 7.4).

When we examined the effect of childhood sexual abuse on sexual relationships with clients by gender and discipline, we found no statistically significant effect for females of any discipline or for male social workers, psychiatrists, or pediatricians. We did, however, find a significant effect for male psychologists ($p = .02$, Fisher's

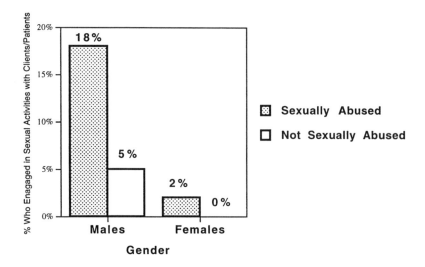

Figure 7.4. Relationship Between Having Been Sexually Abused and Engaging in Sex With Clients or Patients
NOTE: This reflects follow-up survey data.

Exact Test; Siegel, 1956). Of the five male psychologists who had been sexually abused as children, three (60%) reported that they had engaged in sexual activities with clients. In contrast, of the 33 male psychologists who had not been sexually abused as children, only 9% ($N = 3$) had reported such activities.[6] A similar examination of age category and gender showed no differences in the relationship of previous history of sexual abuse and sexual contact with clients by age or gender.

Our frequencies for the total sample are consistent with the overall estimates of prevalence of 5% to 10% for psychotherapists who engage in sexual activity with their clients (Brooks, 1990; Pope, 1988; Pope, Keith-Spiegel, & Tabachnick, 1986). Because it is unlikely that professionals exaggerate sexual boundary violations with their clients, it is probable that these frequencies underestimate the scope of the problem (Holroyd & Brodsky, 1977; Thoreson, Shaugnessy, Heppner, & Cook, 1993).

We speculated that many of the respondents who reported physically or sexually abusing another person (or both) had also engaged in sexual activities with their clients. A cross-tabulation of our 389 respondents revealed a significant association between the two types of reported behavior ($\chi^2 p < .01$).

As expected, the majority of respondents reported neither activity (92%). However, of the 22 respondents who reported abusing another person, 14% ($N = 3$) reported engaging in sexual activity with a client. This ratio is close to 5 times greater than the 3% who reported sex with a client but had not reported sexually or physically abusing another person. Similarly, we found that respondents who reported having engaged in sexual activity with a client were 4 times as likely to have abused another person (21% vs. 5%). A series of cross-tabulation analyses revealed that a history of both physical and sexual abuse, as opposed to a history of sexual abuse only, further increased the likelihood of engaging in sexual activity with clients (15% vs. 6%).

Thus, our findings demonstrate a strong relationship between a history of sexual abuse as a child and sexual boundary violations as an adult professional. Surprisingly, we found only one reference in the literature to such an association. Gartrell et al. (1989), in their anecdotal description of a therapist who had engaged in sexual activities with his clients, make passing reference to his history of childhood abuse. Clearly, this association needs further study.

As early as the 4th century B.C.E., the Hippocratic Oath prohibited sexual contact with a patient (Moore, 1978). Recently called "a crime protected by the profession and society" (Armsworth, 1990, p. 553), sexual exploitation of clients continues to create anxiety and discomfort among some mental health practitioners (Pope et al., 1986). Consequently, such professionals may greet such disclosures with suspicion, often attributing blame to the victim (Borys & Pope, 1989; DeYoung, 1981). Little if any guidance is provided to those who discover that one of their peers has violated sexual boundaries with clients (Levenson, 1986). Yet this issue presents major ethical and teaching concerns for both health and mental health professionals (American Psychological Association, 1992; Borys & Pope, 1989; National Association of Social Workers [NASW], 1995; Pope & Vetter, 1991).

Reports of substantiated cases of sexual boundary violations by professionals have emerged in both lay and professional publications (Goldberg, 1995; NASW, 1995). They have been reported across all disciplines (Armsworth, 1990; Sonne & Pope, 1991) and account for the majority of ethical complaints in some mental health professions (Pope et al., 1986).

According to Berliner (1989), estimates of sexual misbehavior by helping professionals are uniformly underreported. The major impediment to addressing the problem is the unwillingness of clients and professionals to report (Moore, 1985). Therapist-client sexual boundary violations are particularly difficult to identify. In contrast to medical infractions that are likely to be discovered from reviewing hospital charts, the secret nature of sexual activity between a therapist and a client makes its detection difficult (Gartrell et al., 1989).

Clearly, identification of such ethical violations depends on disclosure by the abused client or subsequent therapists (Gartrell, Herman, Olarte, Feldstein, & Localio, 1988). Yet most clients and professionals are hesitant to report or bring charges because such action can be awkward and frustrating (Moore, 1985). "Reporting a colleague is a very difficult and often lonely step . . . [I]t requires that professionals deal with ambivalence and resistance in both [their] clients and themselves while simultaneously respecting clients' confidentiality and autonomy" (Levenson, 1986, p. 317). Cases that are reported are rarely substantiated. Hearings, and their outcomes, often remain confidential, providing protection for the offender and increasing the risk of further abuse.

One of the earlier studies of sexual exploitation of clients was conducted by Kardener, Fuller, and Mensh (1973). They surveyed 460 male physicians (psychiatrists, obstetrician-gynecologists, surgeons, internists, and general practitioners) to determine attitudes and behaviors related to erotic and nonerotic contact with clients. Although we find the distinction between nonerotic and erotic contact to be ambiguous, two thirds of the total sample in the Kardener et al. study believed that nonerotic contact with clients could be helpful (58% had actually engaged in such behavior). Of the male physicians who participated in the study, 19% believed that sexually stimulating contact with clients could, at times, be helpful, whereas 13% of the total sample reported that they had engaged in some form of erotic behavior.

A similar study (Holroyd & Brodsky, 1977) examined male and female psychologists' ($N = 703$) attitudes and behaviors concerning sexually stimulating and nonsexually stimulating touching with clients. Those who endorsed a psychodynamic orientation were least likely to accept the notion that erotic contact could be beneficial to clients (86%; perhaps because of the training emphasis on transference and countertransference phenomena), followed by those who had an eclectic orientation (78%), humanistic orientation (71%), rational-cognitive orientation (68%), and behavior modification orientation (61%).

The Holroyd and Brodsky (1977) study showed that 4% of the participating psychologists sanctioned erotic contact with clients and believed it might be helpful with clients of the opposite sex; 2% believed such contact might be helpful in same-sex relationships. Consistent with our study, Holroyd and Brodsky found strong gender differences. Men were 5 times more likely than women to engage in erotic behavior with their clients (10.9% male; 1.9% female) and to have had sexual intercourse with their clients during treatment (5.5% for males; 0.6% for females), often more than once. When the combined frequencies of reported intercourse at the time of the study, during therapy, and posttermination were calculated, the data showed that 8.1% of the men and 1.0% of the women reported engaging in intercourse with their clients.

Sexual feelings that naturally arise in therapist-client relationships have only begun to be acknowledged (Borys & Pope, 1989; deYoung, 1981). According to Borys & Pope (1989), therapists need to be trained to deal with sexual feelings toward clients and use them as they would any countertransference feeling. These emotional responses should "become a therapeutic resource rather than a push toward revictimizing the patient" (p. 185). Pope et al. (1986) surveyed 585 male and female psychologists in private practice to determine the prevalence of sexual feelings toward clients. Whereas a large majority of both male and female respondents (95% males; 76% females) reported having sexual feelings toward their clients, a minority (9.4% of the men and 2.5% of the women) actually acted on their sexual impulses. Note that most respondents (82%) had not considered acting on their attraction and that 93.5% had never engaged in sexual activity with their clients.

In a survey of psychiatrists (N = 1,423), Gartrell, Herman, Olarte, Feldstein, and Localio (1987) found that 6.4% of their respondents (N = 84) admitted to engaging in sexual activity with their clients. Although 65% of the respondents reported having treated patients who had reported exploitation by former therapists (psychiatrists, psychologists, social workers, and lay therapists), only 8% (of the 65%) had reported such activity to the authorities. Reasons given for not reporting included issues of confidentiality, disbelief, patient's unwillingness, fear of reprisal, and frustration with and lack of confidence in professional organizations and the legal system.

Pope and Feldman-Summers (1992) conducted a national survey to determine the prevalence of abuse among 500 psychologists, equally divided by gender. Respondents were asked about their personal history of abuse, the quality of their training, and their perceived ability to help clients who had been abused. About one third reported some form of child or adolescent sexual or physical abuse (the high prevalence rate may be the result of allowing the respondents to define abuse). Although, on average, the abused psychologists felt competent to work with the abused, they rated their graduate programs as very poor in the area of sexual abuse.

In a national, random sample of master's and doctoral level male counselors and educators ($N = 366$) to investigate sexual boundary violations between clients and therapists, Thoreson et al. (1993) found that about 2% of their respondents reported having engaged in sexual activity with a client one or more times during the course of counseling. A larger number (7%) reported such contact following termination.

In a study of the impact of therapist-client sexual contact, Feldman-Summers and Jones (1984) compared three groups of women: (a) those who had been sexually exploited by their therapists ($N = 14$), (b) those who had been sexually exploited by other health professionals ($N = 7$), and (c) those who had not been sexually exploited by their therapists ($N = 10$). They sought the factors that determined the psychological problems experienced by clients who had been sexually exploited. They found, not surprisingly, that women who had been sexually exploited by their therapists were more likely than those who had not, to express anger and doubts about men in general and therapists in particular. They were also more likely to have psychosomatic symptoms a month following the termination of therapy.

In the same study, Feldman-Summers and Jones (1984) found no significant differences in psychological impact between a client's sexual relationship with a therapist and a sexual relationship with another type of helping professional. Their finding supports the speculation that it is the shattering of the dependency and protective aspect of the relationship that generates the damaging consequences. Women experienced the most severe impact when the offender was married and when they had an earlier history of sexual victimization and serious symptomatology prior to therapy.

Pope et al. (1986) propose a therapist-patient sex syndrome that is similar to other traumatic responses and to borderline personality disorders. The syndrome includes ambivalence toward the therapist, suicidality, cognitive dysfunction (flashbacks, dissociation, depersonalization, and other PTSD symptoms), lack of trust, sexual dysfunction, anger, and depression.

Although sexual activity with a therapist may, in general, have serious consequences for clients, such relationships between an incest survivor and her therapist may have particularly onerous effects (deYoung, 1981). Such exploitation is often experienced as a recreation of the earlier incestuous situation. Armsworth (1990) also draws a parallel between incest and sexual boundary violations with clients, such as abrogation of responsibility by the offender, imbalance of power, confusion of boundaries and roles, deceit, rationalization, false representation, and "depersonalization of [the] victim" (p. 546). According to Armsworth (1990), incest survivors who have been sexually violated by their therapists find it difficult to leave therapy. Feelings of confusion, guilt, shame, and humiliation discourage disclosure. Paradoxically, those who have children are either fearful of losing custody or fearful of not being believed.

Burgess and Hartman (1986) note similarities between professional responses to the sexual victimization of clients and incest and rape. Historically, both have been characterized by denial and avoidance. Although all professional organizations implicitly or explicitly prohibit sexual activity with clients, there are few if any empirically based guidelines to assist helping professionals to recognize, report, or prevent therapist-client sexual involvement. Despite adverse consequences for clients (and therapists; Welfel & Lipsitz, n.d.), only cursory attention is paid to these concerns in graduate curricula (Rhodes, 1984).

Clearly, professionals are ambivalent about their responsibility to report their colleagues for unethical behavior. According to Zitrin and Klein (1976), professionals are unable to monitor their peers due to a lack of investigative capacity, the secret nature of the therapeutic relationship, and hesitancy to judge their colleagues. Furthermore, when informed of therapist-client boundary violations, professionals are confronted with an ethical dilemma that is difficult to resolve without guidance: the obligation to expose the behavior versus the obligation to preserve client confidentiality (Stone, 1982).

Summary and Conclusions

We were surprised by the magnitude of the effects of childhood sexual abuse on the personal lives of our respondents. Those who reported a childhood history of sexual abuse were less likely than their nonabused peers to be married, if they were men, and less likely to have raised children, if they were women (these results were, however, not confirmed in the follow-up survey). Both men and women (in the initial study) who reported a childhood history of sexual abuse were 4 times as likely to have nonmarital relationships with significant others than were those who did not report such a history. Furthermore, we found an inverse relationship between adult sexual satisfaction and childhood sexual abuse.

Of particular clinical relevance was the finding that we could predict with extremely high level of confidence the abuse of others among male respondents who reported a childhood history of physical abuse. Men and women who reported a childhood history of physical or sexual abuse were far more likely than their nonabused peers to acknowledge the physical or sexual abuse of another person.

Clearly, childhood abuse can also have serious repercussions for professional practice. Our data provide strong evidence that a childhood history of sexual and physical abuse is associated with choice of work setting and field of practice. Respondents who reported both types of abuse were more likely to be members of sexual abuse and family violence teams and to work with abused populations. Moreover, male clinicians who reported a history of childhood sexual abuse were more likely to cross professional boundaries in ways that can be seriously damaging to clients. They were far more likely to report having engaged in sexual activity with their clients than their sexually abused female colleagues or their nonsexually abused peers.

Our findings strongly suggest that a history of childhood sexual abuse may be a hidden (and until now, unexamined) factor contributing to sexual exploitation of clients by professionals. Because sexual exploitation of clients by mental health professionals is a major problem that occurs across disciplines, this is an important finding that has major implications for the education and training of all professionals.

Notes

1. We are at a loss to explain the failure of replication here, because the follow-up study gave, essentially, the identical fraction of the sexually abused. Note,

however, that the sample size of the follow-up study was smaller than that of the original survey. Also, the increased rate of child rearing and marital status among our respondents could be a reflection of the passage of time between the first and the follow-up surveys (2 years had passed since the initial study).

2. Neither *force* or *sex* were specifically defined in the Laumann et al. study.

3. Eta is a measure of association between two variables independent of linearity. Eta squared is the proportion of the variance of one variable accounted for by the other variable.

4. For brevity, we use the term *client* to refer to both clients and patients.

5. We have no information on the gender of the clients who experienced sexual activity with their therapists. However, we presume they were primarily female.

6. We do not, on the basis of this fragmentary statistic, distinguish psychologists from the other professions. Clearly, larger samples are needed to draw any conclusions.

8

Implications, Recommendations, and Conclusions

Introduction

The overall prevalence of physical and sexual abuse (21%) found in this population of clinicians is within the range reported in other nonclinical populations. Although respondents, on average, tended to believe the sexual abuse allegations depicted in the 16 vignettes presented, a respondent's history of childhood abuse (among other factors) produced significantly higher levels of belief than nonabused respondents.

We have empirically identified personal and case factors that influence clinicians' judgments of sexual abuse allegations. In addition, we have demonstrated the effects of a history of childhood abuse on the personal and professional lives of clinicians. We do not claim that a history of childhood abuse is the causal factor of these effects. Clearly, the effects of child sexual abuse must be studied in the context of mediating circumstances, such as type, frequency, and duration of abuse, quality of parenting, coping style, poverty, and other potentially pathogenic factors. A childhood history of sexual abuse is clearly one of a variety of factors contributing to later damaging effects.

We have found statistically significant differences between the abused and nonabused clinicians in psychological and personal adjustment—and in professional judgment. Although some effects are modest, the thesis that childhood abuse can have long-term consequences is valid for this professional population and provides further evidence that "the impact of abuse is not simply a phenomenon limited to those who come to the offices of mental health practitioners" (Finkelhor, Hotaling, Lewis, & Smith, 1989, p. 396).

The literature reviewed in this book explains, in part, the confusion and conflict that often surrounds clinical evaluations of allegedly abused children. Despite the increased interest and progress in research on child abuse, there remains a dearth of solid, consistent, empirical research to guide and inform professionals who must make the difficult decisions in the field.

The results presented here are of concern to all professionals dealing with children and families. Our findings provide a foundation that can guide graduate and continuing education and training programs, inform practice, and direct future research. In the following sections, we discuss the implications of our data and make recommendations for professional education, practice, and research.

Implications and Recommendations for Education, Training, and Practice

Our results demonstrate that the clinician, like all of us, is "part of the culture in which he [or she] lives, and . . . never succeeds in freeing himself [or herself] entirely from dependence on the dominant preconceptions and biases of his [or her] environment" (Myrdal, 1944, p. 1035). Because these cultural elements are usually both deep and pervasive, it is not surprising that, when evaluating the same data, individual clinicians arrive at different opinions about the validity of sexual abuse allegations. Nor should it surprise us that disagreement, confusion, and conflict exist among professionals attempting to determine the validity of these allegations.

Some divergence can be attributed to the ambiguity characteristic of sexual abuse allegations and the absence of sound empirically based theories and systematic protocols on which to base clinical judgments. Attitudes and beliefs about sexuality, and the heavy emotional content of child and adolescent sexual abuse, may lead to defensive strategies that distort judgment and produce inaccurate, and sometimes unfortunate, decisions that may damage children and their families. Clearly, without standardized tests of validity, many subjective, and often unconscious, factors compromise objectivity. Because our vignettes were designed to be ambiguous, their hypothetical structure precludes validation. The need for additional research to fill this practice void is compelling.

As expected, we find that a childhood abuse history can affect clinical evaluation of data and clinical decision making. It is not clear whether clinicians with a history of childhood abuse are more empathic than their nonabused peers, and therefore more sensitive to detection of abuse, or are biased as a result of overidentification with the abused. This is an important area for future research.

We expect to find that about 20% of the students (male and female) in professional graduate schools were abused as children. Rates of abuse may be even higher in classes where the focus is on abuse and trauma (Jackson & Nuttall, 1991). Furthermore, we can expect the abuse experience to influence students' information processing on rape, childhood abuse, and family violence and evaluation of sexual abuse allegations in their internships and professional practice. Educators must be sensitive to and address these issues, both in the classroom and in internship and residency programs.

We have demonstrated that race has a large effect on clinical judgment. Indeed, race was the most powerful factor affecting the credibility ratings of the sexual abuse allegations. In evaluations of sexual abuse allegations, factors such as race of the perpetrator or victim are incompatible with reliability, accuracy, or justice. Ironically, clinicians whose intent is to avoid discrimination on the basis of race may show the greatest amount of (reverse) racial bias (Fajardo, 1985). However, when clinicians are faced with the ambiguities typical of sexual abuse allegations, subtle attitudes, often unconscious and prejudicial, may emerge. Because of their complex nature, these influences may be more difficult to identify and eliminate than the more overt patterns of prejudice that we consciously guard against (Fajardo, 1985). Professionals, in spite of efforts to be fair and egalitarian, may thus unwittingly compromise their objectivity.

Although, on average, clinicians relied on many of the case factors shown in the literature to place children at risk for sexual abuse, the weight given to particular factors varied significantly. In addition to misperceptions about the importance of the victim's and perpetrator's race, we found seriously flawed interpretations of the complicated, and often misleading, manifestations of children's trauma. Surprisingly, the average respondent appears unaware that a caretaker's prior history of psychiatric illness and childhood history of sexual abuse or a family's disorganization (as reflected in earlier contact with protective services) indicates increased risk for child sexual abuse.

Most important, professional training and education must be improved to minimize the damage that results, at present, from subjective clinical judgments. Emphasis should be placed on

identification of empirically identified case factors for children at risk,
potential racial biases,
identification and resolution of ethical dilemmas,
self-awareness and self-monitoring, and
the need for feedback, supervision, and consultation.

Continuing education and inservice programs should have an important role in the dissemination of the rapidly accumulating knowledge about sexual abuse. Professional organizations should be urged to lead in efforts to alleviate potential practice biases inherent in stereotypic attitudes and belief systems about race, gender, and age.

Most decisions about sexual abuse allegations are made by multidisciplinary teams. Despite some potential drawbacks, we support the usefulness of the team approach, allowing different disciplines to bring their various perspectives to clinical judgments (DeJong, 1985; Freedman, Rosenberg, Gettman-Felzien, & Van Scoyk, 1993). Our findings, however, show that idiosyncratic personal attributes and professional assumptions may emphasize particular factors and thus influence clinical decisions. Because similar results have been reported for other professional groups (Abramson, 1989), it is clear that the interdisciplinary teams alone cannot minimize the influence of extraneous factors on clinical decision making. Professional education must provide improved training in the methodological evaluation of the complex, ambiguous data characteristic of these cases—and the team approach should be improved, as will be discussed.

Although complete objectivity does not and cannot exist, subjectivity can be minimized by facing our biases rather than avoiding them. To reduce the probability of underreactions or overreactions and the risk of conclusions that are premature and potentially harmful to children and their families, we propose the following:

- Sexual abuse evaluation teams should be composed of both males and females of different ages and disciplines and, of course, should include minority professionals as far as feasible.
- Teams should minimally be composed of five or seven members.
- Initial evaluations of sexual abuse allegations should be made independently (of other team members) and submitted prior to team meetings.
- Team members must support their conclusions with references to the factual data of the case and to relevant literature when available.
- The level of confidence that sexual abuse has or has not occurred should be explicitly acknowledged by each team member (Jones & McGraw, 1987).
- Following initial independent evaluations, team members should meet to discuss their perceptions and arrive at a consensus, if possible.

If consensus is not attained, members should vote to produce a majority and minority report (note the odd number of team members recommended).

Although we recommend the use of interdisciplinary teams as the most objective approach to evaluate allegations of child sexual abuse, their use raises questions that require further investigation. For example,

- What is the effect of high prestige professions on lower prestige team members?
- Are there preferred methods of reaching consensus?
- To what extent does a team member's personal history of abuse affect team decision making?

For the last point, we suggest a study of teams in which some members have personal histories of childhood abuse. Presented with the same set of cases, information about the effect of such histories on team decisions would be valuable.

This study has provided some important guidelines to alert professionals to particular factors that place children at risk for sexual abuse. Knowledge of these factors can improve evaluation of sexual abuse allegations and increase the safety and protection of children. According to our findings, both male and female respondents who, as children, experienced one type of abuse were at significant risk of experiencing another type of abuse. Thus, we recommend that when sexual abuse allegations are being evaluated, the possibility of physical abuse be evaluated as well. Similarly, when physical abuse has been alleged, the probability of sexual abuse should also be evaluated. Our finding that a substantial number of adults physically abused as children subsequently become abusers makes it imperative that when an adult client discloses a history of childhood abuse, the possibility that he or she may be abusing another person must be investigated.[1]

We found that male respondents who reported a childhood history of sexual abuse were more likely to engage in sexual activity with their clients than were respondents who did not report such a history. As evidenced by the increase in research on client-therapist sexual boundary violations, "the old cycle of cover-up within the professional fields seems . . . to have been interrupted" (Gartrell et al., 1989, p. 63). Although Pope (1988) cites the decreased frequency of professional reports of such infringements, he speculates that the decline may, paradoxically, be an artifact of legislation enacted in some states that labels such activity as criminal (as well as unethical), thus discouraging reports of violations.

All professional organizations agree that the use of clients as objects of sexual gratification is unethical and (most agree) immoral. However, the sexual boundary violations reported by respondents in this and other studies (Bartell & Rubin, 1990; Bouhoutsos, Holroyd, Lerman, Forer, & Greenberg, 1983; Gartrell et al., 1989; Holroyd & Brodsky, 1977; Levenson, 1986; Pope, Keith-Spiegel, & Tabachnick, 1986; Thoreson, Shaugnessy, Heppner, & Cook, 1993) suggest that a substantial number of those who seek professional services may "need protection from those who would help them" (deYoung, 1981, p. 99).

Why do some professionals who were victims of childhood abuse subsequently victimize their clients? Why are the violators primarily men? Pope (1988) suggests several routes that may lead to client-therapist sexual activities, such as sexualized transference, masked depression, or neurotic need for attention. Although our study did not seek the characteristics of victims of sexual boundary violations reported by our respondents,[2] there is evidence that clients who were victims of incest as children may present countertransference reactions that make their therapists (particularly those with their own childhood abuse histories) more inclined to engage in client-therapist sexual boundary violations (deYoung, 1981).

The preponderance of males among perpetrators of sexual boundary violations may be explained in part by the observation that men in our society are, in general, discouraged from expressing emotions. Consequently, they may have greater difficulty than do females dealing with transference and countertransference phenomena (Pope, 1988). Another contributing factor may be that the societal education of men as initiators of sexual relationships makes it likely that more men than women will violate client-therapist sexual boundaries. Clearly, more work is needed to explore the scope, dynamics, and implications of client-therapist sexual trespass.

Although the importance of teaching the proper identification and management of sexual attraction to clients is clear, this phenomenon is hardly acknowledged or addressed in professional training. Pope (1988) attributes this lack of focus to professional discomfort with sexual feelings toward clients, denial of its impact (both during treatment and following termination), and power inequity. Because the consequences for clients may include suicide attempts, depression, psychiatric hospitalizations, and marital disintegration, therapists must be trained to deal with their sexual attraction to clients and the use of these feelings as they do for any countertransference phenomenon (Borys & Pope, 1989).

The taboo surrounding this common reaction is reflected in a review of psychiatric texts (Pope et al., 1986) in which no mention of client-therapist boundary violations was noted. We join with many who call for graduate programs to address these issues (Borys & Pope, 1989; Gartrell et al., 1989; Holroyd & Brodsky, 1977; Pope, 1988; Pope & Feldman-Summers, 1992; Pope et al., 1986; Thoreson et al., 1993).

Borys and Pope (1989) propose a graduate education and training program designed to decrease the possibility of therapist-client boundary transgressions. Their principal points are to encourage research related to boundary violations to stimulate a dialogue about the impact of such behavior on clients and therapists,

integrate relevant content throughout the curricula and offer specific courses related to these issues,

sensitize faculty and students to the issues related to boundary violations,

request leadership from professional organizations,

provide clear and unambiguous responses to professional boundary violations.

And in the classroom, to

address the risks of reporting violations honestly,

provide a safe environment for students to explore their attitudes and feelings about sexual boundary violations,

assign readings in which victims give accounts of the impacts of their experiences,

address the issue of the influence of gender bias on the professional response to boundary violations.

We agree with Haas, Malouf, and Mayerson (1986) who submit that education and training in this area should not be limited to graduate students. We encourage students and professionals alike to explore and analyze their own erotic countertransference (Silverstein, 1991). Borys and Pope (1989) recommend that experienced clinicians be apprised of their "needs, motives, and desires." The importance of recognizing and avoiding potentially "exploitive relationships that advance the welfare or pleasure of the therapist at the expense of the client" cannot be overemphasized (p. 290).

Recommendations for Research

Pope and Feldman-Summers (1992) have presented a number of research questions to further understanding of how childhood abuse may affect professional behavior:

- Does a history of abuse influence a clinician's choice of population to serve?
- Does a history of abuse enable professionals to be more empathic to clients who have been abused?

- Does unresolved conflict about the therapists' own childhood abuse affect their ability to work with others who have experienced such abuse?

In response to the first question, clinicians in our study who as children had been both physically and sexually abused were more likely than their peers who had not experienced such abuse to work on family violence and sexual abuse teams. In addition, they were likely to spend more time working directly with clients who were sexually abused. In response to the second question, our finding that abused clinicians rated the sexual abuse allegations to be more credible than did their nonabused peers suggests that a history of abuse may contribute to a more empathic stance toward those alleged to have been abused.[3] Clearly, further research is needed in this important area.

The relative lack of statistical power available to analyze crossbreaks is a major limitation of our follow-up study. For example, when we examined abused versus nonabused respondents by gender and discipline, the cell sizes became so small that only extremely large effects could be found statistically significant. Therefore, we are at risk of a Type II statistical error where we mistakenly fail to reject the null hypothesis.

Thus, we strongly argue for empirical research that can identify risk factors and the short-term and long-term effects specific to a childhood history of sexual abuse. These goals will require prospective and longitudinal studies that use control and comparison groups, studies with sufficient sample sizes to allow adequate statistical power (Cohen, 1969), and designs that have their roots in the real world of practice.

The consistent use of accepted definitions of sexual abuse, standardized psychological instruments that have proven sensitivity to the short-term and long-term effects of abuse, and use of strict diagnostic criteria to assess the presence or absence of mental illness will allow meta-analyses that have the potential to clarify the many contradictory findings reported in the literature. Thus, we recommend the formation of a group of both researchers and practitioners with expertise in the field of child abuse whose task will be to obtain both narrow and broad definitions of sexual abuse. Nominated by their peers, the task force work should be sponsored by agencies such as the National Institute of Mental Health and the National Center for Child Abuse and Neglect and by professional groups, such as American Professional Society on the Abuse of Children, American Psychological Association, American Psychiatric Association, American Medical Association, National Association of Social Workers, and so forth. Once agreed on, use of these definitions could become an important criterion for funding.

Our finding that young male and female respondents in this study reported similar rates of childhood sexual abuse suggests the need to explore further the prevalence of childhood sexual abuse among males. That abused males are the primary perpetrators in abusing others and in sexual activity with their clients suggests the need for more research to determine the effects of gender differences in the damaging sequelae of childhood sexual victimization.

It has been suggested that sexual and physical abuse may cause changes in brain structure (Mukerjee, 1995; van der Kolk & Greenberg, 1987) and that these changes may be related to the intensity of post-traumatic stress symptoms experienced by many survivors of abuse. These findings again underscore the importance of continued research in this area.

How decisions are made by members of interdisciplinary teams is clearly an important area for further exploration, as are studies to determine the differential effects of child abuse at different stages of development and the relationship between different attributes of abuse and specific diagnoses. Research using different types of interviewing techniques (face-to-face, mail survey, telephone survey) and various types of questionnaires as independent variables are necessary to determine how these tools differentially affect the data.

Currently, we cannot distinguish those children at risk for the damaging psychological sequelae of abuse from those who will not suffer serious consequences. Longitudinal studies of children who have been abused could identify some of the protective and vulnerability factors that determine differential outcomes. We also need to study the effects of abuse on adult functioning and symptomatology as a function of the child's developmental cycle to allow comparison of the differential effects of abuse. Such research requires longitudinal studies of children whose initial abuse occurred at different stages of development. Furthermore, prospective studies of children identified as at risk for abuse are needed to differentiate symptoms developed prior to the abuse from those developed following the abuse

As demonstrated by our results and the sexual abuse literature, data about the factors indicative of sexual abuse are contradictory and confusing. A study designed to obtain a random sample of cases of sexual abuse allegations that have been proven valid, either by the perpetrator's confession or by physical evidence, would provide a set of gold standard cases of sexual abuse allegations. These cases could be used to train future clinicians and to evaluate the performance of practicing clinicians. By changing some of the case attributes, such as the race of the alleged perpetrator, the effect of such changes on ratings of the credibility of the allegations could be examined. Statistical analyses of case factors would yield a profile of positive cases. Similarly, Jones and McGraw (1987) suggest having clinicians, blind to the outcome of a sexual abuse allegation, view and rate videotapes of investigatory interviews with sexually abused children to determine the validity and reliability of the factors used in evaluating the case.

The psychological scales used in our study, although showing statistically significant differences between abused and not abused respondents, were not sensitive enough to detect such abuse when used in a predictive mode. Other scales, such as those measuring dissociation, brain alterations, and sexualized behavior, should be used in further research to determine the effects on adults of a history of child sexual abuse.

The phenomenon of reverse racism and its apparent effects on clinical judgment needs further research. Our results raise serious questions:

- Would such an effect be replicated with a different set of vignettes?[4]
- Is the main effect of race confounded by an interaction with other variables?
- Is there such an effect when clinicians judge real allegations of childhood abuse in their practice?

Conclusions

The sample for this study was drawn from the registers of four disciplines: clinical social work, pediatrics, psychiatry, and psychology. Although more than 70% of the respondents reported direct experience with child or adolescent sexual abuse cases or both, these clinicians should not be viewed as representative of experts in the field of child sexual abuse. It is important to note, however, that most evaluations of sexual abuse allegations are done by nonexperts. Thus, results of this study have broad applicability and major implications for professional education and training, practice, and research. How clinicians with special training, qualifications, and expertise in this area would rate the vignettes used in this study remains to be determined.

To achieve clinical objectivity and accuracy, professionals entrusted with the safety of children must keep abreast of rapidly accumulating knowledge about the psychosocial factors and behavioral signs that predict possible sexual abuse. Our findings support earlier work (Hibbard, Serwint, & Connolly, 1987; Johnson, 1989; Oates, 1989) concluding that professionals can benefit from better education and training in the evaluation of sexual abuse cases in particular and in self-awareness in general. Primarily, this educational process should make practitioners aware of the many subtle areas of potential bias and their implications for children and families. "Unfortunate results of concealed valuations . . . insinuate themselves [into practice] in all stages, from its planning to its final presentation" (Myrdal, 1944, p. 1043).

The wide variations found in the reported rates of sexual abuse and the rapid increase in the rates found in recent years clearly requires much additional investigation to obtain objective professional and scientific consensus for the various populations at risk.

In the past decade, professional education and training has made significant progress addressing societal racism, oppression, poverty, and the biases introduced by client and therapist differences in race, culture, SES, and ethnicity. We have demonstrated additional requirements to educate students about reverse racism and other factors, such as gender, age, and a childhood history of abuse, that may influence clinical perceptions, judgments, and the boundaries of the therapist-client relationship. We hope our work will provide a stimulus for this much-needed effort.

Notes

1. Clearly, as in all client-professional relationships, the issue of confidentiality must be clarified to be consistent with the mandated reporting laws of each state.

2. This is an important area for future research.

3. We have in this and in a previous chapter speculated that the tendency toward greater credulity may also be related to an overidentification with the abused.

4. HJ has begun to replicate the initial study with groups of social work students. Preliminary results show effects of the case factors to be similar to those reported here.

Appendix A:
Sixteen Vignettes

Vignette 1: Juan A.

Juan A., 8 years old, and his Hispanic mother came to the emergency room of a large city hospital. The court requested that Juan be given medical tests for sexually transmitted disease.

According to Mrs. A., Steve, her 26-year-old Caucasian brother-in-law, an accountant who lives next door, told her that he had been having a sexual relationship with Juan for the past year. On learning this, Mrs. A. became very upset, called the police, and went to court on the matter.

Juan, who appeared older than his age, said he had never had any sexual contact with Steve. Mrs. A. reported that since the allegation, she noticed that Juan had become increasingly withdrawn and sullen, often spending hours alone in his room.

Mrs. A., when asked about her own childhood, denied any personal history of abuse or psychiatric illness. She reported coming to this country with her sister from Guatemala 15 years ago. She was divorced 6 years ago because, according to Mrs. A., "We didn't get along."

Juan calmly and consistently denied any sexual contact with Steve. He seemed unaffected by Steve's allegations. He did acknowledge that he has spent time at Steve's apartment because "he's smart."

Neither Juan nor his mother could think of any reason that Steve would say such things. Juan's mother, anxious and tearful, hoped that the interviewer could "tell me whether this really happened." Juan calmly continued to deny having had any sexual contact with Steve.

On a scale of 1 to 6, how confident are you that the sexual abuse did occur? Please circle one number:

1	2	3	4	5	6
Very confident it did not occur	Fairly confident it did not occur	Slightly confident it did not occur	Slightly confident it did occur	Fairly confident it did occur	Very confident it did occur

181

Vignette 2: Joey B.

Ms. B., a black, 21-year-old single mother and part-time student, came to the emergency room of a large city hospital requesting a sexual abuse evaluation for her son Joey, 4 years old. Ms. B. voiced her suspicion that Joey's maternal grandmother's boyfriend Bill, a 47-year-old Caucasian TV repairman, may have sexually abused Joey. Although Ms. B. has physical custody of Joey, protective services has retained legal custody.

According to Ms. B., she and Joey had been living with grandmother and Bill for about a year. However, she said, about 2 weeks ago, she and Joey left grandmother's home following an argument in which grandmother criticized the way Ms. B. was taking care of Joey. Ms. B. told the interviewer that her suspicions were aroused 10 days ago when Joey came to her crying, "Bill touches my pooh pooh and it hurts." Although Joey had repeated this quite often over the past week and a half, she hadn't noticed any changes in his behavior since the first allegation. When asked why she had waited so long to bring Joey to the hospital, she said, "I was in shock."

Ms. B. reported that her mother's boyfriend Bill has a history of becoming violent when drinking. Ms. B's mother and Bill met at Alcoholics Anonymous about 2 years ago. They have been living together for the past year. Ms. B. said she has been afraid to visit her mother since Joey's allegations, although she described the mother-daughter relationship as "very close." When asked about her own history, Ms. B. said that she had been sexually abused as a child and had been placed in a foster home following a short psychiatric hospitalization. Ms. B. stated that she is particularly sensitive about Joey's possible abuse because she is afraid he will end up in foster care and that she will lose custody completely.

Joey appeared relaxed and calm during the interview. When asked if anyone had ever hurt him or his "pooh pooh," he nodded sadly. When asked who had hurt him on his "pooh pooh," he shrugged his shoulders and said "I don't know."

On a scale of 1 to 6, how confident are you that the sexual abuse did occur? Please circle one number:

1	2	3	4	5	6
Very confident it did not occur	Fairly confident it did not occur	Slightly confident it did not occur	Slightly confident it did occur	Fairly confident it did occur	Very confident it did occur

Vignette 3: Jean C.

Jean C., an 8-year-old Caucasian girl under legal custody of protective service, was referred to the sexual abuse team for evaluation following an alleged rape attempt.

Jean is a tall, attractive female who appeared older and more developed than her chronological age. She and her mother, Mrs. C., appeared anxious. Both expressed many concerns about pressing charges. Jean reported having dreams that no one would believe her and she would end up in jail. According to Jean's mother, the alleged perpetrators, although having reputations of being troublemakers and getting into fights, were from influential, professional families.

When asked about the specific episode, Jean said she was alone in the house when she heard a knock on the door. On opening it, she said, two or three Caucasian boys, ages 16 and 17, pushed their way into the house. According to Jean, the boys then called to several others to come in and she was attacked.

During the interview, Jean's mother, Mrs. C., reported that when she returned home with her friend, the boys fled. When Jean's mother was questioned about her own history, she reported having been raped at age 16 by two police officers. No charges were ever filed.

Jean said she has been very confused since the incident. She has tried hard to keep it out of her mind. She also was concerned that her mother would blame the situation on her. She reported that there was no penetration during this attempt. However, she said there had been penetration during a previous incident, which had occurred 6 weeks ago and was not reported.

On a scale of 1 to 6, how confident are you that the sexual abuse did occur? Please circle one number:

1	2	3	4	5	6
Very confident it did not occur	Fairly confident it did not occur	Slightly confident it did not occur	Slightly confident it did occur	Fairly confident it did occur	Very confident it did occur

Vignette 4: Rita D.

Rita D., a 13-year-old Puerto Rican adolescent, was brought by her foster parents, Mr. and Mrs. S., to the emergency room of a large city hospital after she told them she had been sexually abused by a friend of her cousin Juan.

According to Rita, Juan and his friend Bill, a 25-year-old Caucasian lawyer who works in Juan's law firm, came to visit one evening while Mr. and Mrs. S. were at the movies. Rita cheerfully told the interviewer that Juan and Bill were watching television and having a couple of beers when Juan fell asleep. Deciding she also was tired, Rita said good night and went to her bedroom. A few minutes later, according to Rita, Bill appeared at the doorway, exposing himself and masturbating. Then, she said, he moved to the bed and began to fondle her breasts. She said she was so surprised she didn't know what to do, so she did nothing.

Mr. and Mrs. S. appeared confused over their foster daughter's allegations. They had noticed nothing unusual in her behavior. Mrs. S. expressed particular concern that the incident would upset her husband who had a past history of becoming depressed. Both reported that since Rita had been placed with them, following removal from her biological parents' home, she had been fine. She went to school regularly and had shown no behavioral difficulties.

On hearing his cousin Rita's disclosure, Juan expressed disbelief. He described Bill as a "terrific, decent guy" with whom he had worked for 3 years and who would never do such a thing.

When questioned, Bill acknowledged that he was a heavy drinker as a teenager but that he had given it up when he went to law school. He denied Rita's allegations, saying he couldn't understand why she would make up such a story.

On a scale of 1 to 6, how confident are you that the sexual abuse did occur? Please circle one number:

1	2	3	4	5	6
Very confident it did not occur	Fairly confident it did not occur	Slightly confident it did not occur	Slightly confident it did occur	Fairly confident it did occur	Very confident it did occur

Vignette 5: Eddie E.

Mr. and Mrs. E., foster parents of Eddie, an 8-year-old African American boy, came to the emergency room of a large city hospital after Eddie told them that his Boy Scout leader, Mr. R., a 45-year-old Caucasian carpenter, had been forcing him to perform sexual acts.

Eddie appeared agitated as he reported that the sexual molestation began more than a year ago when Mr. R. invited him to his home for an "initiation" that, according to Eddie, involved Eddie's getting undressed and doing a "voodoo dance." From there, Eddie said, the sexual activity had proceeded to include Mr. R. forcing him to "put my mouth on everything." According to Eddie, other boys in his troop were also being molested. However, when contacted, the other boys denied the allegations. When asked why he had waited so long to tell his parents, he said that he was scared and afraid that nobody would believe him.

The foster parents said they had not noticed any changes in Eddie's behavior over the past year. When asked about her personal history, Mrs. E. reported that she had been sexually abused as a child and had been hospitalized briefly, during adolescence, for depression. Mr. and Mrs. E. told the interviewer that Eddie had been taken from his biological parents 2 years ago and placed with them. Eddie is the E.s' only foster child. They have no children of their own. They are fearful that these allegations will jeopardize their custody of Eddie.

Mr. R. expressed shock when hearing about the allegations. He had been active in the Boy Scouts for many years and was held in high esteem in the community. Children described him as "great and understanding." Parents described him as "like a second father" and "fantastic with the boys." Over the years, Mr. R. had received national and local awards for community service, as well as a number of presidential citations.

On a scale of 1 to 6, how confident are you that the sexual abuse did occur? Please circle one number:

1	2	3	4	5	6
Very confident it did not occur	Fairly confident it did not occur	Slightly confident it did not occur	Slightly confident it did occur	Fairly confident it did occur	Very confident it did occur

Vignette 6: Linda F.

Linda F., a 3-year-old Caucasian girl, was brought to the emergency room of a large city hospital by her father who requested a sexual abuse evaluation. He said he was concerned because of a bright red rash that covered Linda's vaginal and anal areas. An additional source of worry for Mr. F. was that Linda had been more cranky than usual, waking up in the middle of the night crying. According to Mr. F., when he asked Linda about the rash, she became visibly upset and said "Bobby pinches me." Mr. F. told the interviewer he was afraid that Linda was being sexually abused by Bob, Linda's baby-sitters' 27-year-old son.

Mr. and Mrs. F. were separated shortly after Linda's birth. They were divorced a year ago at which time Mrs. F. was given full custody of her daughter. Two months ago, Mr. F. brought suit for full custody, claiming that he could be a better parent to Linda now that he was remarried. He declared he could provide a more stable environment than his ex-wife who is a single parent and has a history of psychiatric illness.

Currently, Mr. F. has visitation rights every weekend. Mrs. F. works 3 days a week, leaving Linda with an elderly, retired black couple, Mr. and Mrs. W., who baby-sit in their own home for a number of neighborhood children. Bob, the W.'s 27-year-old son who is an engineer, has been living with the W.s since he was discharged from an alcohol rehab program about 6 months ago. According to Mrs. F., he has had no responsibility for Linda or the other children.

Linda is a verbal child who was cooperative during her interview. Her preference was to play with the dollhouse and have teatime "like I do with my mommy." When asked about Bob, she said that they play together and that sometimes he pinches her. When asked where Bob pinches her, she became anxious, shrugging and touching herself all over. Asked if she liked Bob, Linda nodded and said "yes." Asked if Bob ever hurts her on her bum, Linda said "no," continuing to play with her toys.

Mr. and Mrs. W. and Bob said they were outraged at Mr. F.'s accusations. Mrs. F. expressed complete trust in the W.s and Bob. They all contended that the charges were motivated by Mr. F.'s wish to gain custody of Linda.

On a scale of 1 to 6, how confident are you that the sexual abuse did occur? Please circle one number:

1	2	3	4	5	6
Very confident it did not occur	Fairly confident it did not occur	Slightly confident it did not occur	Slightly confident it did occur	Fairly confident it did occur	Very confident it did occur

Vignette 7: Billy G.

Billy G., a 3-year-old black child, and his mother were referred by their protective service social worker to the sexual abuse team of a large city hospital for evaluation. Mrs. G. feared that Billy was being sexually molested by his father, a 25-year-old black accountant from whom she had recently separated.

According to Mrs. G., she had arranged, 10 days earlier, to have Mr. G. baby-sit for Billy so that she could attend an Alanon meeting. Arriving home, she said, she heard Billy gagging and choking. Going into his bedroom, she found Mr. G. standing over the crib dressed only in his shorts. When questioned, Mr. G. said, "Don't worry, everything is OK." Mrs. G. said she was afraid her husband may have been forcing Billy to perform fellatio.

The next day, Mrs. G. reported, Billy seemed indifferent to her questions surrounding the alleged event but began to talk about "Daddy's big one" and rubbing himself up against her. According to mother, since the incident, Billy has been clingy and has had repeated emotional outbursts.

Mrs. G. told her interviewer that she had been sexually abused by her mother's boyfriend when she was 13 years old. She also reported a psychiatric history of hearing voices and having suspicious thoughts since childhood. Currently, she is on a low dose of antipsychotic medication that, according to her psychiatrist, controls her symptoms.

Mrs. G. described Mr. G. as an alcoholic who had been physically abusive to her over the course of their 5-year marriage. Two years ago, they were separated after Mrs. G. issued two restraining orders, one due to a nasal fracture she sustained during a fight with Mr. G. Mrs. G. expressed concern about her husband's behavior toward herself and Billy, stating that she had decided Mr. G. should not be allowed to have unsupervised visitation with Billy.

Mr. G. denied his wife's allegations, saying that drinking and violence were never a serious problem in their relationship. He attributed the accusations to his wife's mental illness and said he would fight any effort to limit his visits with Billy.

On a scale of 1 to 6, how confident are you that the sexual abuse did occur? Please circle one number:

1	2	3	4	5	6
Very confident it did not occur	Fairly confident it did not occur	Slightly confident it did not occur	Slightly confident it did occur	Fairly confident it did occur	Very confident it did occur

Vignette 8: Jennifer H.

Jennifer H., a 3-year-old Caucasian girl, was referred to the sexual abuse treatment team from the emergency room where she had been brought by her mother, Mrs. H., for an evaluation of possible sexual abuse.

According to Mrs. H., a few weeks ago, Jennifer had made a number of statements that aroused her suspicions that Jennifer's stepfather, a 25-year-old mechanic, was sexually molesting her. Mrs. H. reported that when she changed Jennifer's diapers, Jennifer said calmly, "Peter (allegedly Jennifer's name for stepfather's penis) spit on my tummy." In addition, Mrs. H. noticed redness in her daughter's vaginal area. Mrs. H. said she was so upset that she demanded that Mr. H. leave the house. He has not seen Jennifer since.

In her interview, Jennifer presented as an engaging, verbal 3-year-old who seemed socially at ease and whose interactions were spontaneous and age appropriate. According to Mrs. H., she had not noticed any major changes in Jennifer's behavior over the past few months.

Mrs. H., a woman with a history of severe anxiety attacks, appeared nervous and genuinely concerned about her daughter. Mr. and Mrs. H. have been married for 2 years. They described their relationship as tumultuous, with ongoing arguments and disagreements that sometimes ended with Mr. H. striking his wife. Although this has been a source of major conflict in the marriage and the cause of previous separations, protective service has never been involved.

According to Mr. H., Mrs. H. had always assumed the major caretaking responsibility for Jennifer. His parenting activities had been limited to reading to Jennifer, watching TV with her, and changing her diapers. He suggested that her reference to "Peter" may have come from the book *Peter Rabbit*, which, he said, he often reads to her. Mr. H. consistently denies that he has abused his stepdaughter in any way and has arranged for legal help to gain unsupervised visitation.

On a scale of 1 to 6, how confident are you that the sexual abuse did occur? Please circle one number:

1	2	3	4	5	6
Very confident it did not occur	Fairly confident it did not occur	Slightly confident it did not occur	Slightly confident it did occur	Fairly confident it did occur	Very confident it did occur

Vignette 9: Nancy I.

Nancy I., a 16-year-old black high school student, was referred to the sexual abuse team for evaluation after she reported to her guidance counselor that she had been sexually assaulted by Mr. S., a 35-year-old black high school teacher. Nancy lives with her mother, Mrs. I. Nancy has a 3-month-old son, Jack, as a consequence of a gang rape that was never reported. Nancy stated her allegations about Mr. S. in a matter-of-fact way, saying that she had gone to his apartment after school to pick up some books and was forced to stay overnight and have sex with him.

Nancy's mother, when contacted, said that she had already notified the police that Nancy was missing, fearing that she may have been raped. Mrs. I. told the interviewer that she had been raped as an adolescent and that she had "lived in fear" that the same thing would happen to Nancy. According to Mrs. I., Nancy often disappeared overnight, leaving her to worry and to take complete responsibility for Jack. She reported that these disappearances were beginning to be a great concern to her and that she had begun to talk to Nancy about the possibility that the baby should be given up for adoption.

Nancy's teacher, Mr. S., when confronted with the allegations, denied them, saying he couldn't understand why Nancy would "tell lies." When the school was asked about Mr. S., they reported that there had been some allegations of his striking male pupils. However, he was respected by the administration, faculty, and students as a good teacher.

On a scale of 1 to 6, how confident are you that the sexual abuse did occur?
Please circle one number:

1	2	3	4	5	6
Very confident it did not occur	Fairly confident it did not occur	Slightly confident it did not occur	Slightly confident it did occur	Fairly confident it did occur	Very confident it did occur

Vignette 10: Jeffrey J.

Jeffrey J., a 13-year-old Caucasian high school student, was brought by his parents, Mr. and Mrs. J., to the emergency room of a large general hospital to be evaluated for suspicion of sexual abuse after he had disclosed to them he had been sexually molested. Jeffrey told his parents that, coming home from school, he had been forced into a car by José, a 25-year-old Hispanic repairman who had recently worked for Jeffrey's parents.

According to Jeffrey, he was brought to the man's apartment and forced to perform oral sex and mutual masturbation. Jeffrey told his parents that José kept him there against his will, threatening to kill him if he tried to leave. It was only when José fell asleep, Jeffrey reported, that he was able to get away and run home.

Mr. and Mrs. J. described Jeffrey as a fairly reasonable and responsible adolescent. They were therefore surprised when after telling Jeffrey that he would be punished for coming home so late, he became frantic, began to cry, and stormed to his room. About 2 hours later, according to Mr. and Mrs. J., Jeffrey came back downstairs and calmly told them what had allegedly happened. Mr. and Mrs. J. became concerned and called the police who told them to bring Jeffrey to the hospital for evaluation. During his interview, Jeffrey continued to appear calm, repeating his story without any apparent emotion or upset.

Mrs. J. appeared particularly distressed, fearing this incident would upset Mr. J., who, according to Mrs. J., had been sexually abused as a child and who had a history of multiple psychiatric hospitalizations.

When the police questioned José, he seemed surprised. He firmly and consistently denied Jeffrey's allegations. From the investigation, the police could find nothing suspicious in José's background or in his current functioning. He had lived in the community for a number of years and was viewed by everyone as honest, responsible, and hardworking.

On a scale of 1 to 6, how confident are you that the sexual abuse did occur? Please circle one number:

1	2	3	4	5	6
Very confident it did not occur	Fairly confident it did not occur	Slightly confident it did not occur	Slightly confident it did occur	Fairly confident it did occur	Very confident it did occur

Vignette 11: Donna K.

Donna K., a 4-year-old Caucasian girl, was referred by her day-care teacher, Ms. S., for evaluation of possible sexual abuse. This was the second time Ms. S. had reported suspicion of sexual abuse. According to Ms. S., she had observed Donna reenacting scenes with dolls in which a male figure was performing oral and anal sex on a girl. When Donna was asked if she had ever seen anyone do that, she replied happily "yes." When asked "to whom?" she replied "me." When asked "who did that?" she said "John." Donna lives with her mother, Alice W., and her black stepfather, John W., a 34-year-old electrician.

When told about Donna's disclosure, Donna's mother and stepfather immediately expressed concern. They said they were deeply puzzled, because to their knowledge, no such incident had ever occurred. According to Mrs. W., Donna was sleeping well and going off to school without incident. Both parents were cooperative, and they encouraged social services to investigate the possibility of sexual abuse, saying they wanted "to get to the bottom of this."

During the interview, Donna's behavior appeared age appropriate. She separated from her parents comfortably and her play and affect appeared benign. There were no remarkable reactions to any of the toys that were introduced. Mrs. W. described Donna's relationship with Mr. W. as "wonderful."

Mr. and Mrs. W. were described by the social worker as "appropriate caretakers." Both were cooperative, answering questions in a straightforward manner. Mrs. W. was candid in saying that she had been sexually abused as a child and had been placed in foster care during her adolescence. Mr. W. was open in acknowledging that he had been under a lot of stress lately and had been drinking "more than usual."

On a scale of 1 to 6, how confident are you that the sexual abuse did occur? Please circle one number:

1	2	3	4	5	6
Very confident it did not occur	Fairly confident it did not occur	Slightly confident it did not occur	Slightly confident it did occur	Fairly confident it did occur	Very confident it did occur

Vignette 12: Scott L.

Scott L., a 13-year-old Caucasian adolescent, and his mother were referred to the sexual abuse team of a large city hospital after Scott allegedly told his father he had been raped by George, his mother's new boyfriend. According to Mr. L., Scott told him that 2 weeks ago, while Mrs. L. was out shopping, George, a 26-year-old Caucasian construction laborer, forced him to have oral and anal sex with him.

Over the past few weekends, according to Mr. L., he had noticed that his son was acting strangely, refusing to do his homework and behaving in a sullen manner. When Scott began to isolate himself in his room, Mr. L. said, he began to suspect that something serious had happened. After questioning him, his father said, Scott told him about his victimization.

Mr. and Mrs. L. are in the throes of an adversarial divorce, with each parent suing for custody of Scott. Father claims that mother is unfit and shows poor parental judgment. He has previously filed with protective services to have another one of Mrs. L.'s boyfriends removed from the home for allegedly mistreating Scott. Mother accused father of getting Scott "to lie so that he [Mr. L.] can get what he wants."

On questioning, Scott repeated his allegation calmly and without obvious emotion. He said that he had been afraid to tell anyone because George was a heavy drinker who sometimes lost his temper when people didn't do what he wanted.

George denied the allegations, saying that everyone knew that Mr. L. would stop at nothing to gain custody of Scott and that Scott would go along because he was afraid of his father and was always jealous of his mother's boyfriends.

On a scale of 1 to 6, how confident are you that the sexual abuse did occur? Please circle one number:

1	2	3	4	5	6
Very confident it did not occur	Fairly confident it did not occur	Slightly confident it did not occur	Slightly confident it did occur	Fairly confident it did occur	Very confident it did occur

Vignette 13: Rose M.

Mr. and Mrs. M., a black couple, and their daughter Rose, 16 years old, were referred for evaluation to the sexual abuse team follow-up clinic following Rose's allegations that her father, Mr. M., had shown her pictures of nude men and women and forced her to have sexual intercourse with him.

In making her disclosure, Rose appeared teary, upset, and nervous. She reported that since her alleged victimization, she was having nightmares and getting up in the middle of the night. She also reported having intrusive thoughts about the alleged event, saying, "I can't stop thinking about it."

The M. family has a history of contact with protective services due to Rose's truancy from school and her delinquent behavior. Rose is the product of a conflicted marital relationship characterized by what Mrs. M. called Mr. M's "excessive and sometimes physically violent demands for her attention." During her interviews, Mrs. M. was open and cooperative. She reported a personal history of psychiatric illness with many somatic symptoms and complaints. She expressed concern for her daughter, but at the same time, agreed with Mr. M. that Rose was troubled and difficult to manage.

Mr. M., a 42-year-old security guard at a local bank, sat quietly as his daughter made her accusations. He consistently denied the allegations, shaking his head as if in disbelief. His report that his reputation at the bank was excellent was substantiated by his employers who stated that he never drank and was reliable and responsible. According to Mr. M., Rose had always been a problem child who lied and who "started fooling around with the boys about 2 years ago."

On a scale of 1 to 6, how confident are you that the sexual abuse did occur? Please circle one number:

1	2	3	4	5	6
Very confident it did not occur	Fairly confident it did not occur	Slightly confident it did not occur	Slightly confident it did occur	Fairly confident it did occur	Very confident it did occur

Vignette 14: Paula N.

Paula N., a 13-year-old Puerto Rican adolescent, and her mother, Mrs. T., 30 years old, were referred for evaluation to the sexual abuse team of a large city hospital. According to the referral, Paula had told Mrs. T. that Mrs. T.'s new husband, a 25-year-old Caucasian garage mechanic, had been sexually molesting her.

A well-developed adolescent, Paula was teary as she told her interviewer that her stepfather had been sexually molesting her for the past 6 months, fondling her breasts and genitals and forcing her to have intercourse. She said that she decided to tell her mother about the abuse when, just a few weeks ago, she began having nightmares, waking up in the middle of the night and finding it impossible to go back to sleep.

According to her mother, Paula's disclosure came as a complete shock. However, she called protective services and following a preliminary interview, was referred for evaluation. Mrs. T. was particularly upset, she said, because she had been sexually abused by her older brother until she was 13. She cried, saying that all she had ever wanted to do was to protect her daughter but that she had failed.

This is a second marriage for Mrs. T., the first ending in divorce 8 years ago when Paula was 5. Mr. and Mrs. T. were married 6 months ago after living together for 1 year.

According to Mrs. T., Mr. T. is a chronic alcoholic whose drinking has become unbearable. Mrs. T. told her interviewer that she had already begun to make plans to divorce Mr. T. so that she could gain full custody of their 3-month-old son, Gary.

Mr. T. claims his wife is lying. He states unequivocally that drinking has never been a problem for him. He adamantly denies his stepdaughter's allegations, saying she and his wife are "making it all up to get me out of the house so that they can take Gary away from me."

On a scale of 1 to 6, how confident are you that the sexual abuse did occur? Please circle one number:

1	2	3	4	5	6
Very confident it did not occur	Fairly confident it did not occur	Slightly confident it did not occur	Slightly confident it did occur	Fairly confident it did occur	Very confident it did occur

Vignette 15: Harry O.

Harry O., a 13-year-old Caucasian male, was brought to the emergency room of a large general hospital by his mother, Mrs. H., and his black stepfather, Dr. H. According to Dr. and Mrs. H., Harry had told them that Tom, his stepfather's son by a previous marriage, had sexually molested him. Dr. and Mrs. H. said they were shocked by Harry's accusations as they "seemed to come out of the blue."

According to Harry, his stepbrother Tom, a 25-year-old black psychologist who had recently finished his graduate studies, had taken him to the movies to see a horror film. When the lights went out, Harry reported, Tom unzipped Harry's fly and fondled his genitals. Agitated and angry, Harry recalled that the attempts he made to push Tom's hand away were to no avail. He said he was too embarrassed to call out for help.

Dr. and Mrs. H. are an interracial couple who have been married for less than a year. Dr. H.'s first wife died early in their marriage. Mrs. H., when she was divorced from her first husband, Mr. O., 3 years ago, was given full custody of their only son, Harry. Dr. H., a black physicist, is on the faculty of a prestigious university and has two boys by his first wife, who also was black.

According to Mrs. H., since her marriage to Dr. H., Mr. O. has filed numerous care and protection complaints against Dr. H. He has also brought suit against Mrs. H. to gain full custody of Harry.

When confronted with Harry's allegations, Tom H. denied them, saying they were fabrications of an unhappy kid in an effort to discredit Dr. H.'s family. An honor student throughout his life, Tom has the reputation of being a fine psychologist and a "great guy." He has no history of violence or of substance abuse.

On a scale of 1 to 6, how confident are you that the sexual abuse did occur? Please circle one number:

1	2	3	4	5	6
Very confident it did not occur	Fairly confident it did not occur	Slightly confident it did not occur	Slightly confident it did occur	Fairly confident it did occur	Very confident it did occur

Vignette 16: David P.

David P., a 16-year-old Caucasian, was brought to the emergency room of a large general hospital by his mother after he had disclosed to her that he had been sexually abused. According to David, he had gone for his yearly holiday to visit his father, a 41-year-old minister who worked and lived in a distant city.

According to Mrs. P., when David returned home, he seemed fine. There were no noticeable changes in his behavior, which characteristically was somewhat quiet and withdrawn. He went to school, did his homework, and participated in his everyday tasks. Consequently, she said she was very surprised when, 2 weeks later, following an argument with his father over the phone, David accused him of sexually molesting him for a prolonged period of time.

When talking about the event, David appeared angry, upset, and fearful. Mrs. P. said it made her very anxious and distraught at the thought that David may have been sexually abused. She said she was extremely sensitive to this issue because she had been sexually abused as an adolescent and had spent 3 months in a psychiatric hospital as a result. David's parents had been divorced 13 years ago when, according to Mrs. P., Mr. P.'s assaultive behavior and his problems with alcohol had become extreme.

According to Mr. P., following the divorce, he had "turned over a new leaf," going back to school to get his advanced degree so that he could use his own experiences to help others. Mr. P. is highly regarded by his peers and members of his parish. He has held the position of minister for more than 10 years.

He firmly and consistently denied his son's allegations. He claimed that David was disturbed, "just like his mother." The only explanation he could think of, he said, was that the disclosure was an expression of David's aggressive fantasies and homosexual wishes.

On a scale of 1 to 6, how confident are you that the sexual abuse did occur? Please circle one number:

1	2	3	4	5	6
Very confident it did not occur	Fairly confident it did not occur	Slightly confident it did not occur	Slightly confident it did occur	Fairly confident it did occur	Very confident it did occur

Appendix B: Initial Survey Demographic Questionnaire

Now we would like to ask you some information about your work:

1. What is your primary theoretical orientation? (Circle no more than three)
   1. Biological
   2. Child development
   3. Cognitive-behavioral
   4. Ecological
   5. Family systems
   6. Feminist
   7. Psychodynamic
   8. Psychosocial
   9. Social learning
   10. Other (Please specify)
2. What best describes your present work? (Please circle the number next to the one category that describes your position.)
   1. Administrator or supervisor
   2. Therapist
   3. Other (Please specify)
3. What is your present work setting? (Circle number)
   1. Inpatient
   2. Public protective service agency

3. Outpatient

4. Other (Please specify)

4. How many hours per week do you spend in your work setting? ____ Hours

5. What percentage of your time is currently spent in client-patient care related to child-adolescent sexual abuse? _____ %

6. What percentage of your time is currently spent in administrative-supervisory work related to child-adolescent sexual abuse? _____ %

7. How many years beyond your final degree have you worked directly with clients-patients? _____ Years

8. How many years beyond your final degree have you worked directly with clients-patients in the area of child sexual abuse? _____ Years

9. Are you a member of a sexual abuse team or clinic? (Circle number)

1. Yes

2. No

10. Are you a member of a family violence team or clinic? (Circle number)

1. Yes

2. No

11. What is your professional discipline? (Circle number)

1. Clinical social work

2. Pediatrics

3. Psychology

4. Psychiatry

5. Other

Next, we would like to ask you some background information:

Child sexual abuse has been defined as "the involvement of dependent, developmentally immature children and adolescents in sex acts that they do not fully comprehend and to which they are unable to give informed consent or that violate the social taboos of family roles."

12. Within this definition, were you ever the victim of sexual abuse? (Circle number)

1. Yes

2. No (If Yes, go to 13; if No, skip from here to 15)

13. (If yes) At what age(s)? (Circle as many numbers as apply)

1 2 3 4 5 6 7 8 9 10 11 12 13 14 15 16 17 18

14. If yes, by whom? (Circle all numbers that apply)
    1. Stranger(s)
        1. Male
        2. Female
    2. Acquaintance(s)
        1. Male
        2. Female
    3. Family Member(s)
        1. Father
        2. Mother
        3. Stepfather
        4. Grandfather
        5. Brother
        6. Uncle
    4. Other Family Member(s)
        1. Male
        2. Female
    5. Other(s) (Please specify)
15. Using the above definition of sexual abuse, have you ever witnessed anyone else being sexually victimized? (Circle number)
    1. Yes
    2. No (If Yes, go to 16; if No, skip from here to 19)
16. (If yes) How old were you? (Circle as many numbers as apply)
    1 2 3 4 5 6 7 8 9 10 11 12 13 14 15 16 17 18
17. If yes, by whom? (Circle all numbers that apply)
    1. Stranger(s)
        1. Male
        2. Female
    2. Acquaintance(s)
        1. Male
        2. Female
    3. Family Member(s)
        1. Father
        2. Mother
        3. Stepfather
        4. Grandfather
        5. Brother
        6. Uncle
    4. Other Family Member(s)
        1. Male
        2. Female

5. Other(s) (Please specify)
18. If yes, how do you think this experience(s) influenced you?
    1. Positively
    2. Negatively
    3. Mixed
    4. Not at all

Physical abuse has been defined as being "inflicted nonaccidentally . . . which causes or creates a substantial risk of causing disfigurement, impairment of bodily functioning, or other serious physical injury."

19. Within this definition, were you ever the victim of physical abuse? (Circle number)
    1. Yes
    2. No (If Yes, go to 20; if No, skip from here to 22)
20. (If yes) At what age(s)? (Circle as many numbers as apply)
    1 2 3 4 5 6 7 8 9 10 11 12 13 14 15 16 17 18
21. If yes, by whom? (Circle all numbers that apply)
    1. Stranger(s)
        1. Male
        2. Female
    2. Acquaintance(s)
        1. Male
        2. Female
    3. Family Member(s)
        1. Father
        2. Mother
        3. Stepfather
        4. Grandfather
        5. Brother
        6. Uncle
    4. Other Family Member(s)
        1. Male
        2. Female
    5. Other(s) (Please specify)
22. Using the above definition of physical abuse, have you ever witnessed anyone else being physically victimized? (Circle number)
    1. Yes
    2. No (If Yes, go to 23; if No, skip from here to 26)

23. (If yes) How old were you? (Please circle as many numbers as apply)

    1 2 3 4 5 6 7 8 9 10 11 12 13 14 15 16 17 18

24. If yes, by whom?
    1. Stranger(s)
        1. Male
        2. Female
    2. Acquaintance(s)
        1. Male
        2. Female
    3. Family Member(s)
        1. Father
        2. Mother
        3. Stepfather
        4. Grandfather
        5. Brother
        6. Uncle
    4. Other Family Member(s)
        1. Male
        2. Female
    5. Other(s) (Please specify)

25. If yes, how do you think this experience(s) influenced you? (Circle number)
    1. Positively
    2. Negatively
    3. Mixed
    4. Not at all

Last, we would like to ask you for some demographic information:

26. Your gender _____
27. Your present age _____
28. Your present marital status: (Circle number)
    1. Never married
    2. Married
    3. Significant other
    4. Divorced
    5. Separated
    6. Widowed
    7. Other (Please specify)

29. Are you currently raising or have you raised children? (Please include either biological, adoptive, or foster children) (Circle number)
    1. Yes
    2. No
30. If yes, please give the number of children who are male and the number who are female.
    1. Male _____
    2. Female _____

Appendix C: Initial Survey Cover Letter

June 14, 1989

Dear Colleague:

Nearly everyone in the United States is alarmed about the rapid increase in reports of child sexual abuse. As concerned clinicians, we need to know more about what factors are involved in evaluating the credibility of these serious allegations. Under the auspices of the National Institute of Mental Health, Children's Hospital, and Boston College Graduate School of Social Work, I am conducting research that will help answer this important question.

As part of the growing effort of researchers and clinicians to deal with the problem of child and adolescent sexual abuse, I am asking you for your assistance. It involves reading vignettes about sexual abuse and completing the enclosed questionnaire. Your participation will help to expand our knowledge about how difficult decisions about credibility are made.

In appreciation for completing and returning the enclosed forms, I would be pleased if you would accept one of the five professional books listed on the enclosed card. Please return the postcard *separately* to assure anonymity.

Your name has been randomly drawn as part of a national sample of clinicians. Consequently, your response is critical to the reliability of this important study. The enclosed vignettes, although disguised, are based on actual cases. They are typical of the sexual abuse cases clinicians are asked to evaluate. They reflect the limited and ambiguous nature of information on which initial decisions about credibility are, necessarily, based. As a professional, I know you will find them interesting and challenging. Please read them, rate them, complete the accompanying questionnaire, and return them to me as soon as possible in the self-addressed, postage-paid envelope.

Remember to fill out the card and mail it *separately*. Only the vignettes and questionnaires should be returned in the postage-paid envelope. I would be most happy to answer any questions you may have. Please write or call. The telephone number is (617) 552-8046. Thank you for your assistance.

Sincerely,

Helene Jackson, PhD
NIMH Faculty Scholar
Children's Hospital, Boston
Boston College, Graduate School of Social Work

Appendix D:
Taguchi Methods
Applied to
Social Research

The Taguchi method employs a particular type of fractional factorial experimental design procedure. In this appendix, we explain briefly what the Taguchi methods are, how they can be applied to social research in general, and how they were applied to the particular study forming the basis of our national survey of allegations of child sexual abuse.

Social science research generally includes a set of independent variables and one or more dependent variables. The research questions to be answered require discovering how the independent variables relate to the dependent variables. One approach is the type of research called *experiments*. In experiments, the independent variables are systematically varied, following an experimental design, and the values of the dependent variables are observed. Vignette research is often conducted this way.

The use of only 16 vignettes to examine the effects of 15 variables in the initial I survey reported in this book illustrates the power and efficiency of Taguchi methods. Genichi Taguchi, a Japanese engineer who specializes in improving the quality of industrial processes (Ross, 1988; Taguchi, 1987), developed a simple set of procedures for designing and conducting fractional factorial experiments. Anyone who has attempted to design an experiment with more than five or six factors knows that traditional procedures (Hinkelmann & Kempthorne, 1994) are complicated and often require an experienced statistician. Although Taguchi methods are simple to apply, they are sufficiently robust to allow complex designs.

Taguchi's method starts with a set of standardized orthogonal arrays, where each row is an experimental treatment combination and each column is a factor, or effect. For the two-level arrays, the numbers "1" and "2" are used in each array. A "1" code means that a particular row (treatment combination) has the "1" level of the factor corresponding with that particular column.

The orthogonal arrays are generally designed to have the columns orthogonal or uncorrelated with each other, although it is possible to reserve columns for interactions. Otherwise, the two-level and higher interactions are confounded with the main effects of each factor. In this experiment, we used an L16 orthogonal array. This array has 16 rows and 15 columns. In our design, the array was fully saturated. We allocated factors to all 15 columns. Implied in such a design is the confounding or mixing in of the two-level and higher interactions' effects with the main effect measures.

To explain the Taguchi approach, we give an example of an L4 orthogonal array with four rows and three columns.

L4 Orthogonal Array

Row-Column	1	2	3
1	1	1	1
2	1	2	2
3	2	1	2
4	2	2	1
	a	b	ab

To apply this orthogonal design to an experiment, we need to allocate a factor to each of the three columns and two levels to each factor. If we wanted to make this a full factorial design, we would allocate one factor "a" to column 1 and another, "b," to column 2 but reserve column 3 for the "ab" interaction.

In vignette research, the stimuli are vignettes that are constructed by following an experimental design; raters respond to each vignette. The ratings can come from a single person, thus allowing the technique to be used by a clinician working with a single client, or the ratings can be group averages.

Let us imagine a simple experiment where we ask social workers to judge the extent of a child's need for services. Accordingly, we would construct several vignettes that describe children's lives and ask the social workers to judge the degree of "need for services" for each child as described in each vignette. For example, we can let column 1 reflect the factor of sexual abuse (1 = *yes sexual abuse*, 2 = *no sexual abuse*) and column 2 reflect the factor of physical abuse (1 = *yes physical abuse*, 2 = *no physical abuse*). We can leave column 3 unassigned, in which case it reflects the interaction between sexual and physical abuse, or we can assign it a third factor. Let us assign the factor of gender to column 3 (1 = *male*, 2 = *female*). The design of the experiment is now as follows:

L4 Orthogonal Array Applied to a Simple Experiment

Row-Column	1 Sexual Abuse	2 Physical Abuse	3 Gender
John	Sexual abuse	Physical abuse	Male
Susan	Sexual abuse	No physical abuse	Female
Mary	No sexual abuse	Physical abuse	Female
Bill	No sexual abuse	No physical abuse	Male
	a	b	ab

Factors other than those included in the design, such as age, should be controlled as much as possible, that is, held about equal. This is rather difficult to accomplish and still keep the vignettes interesting and realistic. Clearly, with only a few columns, many of the subtle conditions of the abuse history cannot be included. Thus the larger designs, such as the L16 used in our initial survey, allow for more realistic vignettes.

We then construct the vignettes by reading across the rows for the construction of each vignette. In this case, our vignettes read as follows:

John described how his father had hit him with a belt anytime he got out of line. John also said that an uncle had touched him in his "private parts."

Please rate how much this child needs services:

0 No need for services	1 Slight need for services	2 Some need for services	3 Great need for services

Susan reported that she had been touched in a sexual way by a handyman visiting her house.

Please rate how much this child needs services:

0	1	2	3
No need for services	Slight need for services	Some need for services	Great need for services

Mary said that her mother slapped her around or severely pinched her whenever she did not behave.

Please rate how much this child needs services:

0	1	2	3
No need for services	Slight need for services	Some need for services	Great need for services

Bill did not report any problems.

Please rate how much this child needs services:

0	1	2	3
No need for services	Slight need for services	Some need for services	Great need for services

Let us assume that a person rated John as needing services at level 3, Susan at level 2, Mary at level 1, and Bill at level 0. To see how this methodology works, we first calculate the overall need for services, which is the average over all four vignettes $(3 + 2 + 1 + 0)/4 = 6/4 = A$ grand average need for services of 1.5.

To calculate the effect of sexual abuse for this rater, we contrast the average ratings for the two children who were sexually abused (John and Susan) (3 and 2; average = 2.5) against the grand average of 1.5. (2.5 - 1.5 = 1.0). The effect of being sexually abused raises the need for services 1.0 units. The effect of not being sexually abused is the average of the two children who were not sexually abused (Mary and Bill: 1 and 0 = 0.5) minus the grand average (0.5 - 1.5 = - 1.0).

On the other hand, the effects of physical abuse on need for services is the average for the two physically abused children (John and Mary) (3 and 1; average = 2.0) minus the grand average of 1.5 giving us an effect of +0.5 for physical abuse on need for service. The effect on need for services of not being physically abused is the average of the two children who were not physically abused minus the grand average (Susan and Bill) [(2 and 0) - 1.5 = 1 - 1.5 = - 0.5].

We can also examine the effect of gender on need for services by comparing the ratings of the two female children (Susan and Mary) (2 and 1) to the grand average (1.5 - 1.5 = 0) to see that there is no effect of gender on need for services. Similarly, the effect of the child being male will be the average need for services of the male children minus the grand average (John and Bill) (3 and 0 = 1.5 - 1.5 = 0).

However, by assigning gender to the third column, we are confounding the effect of gender with the interaction of physical and sexual abuse. That means that if respondents consider a child with both physical and sexual abuse to be more in need of services than would be predicted for just physical abuse or sexual abuse, this strong interaction will appear in our analysis as due to the gender of the child. We could then reach incorrect conclusions.

We can present the findings of this Taguchi-style orthogonal design experiment in graphic form, as shown in Figure D.1

With two factors, each at two levels, then a full factorial design needs 2 * 2 = 4 vignettes. If we are interested in studying three two-level factors, then we need 2 * 2 * 2 = 8 vignettes. When you want to study many factors, then the full factorial approach becomes unworkable. In this survey, for example, we wished to study 15 factors. To use the full-factorial approach would have required 2^{15} vignettes or 32,768 vignettes. Clearly, no respondent would be able (or willing) to read and rate so many vignettes. In our study, we wanted to examine the effects of 15 different factors or independent variables on the dependent variable of the credibility of the allegation of sexual abuse. Table D.1 presents these 15 factors.

The fractional factorial approach provides a solution to this problem. With only 16 vignettes, it is possible to obtain estimates of the effect of each of the 15 factors. What is required is that the experimental design used in constructing the vignettes be set up so that the levels of each factor are equally weighted and that a balance of each level of each factor with the levels of all other factors is obtained. Taguchi has developed and published a set of fractional factorial designs that make it easy to construct such studies. In our study, we used his L16 design (see Table D.2).

Construction of Vignettes

Using the factor levels specified in Table D.1, each vignette was constructed following the design matrix shown in Table D.2. Thus, each row shown in Table D.2 is, essentially, a recipe for the construction of one of the vignettes. For example, the case vignette "Scott" (see Table D.3) was con-

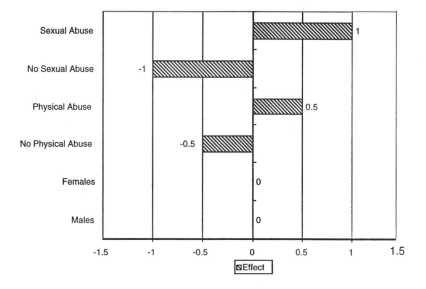

Figure D.1. Effects of Taguchi-Style Experiment

structed by following the sixth row of the design matrix. Thus, Scott is at the 1 level for the first factor (A) (i.e., he is male); the next two factors (B and C) require the 2 level (i.e., Scott is 13 years old and Caucasian). The next two factors (D and E) require the 1 level (i.e., Scott's behavior reportedly changed following the alleged abuse, but he showed no affect when talking about the event).

According to the design matrix, the next four factors (F through I) require the 2 level (i.e., the alleged perpetrator is a nonprofessional, unrelated to Scott. He is over 26 years old and Caucasian). The next two factors (J and K) are at level 1 (i.e., the alleged perpetrator has both a history of violence and substance abuse). The next two factors (L and M) are, according to the design matrix, at level 2 (i.e., Scott's caretakers have neither a childhood history of sexual abuse nor a history of psychiatric illness). The remaining factors (N and O) are at level 1 (i.e., Scott's family has had previous contact with protective services and is involved in child custody issues). The other 15 vignettes were similarly constructed following the design matrix requirements.

Table D.1 Factors Used in Constructing Sixteen Vignettes Alleging Child Sexual Abuse

Factor	Level 1	Level 2
Alleged Victim		
A Gender	Male	Female
B Age	3 to 8 years	13 to 16 years
C Race	Minority	White
D Behavioral changes	Yes	No
E Affect about event	No affect	Affect
Alleged Perpetrator		
F Socioeconomic status	Professional	Nonprofessional
G Relationship to alleged victim	Familial	Nonfamilial
H Age	16 to 25 years	26+ years
I Race	Minority	White
J History of violence	Yes	No
K History of substance abuse	Yes	No
Alleged Victim's Caretaker(s)		
L Childhood history of sexual abuse	Yes	No
M History of psychiatric illness	Yes	No
Family		
N Prior contact with protective service agencies	Yes	No
O Child custody-visitation issues	Yes	No

Table D.2 Taguchi Methods L16 Orthogonal Array: Factor Levels by Variables by Case

Factor	A	B	C	D	E	F	G	H	I	J	K	L	M	N	O
Case															
Billy	1	1	1	1	1	1	1	1	1	1	1	1	1	1	1
Juan	1	1	1	1	1	1	1	2	2	2	2	2	2	2	2
Eddie	1	1	1	2	2	2	2	1	1	1	1	2	2	2	2
Joey	1	1	1	2	2	2	2	2	2	2	2	1	1	1	1
Jeff	1	2	2	1	1	2	2	1	1	2	2	1	1	2	2
Scott	1	2	2	1	1	2	2	2	2	1	1	2	2	1	1
Harry	1	2	2	2	2	1	1	1	1	2	2	2	2	1	1
David	1	2	2	2	2	1	1	2	2	1	1	1	1	2	2
Jean	2	1	2	1	2	1	2	1	2	1	2	1	2	1	2
Linda	2	1	2	1	2	1	2	2	1	2	1	2	1	1	2
Jenny	2	1	2	2	1	2	1	1	2	1	2	2	1	2	1
Donna	2	1	2	2	1	2	1	2	1	2	1	1	2	1	2
Paula	2	2	1	1	2	2	1	1	2	2	1	1	2	2	1
Rose	2	2	1	1	2	2	1	2	1	1	2	2	1	1	2
Rita	2	2	1	2	1	1	2	1	2	2	1	2	1	1	2
Nancy	2	2	1	2	1	1	2	2	1	1	2	1	2	2	1

Table D.3 Example of a Sexual Abuse Allegation Vignette

Scott

Scott L., a 13-year-old Caucasian adolescent, and his mother were referred to the sexual abuse team of a large city hospital after Scott allegedly told his father he had been raped by George, his mother's new boyfriend. According to Mr. L., Scott told him that 2 weeks ago, while Mrs. L. was out shopping, George, a 26-year-old Caucasian construction laborer, forced him to have oral and anal sex with him.

Over the past few weekends, according to Mr. L., he had noticed that his son was acting strangely, refusing to do his homework, and behaving in a sullen manner. When Scott began to isolate himself in his room, Mr. L. said, he began to suspect that something serious had happened. After questioning him, his father said, Scott told him about his victimization.

Mr. and Mrs. L. are in the throes of an adversarial divorce, with each parent suing for custody of Scott. Father claims that mother is unfit and shows poor parental judgment. He has previously filed with protective services to have another one of Mrs. L.'s boyfriends removed from the home for allegedly mistreating Scott. Mother accused father of getting Scott "to lie so that he [Mr. L.] can get what he wants."

On questioning, Scott repeated his allegation calmly and without obvious emotion. He said that he had been afraid to tell anyone because George was a heavy drinker who sometimes lost his temper when people didn't do what he wanted.

George denied the allegations, saying the everyone knew that Mr. L. would stop at nothing to gain custody of Scott and that Scott would go along because he was afraid of his father and was always jealous of his mother's boyfriends.

What is lost with fractional factorial designs is information on possible interactions between two or more factors. Only the main effects are found. It is possible that interactions exist between two or more factors. If they do exist, their effects are confounded or mixed up with the effects observed for the main effects. Thus, when a research study uses a fractional factorial design, there must always be a level of uncertainty about the findings until the study has been replicated with a different design or possible interactions have been explicitly taken into account.

Appendix E:
Response Bias
Cover Letter and
Questionnaire

Cover Letter

Dear Colleague:

A year ago, under the auspices of the National Institute of Mental Health, Children's Hospital, and Boston College, we sent you a questionnaire about sexual abuse. We are now conducting a study to compare the subjects who did respond to the sexual abuse study with those who did not. Over 36% of the respondents to the sexual abuse study reported a history of sexual abuse, physical abuse, or both.[1] We need your help to determine whether or not we can generalize these findings to the general population of clinicians from which our sample was drawn.

All we are asking you to do is circle the correct numbers on the questionnaire on the back of this page and return it in the enclosed self-addressed, postage-paid envelope. *It will take less than 1 minute of your time and will be completely anonymous.* Your response is critical to the success of our research.

We have enclosed a summary of the results of the original study. The findings have important implications for clinical practice and for the education and training of all health and mental health professionals. They are being disseminated at national conferences and will be published in professional journals.

Please complete the questionnaire on the back of this page and return it to us today. If you would like a summary of the results of *this* study, please print your name on the outside of the postage-paid envelope, *not on the questionnaire.* Thank you for your participation.

Sincerely,

Helene Jackson, PhD
NIMH Faculty Scholar
Boston College
Graduate School of Social Work

Ronald Nuttall, PhD, MPH
Professor
Boston College
Graduate School of Arts and Sciences

Questionnaire

Child sexual abuse has been defined as the involvement of dependent, developmentally immature children and adolescents in sex acts that they do not fully comprehend and to which they are unable to give informed consent or that violate the social taboos of family roles.

Within this definition, were you ever, as a child up to age 18, the victim of sexual abuse? (Please circle number.)

1. Yes   0. No

Within this definition, did you ever, as a child up to age 18, *witness* sexual abuse? (Please circle number.)

1. Yes   0. No

Child physical abuse has been defined as being inflicted nonaccidentally, causing or creating a substantial risk of disfigurement, impairment of bodily functioning, or other serious injury.

Within this definition, were you ever, as a child up to age 18, the victim of physical abuse? (Please circle number.)

1. Yes   0. No

Within this definition, did you ever, as a child up to age 18, *witness* anyone being physically victimized? (Please circle number.)

1. Yes   0. No

Did you return the original sexual abuse questionnaire? (Please circle number.)

1. Yes   0. No

Please use the space below for any additional comments.

Thank you again for your participation.

1. Thirty-six percent includes both direct and witnessing physical or sexual abuse.

Appendix F: Follow-Up Survey Cover Letter and Questionnaire

Cover Letter

Dear Colleague:

Last year, you participated in a national research project on sexual abuse. Your generous response has led to a better understanding of the factors that influence clinicians' judgments of child and adolescent sexual abuse allegations. As you can see from the enclosed summary, the findings have important implications for clinical practice. Results are being disseminated at national conferences, hospitals, universities, and social service agencies and will be published in professional journals.

Once again, we are asking for your help. Over 36% of you (all professional clinicians) reported a personal history of sexual or physical abuse or both.[1] As a group, you have achieved a high level of professional functioning. Consequently, you present a unique opportunity to learn about

> how professionals who report a history of abuse compare with professionals who do not and
>
> what factors may mitigate the effects of child or adolescent (or both) victimization.

As part of a larger project in which additional groups will be compared, your participation in this follow-up study will expand our knowledge about these critical issues and have important implications for the prevention and treatment of child and adolescent abuse.

Because the questionnaire in the first study was anonymous, we do not know whether you belong to the abused or the nonabused group. (We know your name only because you requested a free book or a summary of the results or both.) It is unavoidable, therefore, that some of the questions in the enclosed questionnaire are similar to those you answered in the earlier study.

To express our gratitude for your participation, we are again offering you the choice of a free book that has been donated for purposes of this study. Please complete the questionnaire and select one of the seven books listed on the enclosed card. Be sure to return it separately to assure anonymity.

Because of the nature of the study, many questions touch on very sensitive issues. However, the critical importance of studying factors that may predict the effects of sexual or physical abuse or both makes these inquiries essential. The success of this project greatly depends on your participation. We appreciate your continued support.

Sincerely,

Helene Jackson, PhD
NIMH Faculty Scholar
Boston College
Graduate School of Social Work

Ron Nuttall, PhD, MPH
Professor
Boston College
Graduate School of Arts and Sciences

Follow-Up Questionnaire

First, we would like to ask you for some information about your work.

D-1. What is your professional discipline? (Please circle one.)
1. Clinical social work
2. Pediatrics
3. Psychiatry
4. Psychology
5. Other

D-2. What is your primary theoretical orientation? (Please circle no more than three.)
1. Biological
2. Child development
3. Cognitive-behavioral
4. Ecological
5. Family systems
6. Feminist
7. Psychodynamic
8. Psychosocial
9. Social learning
10. Other

D-3. Are you a member of a sexual abuse team or clinic? (Please circle your answer.)
1. Yes
0. No

D-4. Are you a member of a family violence team or clinic? (Please circle your answer.)
1. Yes
0. No

D-5. All in all, how satisfied are you with your career choice? (Please circle your answer.)
1. Not at all
2. Slightly
3. Moderately
4. Quite a bit
5. Extremely

Please circle the answer that best describes how you feel about each statement.

MS-1. If I could go into a different profession that paid the same, I would do it.
1. Not at all true
2. Slightly true
3. Somewhat true
4. Very true
5. Extremely true

MS-2. I definitely want a career for myself in the professional discipline I am in currently.
1. Not at all true
2. Slightly true
3. Somewhat true
4. Very true
5. Extremely true

MS-3. If I could do it all over again, I would not choose to work in my professional discipline.
1. Not at all true
2. Slightly true
3. Somewhat true
4. Very true
5. Extremely true

MS-4. If I had all the money I needed without working, I would probably still continue in my professional discipline.
1. Not at all true
2. Slightly true
3. Somewhat true
4. Very true
5. Extremely true

MS-5. I spend a significant amount of personal time reading professional journals or books written for my professional discipline.
1. Not at all true
2. Slightly true
3. Somewhat true
4. Very true
5. Extremely true

Now we would like to ask you two questions about your sexual relationships.

GSS-1. Are you currently in a sexual relationship?
1. Yes
0. No   If no, please skip to question B-1.

GSS-2. Following is a rating scale on which we would like you to record your personal evaluation of how satisfying your sexual relationship is. The rating is simple. Make your evaluation by circling the appropriate number that best describes your present sexual relationship.
8. Could not be better
7. Excellent
6. Good
5. Above average
4. Adequate
3. Somewhat inadequate
2. Poor
1. Highly inadequate
0. Could not be worse

Sexual Abuse

Now we would like to ask you some questions about sexual abuse. Child sexual abuse is defined as the involvement of dependent, developmentally immature children or adolescents in sex acts that they do not fully comprehend and to which they are unable to give informed consent or that violate the social taboos of family roles.

B-1. According to this definition, were you, as a child up to age 18, ever sexually abused?
1. Yes
0. No   If no, please skip to question WS-1 on page 12.

B-2. What age(s) were you when this occurred?
Please specify.

B-3. Approximately how many times were you sexually abused?
Please specify.

B-4. Altogether, over what period of time were you sexually abused?
1. Days
2. Months
3. Years

B-5. Type of sexual activity (Please circle all that apply.)
Fondling private parts
    1. Yes
    0. No
Oral sex
    1. Yes
    0. No
Penetration by finger(s)
    1. Yes
    0. No
Attempted penile penetration
    1. Yes
    0. No
Penile penetration
    1. Yes
    0. No
Other
    1. Yes
    0. No
    If other, please specify.

B-6. How do you think this experience(s) influenced you?
    1. Positively
    2. Negatively
    3. Mixed
    4. Not at all
    5. Unsure

B-7. Do you believe your experience(s) influenced your choice of profession?
    1. Yes
    0. No
    2. Unsure

B-8. By whom were you sexually abused? (Please circle all that apply.)
    1. Stranger(s)
        1. Male
        2. Female
    2. Caretaker(s)
        1. Male
        2. Female
    3. Acquaintance(s)
        1. Male
        2. Female

4. Family member(s)
   1. Male
   2. Female
   If other or family member(s), please specify:

B-9. Were you aware of any coercion or threat of violence connected with the sexual abuse?
   1. Yes
   0. No

B-10. Did you ever tell anyone about the sexual abuse?
   1. Yes
   0. No   If no, please skip to question WS-1.

B-11. How long after you were first sexually abused did you tell anyone? (Please circle.)
   1. Hours
   2. Days
   3. Months
   4. Years

B-12. Whom did you tell? (Please specify as many as apply.)

B-13. Did anyone believe you?
   1. Yes
   0. No
   2. Unsure

B-14. Did you receive any assistance?
   1. Yes
   0. No
   Please specify.

Witnessing Sexual Abuse

Now, we would like to ask you some questions about witnessing sexual abuse.

WS-1. According to the earlier given definition of sexual abuse, did you, as a child up to age 18, ever witness anyone being sexually abused?
   1. Yes
   0. No   If no, please skip to question P-1.

WS-2. What age(s) were you when this occurred?
   Please specify.

WS-3. Approximately how many times did you witness sexual abuse? Please specify.

WS-4. Altogether, over what period of time did you witness sexual abuse?

    1. Days

    2. Months

    3. Years

WS-5. Type of sexual abused you witnessed (Please circle all that apply.)

Fondling private parts

    1. Yes

    0. No

Oral sex

    1. Yes

    0. No

Digital penetration

    1. Yes

    0. No

Attempted penile penetration

    1. Yes

    0. No

Penile penetration

    1. Yes

    0. No

Other

    1. Yes

    0. No

If other, please specify:

WS-6. How do you think the experience(s) of witnessing sexual abuse influenced you?

    1. Positively

    2. Negatively

    3. Mixed

    4. Not at all

    5. Unsure

WS-7. Do you believe witnessing sexual abuse influenced your choice of profession?

    1. Yes

    0. No

    2. Unsure

WS-8. Whom did you witness being sexually abused? (Please circle all that apply.)
1. Stranger(s)
   1. Male
   2. Female
2. Caretaker(s)
   1. Male
   2. Female
3. Acquaintance(s)
   1. Male
   2. Female
4. Family member(s)
   1. Male
   2. Female
If other or family member(s), please specify:

WS-9. When you witnessed the sexual abuse, who was (were) the abuser(s)? (Please circle all that apply.)
1. Stranger(s)
   1. Male
   2. Female
2. Caretaker(s)
   1. Male
   2. Female
3. Acquaintance(s)
   1. Male
   2. Female
4. Family member(s)
   1. Male
   2. Female
If other or family member(s), please specify:

WS-10. Were you aware of any coercion or threat of violence connected with the sexual abuse you witnessed, either to you or to the victim?
1. Yes
0. No

WS-11. Did you ever tell anyone about the sexual abuse?
1. Yes
0. No   If no, please skip to question P-1.

WS-12. How long after you first witnessed the sexual abuse did you tell anyone? (Please circle.)
  1. Hours
  2. Days
  3. Months
  4. Years

WS-13. Whom did you tell? (Please specify all that apply.)

WS-14. Did anyone believe you?
  1. Yes
  0. No
  2. Unsure

WS-15. Did you receive any assistance?
  1. Yes
  0. No
  Please specify.

Physical Abuse

Now we would like to ask you some questions about physical abuse. For purposes of this study, physical abuse is defined as inflicting on children or adolescents nonaccidental injury that causes or creates a substantial risk of causing disfigurement, impairment of bodily functioning, or other serious physical injury.

P-1. According to this definition, were you, as a child up to age 18, ever the victim of physical abuse?
  1. Yes
  0. No   If no, please skip to question WP1.

P-2. What age(s) were you when this occurred?
  Please specify.

P-3. Approximately how many times were you physically abused?
  Please specify.

P-4. Altogether, over what period of time were you physically abused?
  1. Days
  2. Months
  3. Years

P-5. Type of physical abuse (Please circle all that apply.)

Pinching
1. Yes
0. No

Biting
1. Yes
0. No

Burning
1. Yes
0. No

Smothering
1. Yes
0. No

Strangling
1. Yes
0. No

Hitting *without* an object
1. Yes
0. No

Hitting *with* an object
1. Yes
0. No

Beating *without* an object
1. Yes
0. No

Beating *with* an object
1. Yes
0. No

If other, please specify
1. Yes
0. No

P-6. How do you think your physical victimization influenced you?
1. Positively
2. Negatively
3. Mixed
4. Not at all
5. Unsure

P-7. Do you believe your physical victimization influenced your choice of profession?

    1. Yes

    0. No

    2. Unsure

P-8. By whom were you physically abused? (Please circle all that apply.)

    1. Stranger(s)

        1. Male

        2. Female

    2. Caretaker(s)

        1. Male

        2. Female

    3. Acquaintance(s)

        1. Male

        2. Female

    4. Family member(s)

        1. Male

        2. Female

    If other or family member(s), please specify.

P-9. Were you aware of any coercion or threat of further violence?

    1. Yes

    0. No

P-10. Did you ever tell anyone about the physical abuse?

    1. Yes

    0. No   If no, please skip to question WP-1.

P-11. How long after you were first physically abused did you tell anyone? (Please circle.)

    1. Hours

    2. Days

    3. Months

    4. Years

P-12. Whom did you tell? (Please specify as many as apply.)

P-13. Did anyone believe you?

    1. Yes

    0. No

    2. Unsure

P-14. Did you receive any assistance?

1. Yes

0. No

Please specify.

Witnessing Physical Abuse

Now we would like to ask you for some information about witnessing physical abuse.

WP-1. According to the earlier given definition of physical abuse, did you, as a child up to age 18, ever *witness* anyone being physically abused?

1. Yes

0. No   If no, please skip to question BK-1.

WP-2. What age(s) were you when you witnessed the physical abuse? Please specify.

WP-3. Approximately how many times did you witness physical abuse? Please specify.

WP-4. Altogether, over what period of time did you witness physical abuse?

1. Days

2. Months

3. Years

WP-5. Type of physical abuse you witnessed (please circle all that apply):

Pinching

1. Yes

0. No

Biting

1. Yes

0. No

Burning

1. Yes

0. No

Smothering

1. Yes

0. No

Strangling

1. Yes

0. No

Hitting *without* an object
   1. Yes
   0. No
Hitting *with* an object
   1. Yes
   0. No
Beating *without* an object
   1. Yes
   0. No
Beating *with* an object
   1. Yes
   0. No
If other, please specify
   1. Yes
   0. No

WP-6. How do you think the experience(s) of witnessing physical abuse influenced you?
   1. Positively
   2. Negatively
   3. Mixed
   4. Not at all
   5. Unsure

WP-7. Do you believe witnessing physical abuse influenced your choice of profession?
   1. Yes
   0. No
   2. Unsure

WP-8. Whom did you witness being physically abused? (Please circle all that apply.)
   1. Stranger(s)
      1. Male
      2. Female
   2. Caretaker(s)
      1. Male
      2. Female
   3. Acquaintance(s)
      1. Male
      2. Female
   4. Family member
      1. Male
      2. Female
   If other or family member(s), please specify:

WP-9. When you witnessed the physical abuse, who was the abuser(s)? (Please circle all that apply.)
1. Stranger(s)
   1. Male
   2. Female
2. Caretaker(s)
   1. Male
   2. Female
3. Acquaintance(s)
   1. Male
   2. Female
4. Family member(s)
   1. Male
   2. Female
If other or family member(s), please specify:

WP-10. Were you aware of any further coercion or threat of violence connected with the physical abuse either to you or to the victim?
1. Yes
0. No

WP-11. Did you ever tell anyone about the physical abuse you witnessed?
1. Yes
0. No   If no, please skip to question BK-1.

WP-12. How long after you first witnessed the physical abuse did you tell anyone? (Please circle number.)
1. Hours
2. Days
3. Months
4. Years

WP-13. Whom did you tell? (Please specify all that apply.)

WP-14. Did anyone believe you?
1. Yes
0. No
2. Unsure

WP-15. Did you receive any assistance?
1. Yes
2. No
Please specify.

Background Questions

As a professional, you are familiar with theories that propose that individuals who were abused as children are at higher risk to become abusers than those who were never abused. The following questions address this issue. We appreciate your response to these very personal questions.

BK-1. Have you ever sexually or physically abused another person?
1. Yes
0. No

BK-2. Have you ever engaged in sexual activities with your clients or patients?
1. Yes
0. No

Last, we would like to ask you for some demographic information.

BK-3. Your gender (Please circle number.)
1. Male
2. Female

BK-4. Your present age:

BK-5. Your racial background:

BK-6. Your sexual preference (Please circle.)
1. Asexual
2. Bisexual
3. Heterosexual
4. Homosexual

BK-7. Your present marital status (Please circle.)
1. Never married
2. Married
3. Significant other
4. Divorced
5. Separated
6. Widowed
If other, please specify:

BK-8. Are you currently raising or have you raised children? (Please include biological, adoptive, or foster children.)
1. Yes
0. No

BK-9. For most of the time when you were growing up, were you in a one-parent or a two-parent family?
1. One-parent
2. Two-parent

BK-10. In your family of origin, were you first-born, second-born, or other?
1. First-born
2. Second-born
3. Other

If other, please specify.

References

Aarens, M., Cameron, T., Roizen, J., Schnerberk, D., & Wingard, D. (1978). *Alcohol, casualties and crime.* Berkeley, CA: Social Research Group.

Abramson, J. (1989). Making teams work. *Social Work With Groups, 12*(4), 45-63.

Abramson, J. (1993). Orienting social work employees in interdisciplinary settings: Shaping professional and organizational perspectives. *Social Work, 38*(2), 152-157.

Achenbach, T. M., & Edelbrock, C. (1983). *Manual for the child behavior checklist.* Burlington: University of Vermont.

Aiosa-Karpas, C. J., Karpas, R., Pelcovitz, D., & Kaplan, S. (1991). Gender identification and sex-role attribution in sexually abused adolescent females. *Journal of the American Academy of Child and Adolescent Psychiatry, 30,* 266-271.

Alexander, C. S., & Becker, H. J. (1978). The use of vignettes in survey research. *Public Opinion Quarterly,* 93-104.

Alexander, P. C. (1993). The differential effects of abuse characteristics and attachment in the prediction of long-term effects of sexual abuse. *Journal of Interpersonal Violence, 8*(3), 346-362.

American Association for Protecting Children. (1986). *Highlights of official child neglect and abuse reporting, 1984.* Denver, CO: American Humane Association.

American Association for Protecting Children. (1988). *Highlights of official child neglect and abuse reporting, 1986.* Denver, CO: American Association for Protecting Children.

American Professional Society for the Abuse of Children. (1990). *Guidelines for psychosocial evaluation of suspected sexual abuse in young children.* Chicago: Author.

American Psychiatric Association. (1980). *Diagnostic and statistical manual of mental disorders* (3rd ed.). Washington, DC: Author.

American Psychological Association. (1992). Ethical principles of psychologists and codes of conduct. *American Psychologist, 47,* 1597-1611.

Anderson, J., Martin, J., Mullen, P., Romans, S., & Herbison, P. (1993). Prevalence of childhood sexual abuse experiences in a community sample of women. *Journal of the Academy of Child and Adolescent Psychiatry, 32*(5), 911-919.

Araji, S., & Finkelhor, D. (1986). Abusers: A review of the research. In D. Finkelhor & Associates (Eds.), *A sourcebook on child sexual abuse* (pp. 89-118). Newbury Park, CA: Sage.

Armsworth, M. E. (1990). A qualitative analysis of adult incest survivors' responses to sexual involvement with therapists. *Child Abuse & Neglect, 14,* 541-554.

Attias, R., & Goodwin, J. (1985). Knowledge and management strategies in incest cases: A survey of physicians, psychologists, and family counselors. *Child Abuse & Neglect, 9,* 527-533.

Bagley, C., & Ramsay, R. (1986). Sexual abuse in childhood: Psychosocial outcomes and implications for social work practice. *Journal of Social Work and Human Sexuality, 4,* 33-47.

Bagley, C., & Sewchuk-Dann. (1991). Characteristics of 60 children and adolescents who have a history of sexual assault against others. *Journal of Child and Youth Care,* Special Issues, 43-52.

Bagley, C., Wood, M., & Young, L. (1994). Victim to abuser: mental health and behavioral sequels of child sexual abuse in a community survey of young adult males. *Child Abuse & Neglect, 18*(8), 683-697.

Barringer, F. (1989, September 26). Prison releases defiant mother. *New York Times,* p. A18.

Bartell, P. A., & Rubin, L. J. (1990). Dangerous liaisons: Sexual intimacies in supervision. *Professional psychology: Research and practice, 21*(6), 442-450.

Beck, A. (1978). *Beck inventory.* Philadelphia, PA: Center for Cognitive Therapy.

Beck, A. (1990). *Cognitive therapy of personality disorders.* New York: Guilford.

Beitchman, J. H., Zucker, K. J., Hood, J. E., DaCosta, G. A., & Akman, D. (1991). A review of the short-term effects of child sexual abuse. *Child Abuse & Neglect, 15,* 537-556.

Bender, L., & Blau, A. (1937). The reaction of children to sexual relations with adults. *American Journal of Orthopsychiatry, 7,* 500-518.

Benedek, E. P. (1985). Children and psychic trauma: A brief review of contemporary thinking. In S. Eth & R. Pynoos (Eds.), *Post-traumatic stress disorder in children* (pp. 3-16). Washington, DC: American Psychiatric Association.

Benedek, E. P., & Schetky, D. H. (1987a). Problems in validating allegations of sexual abuse: Part 2. Clinical experience. *Journal of American Academy of Child and Adolescent Psychiatry, 26*(6), 916-921.

Benedek, E. P., & Schetky, D. H. (1987b). Problems in validating allegations of sexual abuse: Part 1. Factors affecting perception and recall of events. *Journal of the American Academy of Child and Adolescent Psychiatry, 26*(6), 912-915.

Benson, D. E., Swann, A., O'Toole, R., & Turbett, J. P. (1991). Physicians' recognition of and response to child abuse: Northern Ireland and the U.S.A. *Child Abuse & Neglect, 15,* 57-67.

Berliner, L. (1988). Deciding whether a child has been sexually abused. In E. B. Nicholson & J. Bulkley (Eds.), *Sexual abuse allegations in custody and visitation cases: A resource book for judges and court personnel* (pp. 48-69). Washington, DC: American Bar Association.

Berliner, L. (1989, January). Misconduct in social work practice. *Social Work,* 69-71.

Berliner, L., & Barbieri, M. K. (1984). The testimony of the child victim of sexual assault. *Journal of Social Issues, 40*(2), 125-137.

Berliner, L., & Conte, J. R. (1993). Sexual abuse evaluations: Conceptual and empirical obstacles. *Child Abuse & Neglect, 17,* 111-125.

Bernet, W. (1993). False statements and the differential diagnosis of abuse allegations. *Journal of the American Academy of Child and Adolescent Psychiatry, 32*(5), 903-910.

Bernstein, E. M., & Putnam, F. W. (1986). Development, reliability, and validity of a dissociation scale. *Journal of Nervous and Mental Disease, 174*(12), 727-735.

Black, M., Dubowitz, H., & Harrington, D. (1994). Sexual abuse: Developmental differences in children's behavior and self-perception. *Child Abuse & Neglect, 18,* 85-95.

Boat, B. W., & Everson, M. D. (1988a). Interviewing young children with anatomical dolls. *Child Welfare, 67*(4), 337-352.

Boat, B. W., & Everson, M. D. (1988b). Use of anatomical dolls among professionals in sexual abuse evaluation. *Child Abuse & Neglect, 12,* 171-179.

Bolton, F. G. (1987). The father in the adolescent pregnancy at risk for child maltreatment: Helpmate or hindrance? *Journal of Family Violence, 2*(1), 67-80.

Boney-McCoy, D., & Finkelhor, D. (1995). Prior victimization: A risk factor for child sexual abuse and for PTSD-related symptomatology among sexually abused youth. *Child Abuse & Neglect, 19*(12), 1401-1421.

Borys, D. S., & Pope, K. S. (1989). Dual relationships between therapist and client: A national study of psychologists, psychiatrists, and social workers. *Professional Psychology: Research and Practice, 20,* 283-292.

Bouhoutsos, J., Holroyd, J., Lerman, H., Forer, B. R., & Greenberg, M. (1983). Sexual intimacy between psychotherapists and patients. *Professional Psychology: Research and Practice, 14*(2), 185-196.

Brant, R. S. T., & Tisza, V. B. (1977). The sexually misused child. *American Journal of Orthopsychiatry, 47,* 80-90.

Brazelton, B. (1990, September 9). Why is America failing its children? *New York Times Magazine,* p. 41.

Brekke, J. S. (1987). Detecting wife and child abuse in clinical settings. *Social Casework: The Journal of Contemporary Social Work, X*(x), 332-338.

Bressee, J. D., Stearns, G. B., Bess, B. H., & Packer, L. S. (1986). Allegations of child sexual abuse in child custody disputes: A therapeutic assessment model. *American Journal of Orthopsychiatry, 56*(4), 560-569.

Briere, J. (1992). Methodological issues in the study of sexual abuse effects. *Journal of Consulting and Clinical Psychology, 60*(2), 196-203.

Briere, J., & Elliott, D. M. (1994). Immediate and long-term impacts of child sexual abuse. *The Future of Children: Sexual Abuse of Children, 4*(2), 54-69.

Briere, J., & Runtz, M. (1988). Symptomatology associated with childhood sexual victimization in a nonclinical adult sample. *Child Abuse & Neglect, 12*(Suicide), 51-59.

Briere, J., & Runtz, M. (1989). The Trauma Symptom Checklist (TSC-33): Early data on a new scale. *Journal of Interpersonal Violence, 2,* 151-163.

Briere, J., & Runtz, M. (1990). Differential adult symptomatology associated with sexual victimization in children. *Child Abuse & Neglect, 14,* 357-364.

Brooks, G. R. (1990). The inexpressive male and vulnerability to therapist-patient sexual exploitation. *Psychotherapy, 27,*(3), 344-349.

Broussard, S. D., & Wagner, W. G. (1988). Child sexual abuse: Who is to blame? *Child Abuse & Neglect, 12,* 563-569.

Broussard, S., Wagner, W. G., & Kazelskis, R. (1991). Undergraduate students' perceptions of child sexual abuse: The impact of victim sex, perpetrator sex, respondent sex, and victim response. *Journal of Family Violence, 6*(3), 267-278.

Browne, A., & Finkelhor, D. (1986a). Impact of child sexual abuse: A review of the research. *Psychological Bulletin, 99*(1), 66-77.

Browne, A., & Finkelhor, D. (1986b). Initial and long-term effects: A review of the research. In D. Finkelhor & Associates (Eds.), *A sourcebook on child sexual abuse,* (pp. 143-179). Newbury Park, CA: Sage.

Bryer, J. B., Nelson, B. A., Miller, J. A., & Krol, P. A. (1987). Childhood sexual and physical abuse as factors in adult psychiatric illness. *American Journal of Psychiatry, 144,* 1426-1430.

Burgess, A., & Hartman, C. (1986). *Sexual exploitation of patients by health professionals.* New York: Praeger.

Bybee, D., & Mowbray, C. T. (1993). An analysis of allegations of sexual abuse in a multi-victim day care center case. *Child Abuse & Neglect, 17,* 767-783.

Cameron, E. (1994). Veterans of a secret war: Survivors of childhood sexual trauma compared to Vietnam War veterans with PTSD. *Journal of Interpersonal Violence, 9*(1), 117-132.

Carmen, E. H., Reiker, P. P., & Mills, T. (1984). Victims of violence and psychiatric illness. *American Journal of Psychiatry, 141,* 378-383.

Carson, R. C. (Ed.). (1969). *Interpretive manual to the MMPI.* New York: McGraw-Hill.

Cattell, R. B. (1966). The scree test of the number of significant factors. *Multivariate Behavioral Research, 1,* 140-161.

Chu, J. A., & Dill, D. L. (1990). Dissociative symptoms in relation to childhood physical and sexual abuse. *American Journal of Psychiatry, 147,* 887-892.

Cohen, E. (1993, Spring). The doubtful male. *AKRON: The Magazine of the University of Akron, 7.*

Cohen, J. (1969). *Statistical power analysis for the behavioral sciences.* New York: Academic.

Collings, S. J., & Payne, M. F. (1991). Attribution of causal and moral responsibility to victims of father-daughter incest: An exploratory examination of five factors. *Child Abuse & Neglect, 15,* 513-521.

Conte, J. R. (1984). Progress in treating the sexual abuse of children. *Social Work, 29*(3), 258-263.

Conte, J. R., & Schuerman, J. R. (1987). Factors associated with an increased impact of child sex abuse. *Child Abuse & Neglect, 11,* 201-1.

Conte, J. R., Sorenson, E., Fogarty, L., & Rosa, J. D. (1991). Evaluating children's reports of sexual abuse: Results from a survey of professionals. *American Journal of Orthopsychiatry, 61*(13), 428-437.

Coons, P. (1986). Child abuse and personality disorder: Review of the literature and suggestions for treatment. *Child Abuse & Neglect, 10,* 455-462.

Coons, P., Bowman, E. S., Pellow, T. A., & Schneider, P. (1989). Post-traumatic aspects of child sexual abuse and incest. *Psychiatric Clinics of North America, 12*(2), 325-335.

Coopersmith, S. (1981). *Manual of the adult self-esteem scale.* Palo Alto, CA: Consulting Psychologists Press.

Corder, B. F., & Whiteside, R. (1988). A survey of jurors' perception of issues related to child sexual abuse. *American Journal of Forensic Psychology, 6*(3), 37-43.

Corwin, D. L. (1995). Child sexual abuse assessment and professional ethics: Commentary on controversies, limits and when to just say no. *Journal of Child Sexual Abuse, 4,* 115-122.

Corwin, D., Berliner, L., Goodman, L., Goodwin, G., & White, S. (1987). Child sexual abuse and custody disputes: No easy answers. *Journal of Interpersonal Violence, 2,* 91-105.

Cosentino, C. E., Meyer-Bahlburg, H. F. L., Alpert, J. L., & Gaines, R. (1993). Cross-gender behavior and gender conflict in sexually abused girls. *Journal of the American Academy of Child and Adolescent Psychiatry, 32,* 940-947.

Courtois, C. A. (1979). The incest experience and its aftermath. *Victimology: An International Journal, 4*(4), 337-347.

Cronbach, L. J. (1951). Coefficient alpha and the internal structure of tests. *Psychometrika, 16,* 297-334.

Crosby, F., Bromley, S., & Saxe, L. (1980). Recent unobtrusive studies of black and white discrimination and prejudice: A literature review. *Psychological Bulletin, 87*(3), 546-563.

Cross, T. P., DeVos, E., & Whitcomb, D. (1994). Prosecution of child sexual abuse: Which cases are accepted? *Child Abuse & Neglect, 18*(8), 663-677.

CSWE. (1994). Current research initiatives in the field of child mental health. *Social Work Education Reporter, 42*(1).

Daniel, J., Hampton, R., & Newberger, E. (1983). Child abuse and childhood accidents in Black families: A controlled comparative study. *American Journal of Orthopsychiatry, 53,* 643-653.

Daro, D. (1988). *Confronting child abuse: Research for effective program design.* New York: Free Press.

Davey, R. I., & Hill, J. (1995). A study of the variability of training and beliefs among professionals who interview children to investigate suspected sexual abuse. *Child Abuse & Neglect, 19*(8), 933-942.

Davis, L. E., & Proctor, E. K. (1989). *Race, gender & class: Guidelines for practice with individuals, families, and groups.* Englewood Cliffs, NJ: Prentice Hall.

Deblinger, E., Lippmann, J., Stauffer, L., & Finkel, M. (1994). Personal versus professional responses to child sexual abuse allegations. *Child Abuse & Neglect, 18*(8), 679-682.

Deblinger, E., McLeer, S. V., Atkins, M. S., Ralphe, D., & Foa, E. (1989). Post-traumatic stress in sexually abused, physically abused, and non abused children. *Child Abuse & Neglect, 13,* 403-408.

DeJong, A. (1985). The medical evaluation of sexual abuse in children. *Hospital and Community Psychiatry, 36*(5), 509-512.

DeJong, A. R., & Emmet, G. A. (1983). Epidemiologic variations in childhood sexual abuse. *Child Abuse & Neglect, 7,* 155-162.

deJonge, J. (1995). On breaking wills: The theological roots of violence in families. *Journal of Psychology and Christianity, 14*(1), 26-37.

Deltaglia, L. (1990). Victims and perpetrators of sexual abuse: A psychosocial study from France. *Child Abuse & Neglect, 14,* 445-447.

de Mause, L. (Ed.). (1974). *The history of childhood.* New York: Psychohistory Press.

Dembo, R., Williams, L., & Schmeidler, J. (1993). Gender differences in mental health service needs among youths entering a juvenile detention center. *Journal of Prison & Jail Health, 12*(2), 73-101.

Derogatis, L. (1983). *SCL-90-R administration, scoring and procedures manual* (2nd ed.). Towson, MD: Clinical Psychometric Research.

Derogatis, L. (1993). *BSI: Brief Symptom Inventory. Administration, scoring, and procedures manual.* Minneapolis, MN: National Computer Systems.

Derogatis, L., Lipman, R., & Covi, L. (1973). The SCL-90: An outpatient rating scale. *Psychopharmacology Bulletin, 9,* 13-28.

Derogatis, L., Rickels, K., & Rock, A. F. (1976). The SCL-90 and the MMPI: A step in the validation of a new self-report scale. *British Journal of Psychiatry, 128,* 280-289.

DeVellis, R. F. (1991). *Scale development: Theory and applications* (Vol. 26). Newbury Park, CA: Sage.

deYoung, M. (1981). Case reports: The sexual exploitation of incest victims by helping professionals. *Victimology: An International Journal, 5*(1-4), 92-101.

deYoung, M. (1984). Counterphobic behavior in multiply molested children. *Child Welfare, 63*(4), 333-339.

deYoung, M. (1986). A conceptual model for judging the truthfulness of a young child's allegation of sexual abuse. *American Journal of Orthopsychiatry, 56,* 550-559.

Dienstbier, R. A. (1970). Positive and negative prejudice: Interactions of prejudice with race and social desirability. *Journal of Personality, 38,* 198-215.

Dillman, D. A. (1978). *Mail and telephone surveys: The total design method.* New York: John Wiley.

Doueck, H., Levine, M., & Bronson, D. E. (1993). Risk assessment in child protective services: An evaluation of the child at risk field system. *Journal of Interpersonal Violence, 8*(4), 446-467.

Douglas, M., & Wildavsky, A. (1983). *Risk and culture*. Berkeley: University of California Press.

Dubowitz, H., Black, M., Harrington, D., & Verschoore, A. (1993). A follow-up study of behavior problems associated with child sexual abuse. *Child Abuse & Neglect, 17*, 743-754.

Dutton, D. G. (1976). Tokenism, reverse discrimination, and egalitarianism in interracial behavior. *Journal of Social Issues, 32*(2), 93-107.

Dutton, D. G., & Lake, R. A. (1973). Threat of own prejudice and reverse discrimination in interracial situations. *Journal of Personality and Social Psychology, 28*(1), 94-100.

Dutton, D. G., & Yee, P. (1974). The effect of subject liberalism, anonymity, and race of experimenter on subjects' ratings of Oriental and White photographs. *Canadian Journal of Behavioral Science Review, 5*(1), 34-45.

Eckenrode, J., Powers, J., Doris, J., Munsch, J., & Bolger, N. (1988). Substantiation of child abuse and neglect reports. *Journal of Consulting and Clinical Psychology, 56*(1), 9-16.

Egeland, B., & Jacobvitz, D. (1984). *Intergenerational continuity of parental abuse: Causes and consequences*. Paper presented at the Conference on Biosocial Perspectives in Abuse and Neglect, York, ME.

Eisenberg, N., Owens, R. G., & Dewey, M. E. (1987). Attitudes of health professionals to child sexual abuse and incest. *Child Abuse & Neglect, 11*, 109-116.

Ellerstein, N. S., & Canavan, J. W. (1980, March). Sexual abuse of boys. *American Journal of Diseases of Children, 134*, 255-257.

Elliott, D. M. (1994). The impact of Christian faith on the prevalence and sequelae of sexual abuse. *Journal of Interpersonal Violence, 9*(1), 95-107.

Elliott, D. M., & Briere, J. (1992). Sexual abuse trauma among professional women: Validating the trauma symptom checklist-40. *Child Abuse & Neglect, 16*, 391-398.

Elliott, D. M., & Guy, J. D. (1993). Mental health professionals versus non-mental-health professionals: Childhood trauma and adult functioning. *Professional Psychology: Research and Practice, 24*(1), 83-90.

Elwell, M. E., & Ephross, P. H. (1987). Initial reactions of sexually abused children. *Social Casework, 68*, 109-116.

Elwood, R. W. (1992). Clinical discriminations and neuropsychological tests: An appeal to Bayes' theorem. *The Clinical Neuropsychologist, 7*, 224-233.

Enzer, N. B. (1988). The real problem: Human pain. In J. Looney (Ed.), *Chronic mental illness in children and adolescents*. Washington, DC: American Psychiatric Press.

Fajardo, D. M. (1985). Author, race, essay quality, and reverse discrimination. *Journal of Applied Social Psychology, 15*(3), 255-268.

Faller, K. C. (1990). *Understanding child sexual maltreatment*. Newbury Park, CA: Sage.

Feldman-Summers, S., & Jones, G. (1984). Psychological impacts of sexual contact between therapists or other health care practitioners and their clients. *Journal of Consulting and Clinical Psychology, 52*(6), 1054-1061.

Feldman-Summers, S., & Pope, K. (1994). The experience of "forgetting" childhood abuse: A national survey of psychologists. *Journal of Consulting and Clinical Psychology, 62*(3), 630-639.

Felsen, R. B. (1991). Blame analysis: Accounting for the behavior of protected groups. *The American Sociologist, 22*(1), 5-23.

Ferenczi, S. (1949). Confusion of tongues between adults and the child. *International Journal of Psychoanalysis, 30*, 225-230.

Ferenczi, S. (1955). Confusion of tongues between adults and the child: The language of tenderness and passion. Paper read before the International Psycho-Analytic Congress, Wiesbaden, September, 1932. In M. Balint (Ed.), *Final contributions to the problems and methods of psycho-analysis* (pp. 156-167). London: Hogarth. (Original work published 1932)

Festinger, L. (1957). *A theory of cognitive dissonance.* Evanston, IL: Row, Peterson.

Finkelhor, D. (1979a). *Sexually victimized children.* New York: Free Press.

Finkelhor, D. (1979b). What's wrong with sex between adults and children? Ethics and the problem of sexual abuse. *American Journal of Orthopsychiatry, 49*(4), 692-697.

Finkelhor, D. (1980). Risk factors in the sexual victimization of children. *Child Abuse & Neglect, 4,* 265-273.

Finkelhor, D. (1984). *Child sexual abuse: New theory and research.* New York: Free Press.

Finkelhor, D. (1985). Some critical differences between physical and sexual abuse. In E. Newberger & D. Bourne (Eds.), *Unhappy families.* Livingston, MA: JSL.

Finkelhor, D., & Associates (1986). *A sourcebook on child sexual abuse.* Newbury Park, CA: Sage.

Finkelhor, D. (1993). Epidemiological factors in the clinical identification of child sexual abuse. *Child Abuse & Neglect, 17*(1), 67-70.

Finkelhor, D. (1994). The international epidemiology of child sexual abuse. *Child Abuse & Neglect, 18*(5), 409-417.

Finkelhor, D., & Baron, L. (1986). Risk factors for child sexual abuse. *Journal of Interpersonal Violence, 1*(1), 43-71.

Finkelhor, D., & Browne, A. (1985). The traumatic impact of child sexual abuse. *American Journal of Orthopsychiatry, 55*(4), 530-541.

Finkelhor, D., & Hotaling, G. T. (1984). Sexual abuse in the national incidence study of child abuse and neglect: An appraisal. *Child Abuse & Neglect, 1,* 23-32.

Finkelhor, D., Hotaling, G. T., Lewis, I. A., & Smith, C. (1989). Sexual abuse and its relationship to later sexual satisfaction, marital status, religion, and attitudes. *Journal of Interpersonal Violence, 4*(4), 379-399.

Finkelhor, D., Hotaling, G., Lewis, I. A., & Smith, C. (1990). Sexual abuse in a national survey of adult men and women: Prevalence, characteristics, and risk factors. *Child Abuse & Neglect, 14,* 19-28.

Finkelhor, D., Williams, L. M., Burns, N., & Kalinowski, M. (1988). *Nursery crimes: Sexual abuse in day care.* Newbury Park, CA: Sage.

Finlayson, L. M., & Koocher, G. (1991). Professional judgments and child abuse reporting in sexual abuse cases. *Professional Psychology: Research and Practice, 22,* 464-472.

Fish-Murray, C. C., Koby, E. V., & van der Kolk, B. A. (1987). Evolving ideas: The effect of abuse on children's thought. In B. A. v. d. Kolk (Ed.), *Psychological Trauma,* (pp. 89-110). Washington, DC: American Psychiatric Press.

Freedman, M. R., Rosenberg, S. J., Gettman-Felzien, D., & Van Scoyk, S. (1993). Evaluator countertransference in child custody evaluations. *American Journal of Forensic Psychology, 11*(3), 61-73.

Freeman-Longo, R. E. (1986). The impact of sexual victimization on males. *Child Abuse & Neglect, 10,* 411-414.

Frenken, J., & Stolk, B. V. (1990). Incest victims: Inadequate help by professionals. *Child Abuse & Neglect, 14,* 253-263.

Freud, S. (1989). The Aetiology of hysteria. Paper read before the Society for Psychiatry and Neurology, Vienna, September, 1896. In. P. Gay (Ed.). *The Freud reader* (pp. 96-111). New York: Norton. (Original work published 1896)

Freud, S. (Ed.). (1953). *My views on the part played by sexuality in the aetiology of the neurosis.* (Vol. 7; 1901-1905). London: Hogarth.

Friedrich, W. F., & Reams, R. A. (1987). Course of psychological symptoms in sexually abused young children. *Psychotherapy, 24*(2), 160-170.

Fry, R. (1993). Invited review: Adult physical illness and childhood sexual abuse. *Journal of Psychosomatic Research, 37*(2), 89-103.

Gabel, S., Finn, M., & Ahmed, A. (1988). Day treatment outcome with severely disturbed children. *American Academy of Child and Adolescent Psychiatry, 27*(4), 479-482.

Gaertner, S. L. (1973). Helping behavior and racial discrimination among liberals and conservatives. *Journal of Personality and Social Psychology, 25*(3), 335-341.

Gale, J., Thompson, R. J., Moran, T., & Sack, W. H. (1988). Sexual abuse in young children: Its clinical presentation and characteristic patterns. *Child Abuse & Neglect, 12*, 163-170.

Gambrill, E. (1990). *Critical thinking in clinical practice.* San Francisco: Jossey-Bass.

Garbarino, J., Schellenback, C., & Sebes, J. (1986). *Troubled youth, troubled families.* New York: Aldine.

Gardner, R. (1994). Differentiating between true and false sex-abuse accusations in child-custody disputes. *Journal of Divorce & Remarriage, 21*(3/4), 1-20.

Gartrell, N., Herman, J., Olarte, S., Feldstein, M., & Localio, R. (1987). Reporting practices of psychiatrists who knew of sexual misconduct by colleagues. *American Journal of Orthopsychiatry, 57*(2), 287-295.

Gartrell, N., Herman, J. L., Olarte, S., Feldstein, M., & Localio, R. (1988). Management and rehabilitation of sexually exploitive therapists. *Hospital and Community Psychiatry, 39*(10), 1070-1074.

Gartrell, N., Herman, J., Olarte, S., Feldstein, M., Localio, R., & Schoener, G. (Eds.). (1989). *Sexual abuse of patients by therapists: Strategies for offender management and rehabilitation.* San Francisco: Jossey-Bass.

Gelinas, D. J. (1983, November). The persisting negative effects of incest. *Psychiatry, 46*, 312-332.

Gelles, R. J., & Straus, M. A. (1987). Is violence toward children increasing? A comparison of 1975 and 1985 National Survey rates. *Journal of Interpersonal Violence, 2*(2), 212-222.

German, D. E., Habenicht, D. J., & Futcher, W. G. (1990). Psychological profile of the female adolescent incest victim. *Child Abuse & Neglect, 14*, 429-438.

Gil, D. (1973). *Violence against children: Physical abuse in the United States.* Cambridge, MA: Harvard University Press.

Gilligan G. (1982). *In a different voice.* Cambridge, MA: Harvard University Press.

Giovannoni, J. M., & Becerra, R. M. (1979). *Defining child abuse.* New York: Free Press.

Glass, G. V., & Hopkins, K. D. (1996). *Statistical methods in education and psychology* (3rd ed.). Boston: Allyn & Bacon.

Gold, E. R. (1986). Long-term effects of sexual victimization in childhood: An attributional approach. *Journal of Consulting and Clinical Psychology, 54*(4), 471-475.

Goldberg, C. (1995, Sunday, May 21). When a teacher crosses the line: Sex with students not unusual, but wrong, experts say. *New York Times*, p. 37.

Goldman, R. J., & Goldman, J. D. G. (1988). The prevalence and nature of child sexual abuse in Australia. *Australian Journal of Sex, Marriage & Family, 9*(2), 94-106.

Gomez-Schwartz, B., & Horowitz, J. (1984). Professionals' responses. In D. Finkelhor (Ed.), *Child sexual abuse: New theory and research* (pp. 200-215). New York: Free Press.

Gomez-Schwartz, B., Horowitz, J. M., & Saucier, M. (1985). Severity of emotional distress among sexually-abused preschool, school-age and adolescent children. *Hospital and Community Psychiatry, 36*, 503-508.

Goodwin, J. (1985). Credibility problems in multiple personality disorder patients and abused children. In R. P. Kluft (Ed.), *Childhood antecedents of multiple personality* (pp. 2-19). Washington, DC: American Psychiatric Press.

Gordon, L. (1988). *Heroes of their own lives: The politics and history of family violence.* New York: Penguin.

Green, A. H. (1986). True and false allegations of sexual abuse in child custody disputes. *Journal of the American Academy of Child Psychiatry, 25*(4), 449-456.

Green, A. H. (1993). Child sexual abuse: Immediate and long-term effects and intervention. *Journal of the American Academy of Child and Adolescent Psychiatry, 32*(5), 890-902.

Grevan, P. (1991). *Spare the child: The religious roots of punishment and the psychological impact of physical abuse.* New York: Knopf.

Haaken, J. (1994). Sexual abuse, recovered memory, and therapeutic practice: A feminist-psychoanalytic perspective. *Social Text, 40,* 115-145.

Haas, L. J., Malouf, J. L., & Mayerson, N. H. (1986). Ethical dilemmas in psychological practice: Results of a national survey. *Professional Psychology: Research and Practice, 17*(4), 316-321.

Hall, L. A., Sachs, B., Rayens, M. K., & Lutenbacher, M. (1993, Winter). Childhood physical and sexual abuse: Their relationship with depressive symptoms in adulthood. *IMAGE: Journal of Nursing Scholarship, 25*(4), 317-323.

Hampton, R. L., & Newberger, E. H. (1985). Child abuse incidence and reporting by hospitals: Significance of severity, class, and race. *American Journal of Public Health, 75*(1), 56-60.

Hanson, G. (1988). The sex abuse controversy. *Journal of the Academy of Child and Adolescent Psychiatry, 27,* 258-259.

Hanson, R. F., Lipovsky, J. A., & Saunders, B. E. (1994). Characteristics of fathers in incest families. *Journal of Interpersonal Violence, 9*(2), 155-169.

Haugaard, J. J., & Reppucci, N. D. (1988). *The sexual abuse of children.* San Francisco: Jossey-Bass.

Hawkins, R., & Tiedeman, G. (1975). *The creation of deviance.* Columbus, OH: Merrill.

Hazzard, A. (1993). Trauma-related beliefs as mediators of sexual abuse impact in adult women survivors: A pilot study. *Journal of Child Sexual Abuse, 2*(3), 55-69.

Heiman, M. L. (1992). Annotation: Putting the puzzle together: Validating allegations of child sexual abuse. *Journal of Child Psychology and Psychiatry, 33*(2), 311-329.

Helfer, R. E. (1987). The perinatal period, a window of opportunity for enhancing parent-infant communication: An approach to prevention. *Child Abuse & Neglect, 11*(4), 565-579.

Helmreich, R., & Strapp, J. (1974). Short forms of the Texas Social Behavior Inventory (TSBI), an objective measure of self-esteem. *Bulletin of Psychonomic Sociology, 4*(5a), 473-475.

Henderson, J. (1983). Is sexual abuse harmful? *Canadian Journal of Psychiatry, 28,* 34-39.

Herman, J. (1981). *Father-daughter incest.* Cambridge, MA: Harvard University Press.

Herman, J. (1986). Histories of violence in an outpatient population: An exploratory study. *American Journal of Orthopsychiatry, 56*(1), 137-141.

Herzberger, S. D., & Tennen, H. (1988). Applying the label of physical abuse. In G. T. Hotaling, D. Finkelhor, J. T. Kirkpatrick, & M. A. Smith (Eds.), *Coping with family violence: Research and policy perspectives* (pp. 18-30). Newbury Park, CA: Sage.

Hibbard, R. A., Serwint, J., & Connolly, M. (1987). Educational program on evaluation of alleged sexual abuse victims. *Child Abuse & Neglect, 11*(4), 513-519.

Hibbard, R. A., & Zollinger, T. W. (1990). Patterns of sexual abuse knowledge among professionals. *Child Abuse & Neglect, 14,* 347-355.

Hinkelmann, K., & Kempthorne, O. (1994). *Design and analysis of experiments: Vol. 1. Introduction to experimental design.* New York: John Wiley.

Holroyd, J. C., & Brodsky, A. M. (1977). Psychologists' attitudes and practices regarding erotic and nonerotic physical contact with patients. *American Psychologist, October*, 843-849.

Howe, A. C., Herzberger, S., & Tennen, H. (1988). The influence of personal history of abuse and gender on clinicians' judgments of child abuse. *Journal of Family Violence, 3*(2), 105-119.

Howling, P. T., Wodarski, J. S., Kurtz, P. D., & Gaudin, J. M. (1989, September). Methodological issues in child maltreatment research. *Social Work Research & Abstracts*, 3-7.

Hunter, R., & Kilstrom, N. (1979). Breaking the cycle in abusive families. *American Journal of Psychiatry, 136*, 1320-1322.

Hussey, D. L., & Singer, M. (1993). Psychological distress, problem behaviors, and family functioning of sexually abused adolescent inpatients. *Journal of the American Academy of Child and Adolescent Psychiatry, 32*(5), 954-961.

Jackson, H., & Nuttall, R. (1991). *Prevalence of a history of child abuse among social work students*. Unpublished manuscript.

Jackson, H., & Nuttall, R. (1993). Clinician responses to sexual abuse allegations. *Child Abuse & Neglect, 17*, 127-143.

Jackson, H., & Nuttall, R. (1994). Effects of gender, race and age on social workers' clinical judgments. *Social Work Research, 18*(2), 105-113.

Jackson, T. L., & Ferguson, W. P. (1983). Attribution of blame. *American Journal of Community Psychology, 11*(3), 313-322.

Janus, S. S., & Janus, C. L. (1993). *The Janus report on sexual behavior*. New York: John Wiley.

Jason, J., Andereck, N. D., Marks, J., & Tyler, C. W. (1982). Child abuse in Georgia: A method to evaluate risk factors and reporting. *American Journal of Public Health, 72*, 1353-1358.

Jehu, D. (1989). Mood disturbances among women clients sexually abused in childhood. *Journal of Interpersonal Violence, 4*(2), 164-184.

Jenny, C., & Roesler, T. A. (1993). Quality assurance—a response to the backlash against child sexual abuse diagnosis and treatment. *Journal of Child Sexual Abuse, 2*(3), 89-98.

Johnson, C. P. (1989). Residency training and child abuse (letter). *Pediatrics, 83*(5), 805-806.

Johnson, P. A., Owens, R. G., Dewey, M. E., & Eisenberg, N. E. (1990). Professionals' attributions of censure in father-daughter incest. *Child Abuse & Neglect, 14*, 419-428.

Johnson, R. L., & Schrier, D. K. (1985). Sexual victimization of boys: Experience at an adolescent medicine clinic. *Journal of Adolescent Health Care, 6*, 372-376.

Jones, D. P. H., & Krugman, R. D. (1986). Can a three year old child bear witness to her own sexual assault and attempted murder? *Child Abuse & Neglect, 10*, 253-258.

Jones, D. P. H., & Seig, A. (n.d.). *Fictitious accounts of sexual abuse in child custody and visitation disputes*. Unpublished manuscript.

Jones, D., & McGraw, J. M. (1987). Reliable and fictitious accounts of sexual abuse to children. *Journal of Interpersonal Violence, 2*(1), 27-45.

Jordan, J., Kaplan, A., & Miller, J. B. (1991). *Women's growth in connection: Writings from the Stone Center*. New York: Guilford.

Justice, B., & Justice, R. (1990). *The abusing family*. New York: Plenum.

Kalichman, S. C., Craig, M. E., & Follingstad, D. R. (1988). Mental health professionals and suspected cases of child abuse: An investigation of factors influencing reporting. *Community Mental Health Journal, 24*(1), 43-51.

Kalichman, S. C., Craig, M. E., & Follingstad, D. R. (1990). Professionals' adherence to mandatory child abuse reporting laws: Effects of responsibility attribution, confidence ratings, and situational factors. *Child Abuse & Neglect, 14,* 69-77.

Kameen, M. C., & Thompson, D. L. (1983). Substance abuse and child abuse-neglect: Implications for direct-service providers. *Personnel and Guidance Journal, 61*(5), 269-273.

Kardener, S. H., Fuller, M., & Mensh, I. N. (1973). A survey of physicians' attitudes and practices regarding erotic and nonerotic contact with patients. *American Journal of Psychiatry, 130*(10), 1077-1081.

Katz, I. (1970). Experimental studies of Negro-White relationships. In L. Berkowitz (Ed.), *Advances in experimental social psychology* (pp. 71-115). New York: Academic.

Katz, L., & Benjamin, L. (1960). Effects of White authoritarianism in biracial work groups. *Journal of Abnormal and Social Psychology, 61,* 448-456.

Kaufman, J., & Zigler, E. (1987). Do abused children become abusive parents? *American Journal of Orthopsychiatry, 57*(2), 186-192.

Keane, T. M. (1988). Mississippi scale for combat-related posttraumatic stress disorder: Three studies in reliability and validity. *Journal of Consulting and Clinical Psychology, 56*(1), 85-90.

Kelley, S. J. (1990). Responsibility and management strategies in child sexual abuse: A comparison of child protective workers, nurses, and police officers. *Child Welfare, 69*(1), 43-51.

Kempe, C. H. (1978). Sexual abuse, another hidden pediatric problem: The 1977 C. Anderson Aldrich lecture. *Pediatrics, 62,* 382-389.

Kempe, C. H., & Helfer, R. E. (1974). *The battered child.* Chicago: University of Chicago Press.

Kendall-Tackett, K. A., & Simon, A. F. (1987). Perpetrators and their acts: Data from 365 adults molested as children. *Child Abuse & Neglect, 11,* 237-245.

Kendall-Tackett, K. A., & Watson, M. W. (1991). Factors that influence professionals' perceptions of behavioral indicators of child sexual abuse. *Journal of Interpersonal Violence, 6*(3), 385-395.

Kendall-Tackett, K. A., Williams, L. M., & Finkelhor, D. (1993). Impact of sexual abuse on children: A review and synthesis of recent empirical studies. *Psychological Bulletin, 113*(1), 164-180.

Kercher, G. A., & McShane, M. (1984). The prevalence of child sexual abuse victimization in an adult sample of Texas residents. *Child Abuse & Neglect, 8,* 495-501.

Kinsey, A. C., Pomeroy, W. B., & Martin, C. E. (1953). *Sexual behavior of the human female.* Philadelphia: Saunders.

Kinzl, J., & Biebl, W. (1992). Long-term effects of incest: Life events triggering mental disorders in female patients with sexual abuse in childhood. *Child Abuse & Neglect, 16,* 567-573.

Kolko, D. J., Moser, J. T., & Weldy, S. R. (1988). Behavioral/emotional indicators of sexual abuse in child psychiatric inpatients: A controlled comparison with physical abuse. *Child Abuse & Neglect, 12,* 529-541.

Koverola, C., Pound, J., Heger, A., & Lytle, C. (1993). Relationship of child sexual abuse to depression. *Child Abuse & Neglect, 17,* 393-400.

Lanktree, C., Briere, J., & Zaidi, L. (1991). Incidence and impact of sexual abuse in a child outpatient sample: The role of direct inquiry. *Child Abuse & Neglect, 15,* 447-453.

Lanza, M. L., & Carifo, J. (1992). Use of a panel of experts to establish validity for patient assault vignettes. *Evaluation Review, 17*(1), 82-92.

Lanza, M. L. (1990). A methodological approach to enhance external validity in simulation based research. *Issues in Mental Health Nursing, 11,* 407-422.

Larsen, K. S. (1974). Social cost, belief incongruence, and race-experiments in choice behavior. *The Journal of Social Psychology, 94,* 253-267.

Laumann, E. O., Gagnon, J. H., Michael, R. T., & Michaels, S. (1994). *The social organization of sexuality: Sexual practices in the United States* (1st ed.). Chicago: University of Chicago.

Levenson, J. L. (1986, January). When a colleague practices unethically: Guidelines for intervention. *Journal of Counseling and Development, 64,* 315-317.

Lindberg, F., & Distad, L. (1985). Post-traumatic stress disorders in women who experienced childhood incest. *Child Abuse & Neglect, 9,* 329-344.

Lister, E. D. (1982). Forced silence. *American Journal of Psychiatry, 139*(7), 872-876.

Lutzker, J. R., & Rice, J. M. (1987). Using recidivism data to evaluate Project 12 Ways: An ecobehavioral approach to the treatment and prevention of child abuse and neglect. *Journal of Family Violence, 12*(4), 283-290.

Margolin, L. (1991). Child sexual abuse by nonrelated caregivers. *Child Abuse & Neglect, 15,* 213-221.

Margolin, L. (1994). Child sexual abuse by uncles: A risk assessment. *Child Abuse & Neglect, 18,* 215-224.

Marlow, D., Frager, R., & Nuttall, R. L. (1965). Commitment to action taking as a consequence of cognitive dissonance. *Journal of Personality and Social Psychology, 2*(6), 864-868.

May, J. L. (1974). *Attraction and reverse discrimination: The effects of authoritarianism and the applicant's race and character on social welfare cases.* Unpublished doctoral dissertation, Kansas State University, Manhattan.

Mayer, A. (1983). *Incest: A treatment manual.* Holmes Beach, FL: Learning Publications.

McPherson, K. S., & Garcia, L. L. (1983). Effects of social class and familiarity on pediatricians' responses to child abuse. *Child Welfare, 62*(5), 387-393.

Meiselman, K. (1978). *Incest.* San Francisco: Jossey-Bass.

Melton, G. (1989). Psychologists' involvement in cases of child maltreatment: Limits of role and expertise. *American Psychologist, 44*(9), 1225-1233.

Mennen, F. E. (1993). Evaluation of risk factors in childhood sexual abuse. *Journal of the Academy of Child and Adolescent Psychiatry, 32*(5), 934-937.

Mian, M., Marton, P., LeBaron, D., & Birtwistle, D. (1994). Familial risk factors associated with intrafamilial and extrafamilial sexual abuse of three to five year old girls. *Canadian Journal of Psychiatry, 39,* 348-353.

Mikkelsen, E. J., Gutheil, T. G., & Emens, M. (1992). False sexual-abuse allegations by children and adolescents: Contextual factors and clinical subtypes. *American Journal of Psychotherapy, 46*(4), 556-570.

Moore, D. W., & Schussel, R. (1995). *Disciplining children in America* (A Gallup News Service poll). Princeton, NJ: Gallup.

Moore, R. A. (1978). Ethics in the practice of psychiatry—Origins, functions, models, and enforcement. *American Journal of Psychiatry, 135*(2), 157-163.

Moore, R. A. (1985). Ethics in the practice of psychiatry: Update on the results of enforcement of the code. *American Journal of Psychiatry, 142*(9), 1043-1046.

Morison, S., & Greene, E. (1992). Juror and expert knowledge of child sexual abuse. *Child Abuse & Neglect, 16,* 595-613.

Moynihan, D. P. (1990). Family and nation revisited. *Social Thought, 16,* 49-59.

Mukerjee, M. (1995, October). Hidden scars: Sexual and other abuse may alter a brain region. *Scientific American, 14,* 20.

Murman, D., Dorko, B., Brown, J. G., & Tolley, E. (1991). Child sexual abuse in Shelby County, Tennessee: A new epidemic? *Child Abuse & Neglect, 15,* 523-529.

Murphy, J. M., Jellinek, M., Quinn, D., Smith, G., Poitrast, F. G., & Goshko, M. (1991). Substance abuse and serious child mistreatment: Prevalence, risk, and outcome in a court sample. *Child Abuse & Neglect, 15,* 197-211.

Murphy, S. M., Kilpatrick, D. G., Amick-McMullan, Veronen, L. J., Paduhovich, J., Best, C. L., Villeponteaux, L. A., & Saunders, B. E. (1988). Current psychological functioning of child sexual assault survivors: A community study. *Journal of Interpersonal Violence, 3*(1), 55-79.

Myrdal, G. (1944). *An American dilemma* (Vol. 2.). New York: Harper & Brothers.

Nash, M. R., Zivney, O. A., & Hulsey, T. (1993). Characteristics of sexual abuse associated with greater psychological impairment among children. *Child Abuse & Neglect, 17,* 401-408.

Nasjleti, M. (1980). Suffering in silence: The male incest victim. *Child Welfare, 59,* 269-275.

National Association of Social Workers. (1995). Study cites most-reported ethics breaches. *NASW News, 40*(4), pp. 4.

National Center on Child Abuse & Neglect. (1988). *Study of national incidence and prevalence of child abuse and neglect: 1988.* Washington, DC: Author.

National Research Council. (1993). *Understanding child abuse and neglect.* Washington, DC: National Academy.

Newberger, E. H., Hampton, R. L., Marx, T. J., & White, K. M. (1986). Child abuse and pediatric social illness: An epidemiological analysis and ecological reformulation. *American Journal of Orthopsychiatry, 56*(4), 589-601.

Nunno, M. A., & Motz, J. K. (1988). The development of an effective response to the abuse of children in out-of-home care. *Child Abuse & Neglect, 12,* 521-528.

Nuttall, R., & Jackson, H. (1994). Personal history of childhood abuse among clinicians. *Child Abuse & Neglect, 18*(5), 455-472.

Oates, K. (1989). Medical issues in child abuse. *Child Abuse & Neglect, 13,* 167.

Ogata, S. N., Silk, K. R., Goodrich, S., Lohr, N. E., Westen, D., & Hill, E. M. (1990). Childhood sexual and physical abuse in adult patients with borderline personality disorder. *American Journal of Psychiatry, 147*(8), 1008-1013.

Okami, P. (1991). Self-reports of "positive" childhood and adolescent sexual contacts with older persons: An exploratory study. *Archives of Sexual Behavior, 20*(5), 437-457.

Olafson, E., Corwin, D. L., and Summit, R. C. (1993). Modern history of child sexual abuse awareness: Cycles of discovery and suppression. *Child Abuse & Neglect, 17,* 7-24.

O'Toole, R. E., Turbett, J. P., & Nalepka, C. (Eds.). (1983). *Theories, professional knowledge, and diagnosis of child abuse.* Beverly Hills, CA: Sage.

Parker, S., & Parker, H. P. (1991). Female victims of child sexual abuse: Adult adjustment. *Journal of Family Violence, 6*(2), 183-197.

Pelton, L. H. (1985). *The social context of child abuse and neglect.* New York: Human Sciences Press.

Peters, J. J. (1976). Children who are victims of sexual assault and the psychology of offenders. *American Journal of Psychotherapy, 30*(3), 398-421.

Peterson, C., Semmel, A., von Baeyer, C., Abramson, L., Metalsky, G., & Seligman, M. (1982). The attributional style questionnaire. *Cognitive Therapy and Research, 6,* 287-300.

Pierce, R., & Pierce, L. H. (1985). The sexually abused child: A comparison of male and female victims. *Child Abuse & Neglect, 9,* 191-199.

Pope, K. S. (1988, December). How clients are harmed by sexual contact with mental health professionals: The syndrome and its prevalence. *Journal of Counseling and Development, 67,* 222-226.

Pope, K. S., & Feldman-Summers, S. (1992). National survey of psychologists' sexual and physical abuse history and their evaluation of training and competence in these areas. *Professional Psychology: Research and Practice, 23*(5), 353-361.

Pope, K. S., Keith-Spiegel, P., & Tabachnick, B. G. (1986). Sexual attraction to clients: The human therapist and the (sometimes) inhuman training system. *American Psychologist, February,* 147-157.

Pope, K. S., & Vetter, V. A. (1991). Prior therapist-patient sexual involvement among patients seen by psychologists. *Psychotherapy, 28,* 429-438.

Powers, J. L., & Eckenrode, J. (1988). The maltreatment of adolescents. *Child Abuse & Neglect, 12,* 189-199.

Powers, J. L., Eckenrode, J., & Jaklitsch, B. (1990). Maltreatment among runaway and homeless youth. *Child Abuse & Neglect, 4,* 87-98.

Radloff, L. S. (1977). The CES-D scale: A self-report depression scale for research in the general population. *Applied Psychological Measurement, 1*(3), 385-401.

Reidy, T. J., & Hochstadt, N. J. (1993). Attribution of blame in incest cases: A comparison of mental health professionals. *Child Abuse & Neglect, 17,* 371-381.

Reinhart, M. A. (1987). Sexually abused boys. *Child Abuse & Neglect, 11,* 229-235.

Rhodes, M. (1984). *Ethical dilemmas in social work practice.* Boston: Routledge & Kegan Paul.

Rimsza, M. E., & Berg, R. A. (1988). Sexual abuse: Somatic and emotional reactions. *Child Abuse & Neglect, 12,* 201-208.

Robins, L. N., Helzer, J. E., Ratcliff, K. S., & Seyfried, W. (1982). Validity of the Diagnostic Interview Schedule, Version II: DSM-III diagnoses. *Psychological Medicine, 12,* 855-870.

Rosenberg, M. (1965). *Society and the adolescent self-image.* Princeton, NJ: Princeton University Press.

Rosenfeld, A. A., Nadelson, C. C., & Krieger, M. (1979). Fantasy and reality in patient reports of incest. *Journal of Clinical Psychiatry, 40,* 159-164.

Rosenthal, J. A. (1988). Patterns of reported child abuse and neglect. *Child Abuse & Neglect, 12,* 263-271.

Ross, P. J. (1988). *Taguchi techniques for quality engineering: Loss function, orthogonal experiments, parameter and tolerance design.* New York: McGraw-Hill.

Rowan, A. B., Foy, D. W., Rodriguez, N., & Ryan, S. (1994). Posttraumatic stress disorder in a clinical sample of adults sexually abused as children. *Child Abuse & Neglect, 18,* 51-61.

Roy, J., & Bargman, R. E. (1958). Tests of multiple independence and the associated confidence bounds. *Annals of Mathematical Statistics, 29,* 491-503.

Runyon, D. K., Gould, C. L., Trost, D. C., & Loda, F. A. (1982). Determinants of foster care placement for the maltreated child. *Child Abuse & Neglect, 6,* 343-350.

Russell, D. E. H. (1983). The incidence and prevalence of intrafamilial and extrafamilial sexual abuse of female children. *Child Abuse & Neglect, 7,* 133-146.

Russell, D. E. H. (1984). The prevalence and seriousness of incestuous abuse: Stepfathers vs. biological fathers. *Child Abuse & Neglect, 8,* 15-22.

Russell, D. E. H. (1986). *The secret trauma: Incest in the lives of girls and women.* New York: Basic Books.

Ryan, P., Warren, B. L., & Weincek. (1991). Removal of the perpetrator versus removal of the victim in cases of intrafamilial child sexual abuse. In D. D. Knudsen & J. L. Miller (Eds.), *Abused and battered: Social and legal responses to family violence* (pp. 123-133). New York: Aldine de Gruyter.

Sansonnet-Hayden, H., Haley, G., Marriage, K., & Fine, S. (1987). Sexual abuse and psychopathology in hospitalized adolescents. *Journal of the American Academy of Child and Adolescent Psychiatry, 26,* 753-757.

Saunders, E. J. (1988). A comparative study of attitudes toward child sexual abuse among social work and judicial system professionals. *Child Abuse & Neglect, 12,* 83-90.

Sauzier, M. (1989). Disclosure of child sexual abuse: For better or for worse. *Psychiatric Clinics of North America, 12*(2), 455-469.

Sedney, M. A., & Brooks, B. (1984). Factors associated with a history of childhood sexual experiences in a nonclinical female population. *Journal of the American Academy of Child Psychiatry, 23,* 215-218.

Sgroi, S. M. (1978). Introduction: A national needs assessment for protecting child victims of sexual assault. In A. W. Burgess, A. N. Groth, L. L. Homstrom, & S. M. Sgroi (Eds.), *Sexual assault of children and adolescents* (pp. xiv-xxii). Lexington, MA: Lexington Books, D. C. Heath.

Sgroi, S. M., Porter, F. S., & Blick, L. C. (1982). Validation of child sexual abuse. In S. M. Sgroi (Ed.), *Handbook of clinical intervention in child sexual abuse* (pp. 39-79). Lexington, MA: D. C. Heath.

Siegel, S. (1956). *Nonparametric statistics for the behavioral sciences.* New York: McGraw-Hill.

Silver, R. L., Boon, C., & Stones, M. H. (1983). Searching for meaning in misfortune: Making sense of incest. *Journal of Social Issues, 39*(2), 81-102.

Silverstein, C. (Ed.). (1991). *Psychotherapy and psychotherapists: A history.* New York: Norton.

Sirles, E. A., Smith, J. A., & Kusama, H. (1989). Psychiatric status of intrafamilial child sexual abuse victims. *Journal of the American Academy of Child and Adolescent Psychiatry, 28,* 225-229.

Smith, H., & Israel, E. (1987). Sibling incest: A study of the dynamics of 25 cases. *Child Abuse & Neglect, 11,* 101-108.

Snyder, J. C., & Newberger, E. H. (1986). Consensus and differences among hospital professionals in evaluating child maltreatment. *Violence & Victims, 1*(2), 125-139.

Sonne, J. L., & Pope, K. S. (1991, Spring). Treating victims of therapist-patient sexual involvement. *Psychotherapy, 28,* 174-187.

Steward, M. S., Bussey, K., Goodman, G. S., & Saywitz, K. J. (1993). Implications of developmental research for interviewing children. *Child Abuse & Neglect, 17,* 25-37.

Stiver, I. (1990). *Dysfunctional families and wounded relationships, Part I: Work in progress* (Vol. 41). Wellesley, MA: Wellesley College, Stone Center.

Stone, A. A. (1982). Sexual misconduct by psychiatrists: The ethical and clinical dilemma of confidentiality. *American Journal of Psychiatry, 140*(2), 195-197.

Straus, M. (1979). Family patterns and child abuse in a nationally representative sample. *International Journal of Child Abuse & Neglect, 3,* 213-225.

Sturkie, K., & Flanzer, J. P. (1987). Depression and self-esteem in the families of maltreated adolescents. *Social Work, 32,* 491-496.

Summit, R. (1983). The child sexual abuse syndrome. *Child Abuse & Neglect, 7,* 177-193.

Surrey, J. (1985). *Self-in-relation: A theory of women's development: Work in progress* (Vol. 13). Wellesley, MA: Wellesley College, Stone Center.

Swett, C., & Halpert, M. (1993). Reported history of physical and sexual abuse in relation to dissociation and other symptomatology in women psychiatric inpatients. *Journal of Interpersonal Violence, 8*(4), 545-555.

Szegedy-Maszak, M. (1989, May 21). Who's to judge? *New York Times Magazine Section,* pp. 28-29, 88-91, 118-120.

Taguchi, G. (1987). *System of experimental design: Engineering methods to optimize quality and minimize costs* (Vol.1.). Dearborn, MI: American Supplier Institute.

Taguchi, G., & Konishi, S. (1987). *Taguchi methods orthogonal arrays and linear graphs: Tools for quality engineering.* Dearborn, MI: American Supplier Institute, Center for Taguchi Methods.

Tajfel, H. (1969). Cognitive aspects of prejudice. *Journal of Social Issues, 25*(4), 79-97.

Tedeschi, R. G., & Calhoun, L. G. (1995). *Trauma and transformation.* Thousand Oaks, CA: Sage.

Terr, L. (1986). The child psychiatrist and the child witness, traveling companions by necessity, if not design. *Journal of the Academy of Child and Adolescent Psychiatry, 25,* 462-472.

Thoennes, N., & Tjaden, P. G. (1990). The extent, nature and validity of sexual abuse allegations in custody/visitation disputes. *Child Abuse & Neglect, 14,* 151-163.

Thoreson, R. W., Shaugnessy, P., Heppner, P., & Cook, S. W. (1993, March/April). Sexual contact during and after the professional relationship: Attitudes and practices of male counselors. *Journal of Counseling & Development, 71,* 429-434.

Tierney, J. (1992, February 12). The 1992 campaign: Campaign journal: New Hampshire voters take the high road. *New York Times,* pp. A20.

Tong, L., Oates, K., & McDowell, M. (1987). Personality development following sexual abuse. *Child Abuse & Neglect, 11*(11), 371-383.

Tsai, M., Feldman-Summers, S., & Edgar, M. (1979). Childhood molestation: Variables related to differential impacts on psychosexual functioning in adult women. *Journal of Abnormal Psychology, 88*(4), 407-417.

Tzeng, O. C. S., & Schwarzin, H. J. (1990). Gender differences in child sexual abuse correlates. *Child Abuse & Neglect, 14,* 135-161.

U.S. Department of Health and Human Services. (1988). *Study findings: Study of national incidence and prevalence of child abuse and neglect: 1988.* Washington, DC: Government Printing Office.

U.S. Department of Health and Human Services. (1992). *Child maltreatment 1992: Reports from the states to the National Center on Child Abuse & Neglect.* Washington, DC: Government Printing Office.

UNICEF. (1990). *The state of the world's children 1990.* Oxford, UK: Oxford University Press.

van der Kolk, B. A. (1987). The psychological consequences of overwhelming life experiences. In B. A. v. d. Kolk (Ed.), *Psychological trauma* (pp. 1-30). Washington, DC: American Psychiatric Press.

van der Kolk, B., & Greenberg, M. S. (Eds.). (1987). *The psychobiology of the trauma response: Hyperarousal, constriction, and addiction to traumatic reexposure.* Washington, DC: American Psychiatric Press.

van der May, B. J. (1988). The sexual victimization of male children: A review of previous research. *Child Abuse & Neglect, 12,* 61-72.

Waterhouse, L., & Carnie, J. (1992). Assessing child protection risk. *British Journal of Social Work, 22,* 47-60.

Weissman, M. M., & Bothwell, S. (1976). Assessment of social adjustment by patient self-report. *Archives of General Psychiatry, 33,* 1111-1115.

Welfel, E. R., & Lipsitz, N. E. (n.d.). The ethical behavior of professional psychologists: A critical analysis of the research. *The Counseling Psychologist, 12*(3), 31-41.

White, S., Strom, G. A., Santilli, G., & Halpin, B. M. (1986). Interviewing young sexual abuse victims with anatomically correct dolls. *Child Abuse & Neglect, 10,* 519-529.

Widom, C. (1989a). Child abuse, neglect, and adult behavior: Research design and findings on criminality, violence, and child abuse. *American Journal of Orthopsychiatry, 59,* 355-367.

Widom, C. (1989b). The cycle of violence. *Science, 244,* 160-166.

Wind, T. W., & Silvern, L. (1992). Type and extent of child abuse as predictors of adult functioning. *Journal of Family Violence, 7*(4), 261-281.

Wolfe, D. A. (1987). *Child abuse: Implications for child development and psychopathology.* Newbury Park, CA: Sage.

Wolfe, V. V., Gentile, C., & Wolfe, D. A. (1989). The impact of sexual abuse on children: A PTSD formulation. *Behavior Therapy, 20,* 215-228.

Wyatt, G. E. (1985). The sexual abuse of Afro-American and White American women in childhood. *Child Abuse & Neglect, 9,* 507-519.

Wyatt, G. E., & Peters, S. D. (1986a). Issues in the definition of child sexual abuse in prevalence research. *Child Abuse & Neglect, 10,* 231-240.

Wyatt, G. E., & Peters, S. D. (1986b). Methodological considerations in research on the prevalence of child sexual abuse. *Child Abuse & Neglect, 10,* 241-251.

Yates, A. (1993). Discussion of clinical expertise and the assessment of child sexual abuse. *Journal of the American Academy of Child and Adolescent Psychiatry, 32*(5), 931-933.

Zelizer, V. A. (1985). *Pricing the priceless child.* New York: Basic Books.

Zellman, G., & Bell, K. (1989). *The role of professional background, case characteristics, and protective agency response in mandated child abuse reporting.* Santa Monica, CA: RAND.

Zitrin, A., & Klein, H. (1976). Can psychiatry police itself effectively? The experience of one district branch. *American Journal of Psychiatry, 133,* 853-656.

Name Index

Subject Index

About the Authors

Helene Jackson is Associate Professor at Columbia University School of Social Work. She received her PhD in clinical social work from Smith College School for Social Work in 1982. She was the Director of Field Instruction at Boston College Graduate School of Social Work from 1984 to 1989. As an NIMH Clinical Faculty Scholar, she completed postdoctoral training at Children's Hospital, Boston, MA, and was Principal Investigator of the national survey reported in this book. In addition to teaching social work practice, she conducts research on trauma, sexual abuse, preadolescent suicide, domestic violence, and mental health assessment. She has published widely on these subjects and is editor of and contributor to the book *Using Self Psychology in Psychotherapy*.

Ronald L. Nuttall is Professor at Boston College. A social psychologist with a specialty in methodology, he has four degrees from Harvard University, including an AB in chemistry and physics, AM and PhD in social psychology, and an MPH in biostatistics. He teaches courses in survey research methodology, experimental design, and statistics. He is especially interested in the application of Taguchi-style fractional factorial designs in the social sciences. He is applying the total quality approach to improving processes and in using these concepts in education and in public policy. He has nine than 80 publications in refereed journals.